Zinzendorf

NINE PUBLIC LECTURES

Nicholaus Ludwig Count von Zinzendorf
Bishop of the Church of the Moravian Brethren

NINE PUBLIC LECTURES
ON IMPORTANT SUBJECTS
in *RELIGION*

Preached in Fetter Lane Chapel in London in the Year 1746

Translated & Edited by

GEORGE W. FORELL

Wipf and Stock Publishers
150 West Broadway • Eugene OR 97401
1998

Nine Public Lectures on Important Subjects in Religion

By Nicholaus Ludwig Count von Zinzendorf
Edited by Forell, George W.
Copyright©1998 Forell, George W.

ISBN: 1-57910-152-6

Printed by *Wipf and Stock Publishers* 1998
150 West Broadway • Eugene OR 97401

Contents

Introduction

THE MOST influential German theologian between Luther and Schleiermacher was Nicholaus Ludwig Count von Zinzendorf, who was born May 26, 1700, at Dresden, and who died May 9, 1760, at Herrnhut, and who, by the way, never studied theology.

Adored or despised by his contemporaries, he apparently never produced indifference in the many Europeans and Americans who met him during his lengthy journeys across the western world. A friend of kings and archbishops, Indian braves and British merchants, he had considerable influence on those who got to know him. Some Catholic cardinals and Mennonite lay preachers spoke highly of him, while some of his own fellow Lutherans considered him mad, a circumstance which his occasionally bizarre behavior might explain. He affected John and Charles Wesley in their religious development, yet was personally disliked by John. A man of deep Christian humility, he nevertheless was never able to put off the manners and occasionally the autocratic behavior of an eighteenth-century German imperial count. A child of the Enlightenment, whose favorite secular author was Pierre Bayle, he displayed a simple and profound faith in the "lamb of God" rarely equalled in the history of Christianity. The men of the nineteenth century generally admired him. Johann Gottfried Herder wrote in 1802, that "Zinzendorf departed the world as a conqueror who had few equals and none in the century past." [1] Goethe described Zinzendorf and his movement most positively and wrote in *Dichtung und Wahrheit:* "That I eventually moved further and further away from this confession [the Moravian] was actually because of the great seriousness and passionate love with which I had tried to grasp it." [2] Zinzendorf was one spokesman of the Christian faith who seriously appealed to this generally caustic critic of the religious establishment of his time.

Schleiermacher, born only eight years after Zinzendorf's death and educated from 1783 to 1787 at Niesky and Barby, two educational institutions of the followers of Count Zinzendorf, called himself later in life a *Herrnhuter*

---

1   Herder, *Sämmtliche Werke*, vol. 24 (Berlin: Weidmann, 1886), p. 32.
2   *Goethes Werke* (Hamburg: Wegner, 1963), 10:42.

von einer höheren Ordnung, "a Moravian of a higher order."[3] The count's subtle and pervasive influence on Schleiermacher and the theology that developed after him is one reason for his abiding significance.

In 1866, Ludwig Feuerbach claimed that the assertion that Zinzendorf was *Lutherus vere redivivus,* "Luther come back to life," was quite justified. "Zinzendorf is Luther reborn in the 18th century, therefore not in the form of a miner's son and former Augustinian monk but rather as a great man of the world, an imperial count." [4] Indeed, the question of Zinzendorf's relationship to Luther is not solved by any means in spite of Leiv Aalen's massive effort to drive a deep wedge between the two.[5]

There has been something like a Zinzendorf revival in Europe. A critical review of this development was published by Martin Schmidt in 1953, under the title, "The Picture of Zinzendorf in Recent Research."[6] In 1962, F. W. Kantzenbach in an article in *Lutherische Monatshefte,* "The Picture of the Count,"[7] brought this review up to date.

A number of factors have contributed to the continuing interest in Zinzendorf, particularly in Germany and Scandinavia. He was a truly fascinating personality, fitting into no existing category. Scion of the highest German nobility and stepson of a Prussian General Field Marshal, he was at the same time the friend of all kinds of religious radicals, enthusiasts, and Christian pacifists. He used daring and paradoxical language which tended to charm and bewilder his hearers and readers simultaneously. An original, even seminal thinker, he was unaffected by the technical training of professional theologians and was thus frequently able to see old truths in a new light.

Some contemporary theologians have pointed to his unique contribution to ecumenism, and one of the few books in English dealing with his thought has emphasized this aspect of his work.[8] But it was Karl Barth who juxtaposed Zinzendorf's ecumenism with his Christology when he wrote: "If appearances are not deceptive, it was the prophetic intention of Count Zinzendorf in the founding of his remarkable 'brotherhoods,' not to split the Confessional Churches, not to replace them by a super-Church, but, as they came together freely as loyal members of the particular Churches, to confront them typically with the unity which they had not lost and actually could not lose in Jesus Christ Himself, who remarkably enough was elected their common Elder Brother. It is no accident that the very man who in his preaching and poetry

3 *Aus Schleiermachers Leben,* eds. L. Jonas and W. Dilthey (1858–63), as quoted in Gösta Hök, *Zinzendorfs Begriff der Religion* (Uppsala: 1948), p. 3.
4 Ludwig Feuerbach, *Sämmtliche Werke* (Stuttgart: Frommann, 1960), 2:69.
5 Leiv Aalen, *Die Theologie des jungen Zinzendorf* (Berlin: Lutherisches Verlagshaus, 1966).
6 "Das Bild Zinzendorfs in der neueren Forschung," *Evangelisch Lutherische Kirchenzeitung* 7 (1953):340–43, and 365–69.
7 F. W. Katzenbach, "Das Bild des Grafen," *Lutherische Monatshefte* 1 (1962):384–91.
8 A. J. Lewis, *Zinzendorf the Ecumenical Pioneer* (London: SCM, 1962).

and dogmatics (so far as he had any) was perhaps *the only genuine Christocentric of the modern age* (fools would say: Christomonist), must also perhaps be called the first genuine ecumenist, i.e., the first really to speak and think wholly in terms of the matter itself."[9] No wonder that theologians influenced by Barth have taken a renewed interest in Zinzendorf's theology.

Paul Schütz, emphasizing a different aspect of Zinzendorf's thought, the notion of the "motherhood of the Holy Spirit," calls him, "the lonely reminder of the maternal person in God in post-Reformation times."[10] Even though this statement may not do full justice to the contribution of a Jakob Böhme, it does stress that Zinzendorf's emphasis on the feminine dimension in the Trinity makes him the advocate of a point of view which had not been recognized among Protestants until Tillich raised the question, "whether there are elements in genuine Protestant symbolism which transcend the alternative male-female and which are capable of being developed over against a one-sided male-determined symbolism."[11] And it is Tillich who sees his "ground of being" pointing "to the mother quality of giving birth, carrying and embracing, and, at the same time, of calling back, resisting independence of the created, and swallowing it."[12] Here again Zinzendorf, in his open advocacy of a more inclusive sexual imagery as applied to the Trinity, pointed the way which orthodox Christianity rejected at the cost of its symbolic impoverishment.

But if these theological insights were not enough to justify renewed interest in Zinzendorf in the English-speaking world, there are at least two confrontations in Zinzendorf's life which had made a major impact in England and America and which should draw our attention to this man. It was through Zinzendorf and the Moravians that John Wesley encountered Luther and Lutheranism. Both his positive and negative reactions were shaped by what was essentially a Moravian form of Lutheranism. And it was Zinzendorf's activity in America which finally persuaded the German pietist Lutherans to do something for their dispersed coreligionists in the New World.

Because of John Wesley's massive literary output, we are well-informed about his wavering reactions to Zinzendorf and the Moravians. He began to learn German on his journey to Georgia for the express purpose of conversing with his German-speaking Moravian fellow-passengers.[13] The entry of January 25, 1736, shows how deeply the behavior of these people

---

9 Karl Barth, *Church Dogmatics*, 4 vols. (Edinburgh: T. T. Clark, 1956), 1:683. By permission. Italics mine.

10 Paul Schütz. *Gesammelte Werke* (Hamburg: Furche, 1966), 1:376.

11 Paul Tillich, *Systematic Theology* (Chicago: University of Chicago Press, 1963), 3:293. By permission.

12 *Systematic Theology*, 3:294.

13 *The Journal of the Rev. John Wesley*, ed. Nehemiah Curnock, 8 vols. (London: Epworth Press, 1938), 1:110. By permission.

impressed him: "At seven I went to the Germans. I had long before observed the great seriousness of their behavior. Of their humility they had given a continual proof, by performing those servile offices for the other passengers which none of the English would undertake; for which they desired and would receive no pay, saying 'it was good for their proud hearts,' and 'their loving Saviour had done more for them.' And every day had given them occasion of showing a meekness which no injury could move. If they were pushed, struck, or thrown down, they rose again and went away; but no complaint was found in their mouth. There was now an opportunity of trying whether they were delivered from the spirit of fear, as well as from that of pride, anger, and revenge. In the midst of the psalm wherewith their service began, wherein we were mentioning the power of God, the sea broke over, split the mainsail in pieces, covered the ship, and poured in between the decks, as if the great deep had already swallowed us up. A terrible screaming began among the English. The Germans looked up, and without intermission calmly sang on. I asked one of them afterwards, 'Was you not afraid?' He answered, 'I thank God, no.' I asked, 'But were not your women and children afraid?' He replied mildly, 'No; our women and children are not afraid to die.'" [14]

It was on a little island off Georgia that Wesley had the conversation with Bishop Spangenberg of the Moravians which made him question the sincerity of his own religious conviction. And it was from Spangenberg that he learned at that time about Zinzendorf's community at Herrnhut. [15] From then on Wesley's path frequently crossed that of the Moravians. After his return to England he participated for a while in the community which met at Fetter Lane, the meeting place where Zinzendorf's lectures presented in this volume were later delivered. Indeed, he and his brother Charles came so close to the Moravians in England as to give offense to the mother of one of his friends, James Hutton, who eventually became Zinzendorf's associate and publisher of his writings in England and an important leader in the Moravian movement. It was through John Wesley that Hutton had come into contact with the Moravians and for a while Hutton and Gambold, eventually leading Moravians, worked hand in hand with the Wesleys in their evangelistic outreach. After May 1, 1738, this small band began its services at Fetter Lane. [16] John Wesley describes this development in his *Journal* of May 1, 1738, as follows: "This evening our little society began which afterwards met in Fetter Lane. Our fundamental rules were as follows 'In obedience to the command of God by St. James and by the advice

---

14 *Journal of John Wesley*, 1:142 f.
15 *Journal of John Wesley*, 1:152 ff.
16 See Daniel Benham, *Memoirs of James Hutton* (London: Hamilton, Adams & Co., 1856), p. 27 ff.

of Peter Böhler,[17] it is agreed by us, 1. That we will meet together once a week to 'confess our faults one to another, and pray one for another, that we may be healed.' 2. That the persons so meeting be divided into several bands, or little companies, none of them consisting of fewer than five or more than ten persons. 3. That every one in order speak as freely, plainly, and concisely as he can, the real state of his heart, with his several temptations and deliverances, since the last time of meeting. 4. That all the bands have a conference at eight every Wednesday evening, begun and ended with singing and prayer. 5. That any who desire to be admitted into the society be asked, 'What are your reasons for desiring this? Will you be entirely open; using no kind of reserve? Have you any objection to any of our orders?' (which may then be read). 6. That when any new member is proposed, every one present speak clearly and freely whatever objection he has to him. 7. That those against whom no reasonable objection appears be, in order for their trial, formed into one or more distinct bands, and some person agreed on to assist them. 8. That after two months' trial, if no objections then appear, they may be admitted into the society. 9. That every fourth Sunday be observed as a day of general intercession. 10. That on the Sunday seven-night following be a general love feast, from seven till ten in the evening. 11. That no particular member be allowed to act in anything contrary to any order of the society; and that if any persons, after being thrice admonished, do not conform thereto, they be not any longer esteemed as members.'"[18] While this list shows clearly the authorship of John Wesley, the society itself was neither Methodist nor

---

17 Wesley had met Böhler on February 7, 1738. Curnock, the editor of the *Journal* gives the following information about him: "Peter Böhler, born in 1712 at Frankfort-on-the-Maine, was brought up a Lutheran. In 1731, he entered the University at Jena. The religious influence in Lutheran churches nicknamed 'Pietism' led him to seek experimental religion and to adopt those views of justifying faith which he afterwards pressed upon the Wesleys. Count Zinzendorf, the protector of the Moravian refugees at Herrnhut, visited Jena, and became acquainted with Böhler and Professor Spangenberg. This interview eventually led these two Lutheran Pietists to join the Church of the Moravian Brethren. The Count appointed Böhler tutor to his son; and when he himself became a bishop of the Moravian Church, his first episcopal act was the ordination of Peter Böhler . . . . When Wesley met him in London, Böhler was on his way to America as a missionary to Georgia and the negroes of Carolina." (*The Journal of John Wesley*, vol. I, p. 436) The influence of Böhler on Wesley is further attested by the entry of March 4, 1738: "I found my brother at Oxford recovering from his pleurisy; and with him Peter Böhler, by whom (in the hand of the great God) I was, on Sunday the 5th, clearly convinced of unbelief, of the want of that faith whereby alone we are saved. Immediately it struck into my mind, 'Leave off preaching. How can you preach to others, who have no faith yourself?' I asked Böhler whether he thought I should leave it off or not. He answered, 'By no means'. I asked, 'But what can I preach?' He said, 'Preach faith *till* you have it; and then, *because* you have it, you *will* preach faith.' " (*Ibid.*, p. 442) For the profound influence of Böhler on Wesley cf. also M. Schmidt, *John Wesley, A Theological Biography* (New York: Abingdon, 1962), pp. 224 ff.

18 *Journal of John Wesley*, 1:458 f. See also the modified version, "Orders of a Religious Society Meeting in Fetter Lane," as printed in *Memoirs of James Hutton*, pp. 29–32.

Moravian. Its members considered themselves part of the Church of England and apparently went in a body to St. Paul's Cathedral to receive the Lord's Supper.[19] Both Methodists and the Moravian Church in England can claim that they derived from this society.

The original reaction by more staid members of the Church of England to the rules and activities of this society was mostly negative. The rules were referred to as "so falsely, so twistingly, so pelagianical, and more than papistically servile, etc., that a stone might have felt compassion."[20] And the mother of one of the most active members, James Hutton, became so upset as to write on June 6, 1738, the following letter to the Reverend Samuel Wesley, at Tiverton, Devon, the older brother of John and Charles. It reflects the attitude of the more typical church member, for Mrs. Hutton was the wife of John Hutton, a nonjuring clergyman of the Church of England.

Dear Sir, — You will be surprised to see a letter from me, but Mr. Hutton and I are really under a very great concern, and know not what to apply to, if you cannot help us. After you left London, and your brothers had lost the conveniency of your house, believing them good and pious Christians, we invited them to make the same use of ours, and thought such an offer would not be unacceptable to God, or to them; which they received with signs of friendship, and took up with such accommodations as our house could afford, from time to time, as they had occasion. Mr. Charles at his arrival in England, we received and treated with such tenderness and love, as he could have been in your house, Mr. John the same; and as occasion has offered at different times, ten or twelve of their friends. But your brother John seems to be turned a wild enthusiast, or fanatic, and, to our very great affliction, is drawing our two children into these wild notions, by their great opinion of Mr. John's sanctity and judgment. It would be a great charity to many other honest well-meaning simple souls, as well as to my children if you could either confine, or convert Mr. John when he is with you. For after his behaviour on Sunday the 28th May, when you hear it, you will think him not a quite right man.

Without ever acquainting Mr. Hutton with any of his notions or designs, when Mr. Hutton had ended a sermon of Bishop Blackall's, which he had been reading in his study to a great number of people; Mr. John got up, and told the people, that five days before he was not a Christian, and this he was as well assured of as that five days before he was not in that room, and the way for them all to be christians was to believe, and own, that they were not now christians. Mr. Hutton was much surprised at this unexpected injudicious speech, but only said, 'Have a care Mr. Wesley, how you despise the benefits received by the two sacraments.' I not being in the study when this speech was made, had heard nothing of it when he came into the parlour to supper, where were my two children, two or three others of his deluded followers, two or three ladies who board with me, my niece, and two or three gentlemen of Mr. John's acquaintance, though not got into his new notions.

He made the same wild speech again, to which I made answer, if you was not

19 *Journal of John Wesley*, 1:458 n. 2.
20 *Memoirs of James Hutton*, p. 32.

a christian ever since I knew you, you was a great hypocrite, for you made us all believe you was one. He said, when we had renounced every thing but faith, and then got into Christ, then, and not til then, had we any reason to believe we were christians; and when we had so got Christ, we might keep him, and so be kept from sin. Mr. Hutton said, 'if faith only was necessary to save us, why did our Lord give us that divine sermon?' Mr. John said, that was *the letter that killeth.* 'Hold,' says Mr. Hutton, 'you seem not to know what you say, are our Lord's words the letter that killeth?' Mr. John said, 'if we had no faith.' Mr. Hutton replied, 'I did not ask you how we should receive it? But why our Lord gave it; as also the account of the judgment in the twenty-fifth of St. Matthew, if works are not what he expects, but faith only?'

Now it is a most melancholy thing to have not only our two children, but many others, to disregard all preaching, but by such a spirit as comes to some in dreams, to others in such visions as will surprise you to hear of. If there cannot be some stop put to this, and he can be taught true humility, the mischief he will do wherever he goes among the ignorant, but well meaning christians will be very great.

Mr. Charles went from my son's, where he lay ill for some time, and would not come to our house, where I offered him the choice of two of my best rooms, but he would accept of neither, but chose to go to a poor brazier's in Little Britain, that that brazier might help him forward in his conversion, which was completed on May 22d, as his brother John was praying. Mr. John was converted, or I know not what, or how, but made a christian, on May 25th. . . . Mr. John has abridged the life of one Halyburton, a presbyterian teacher in Scotland. My son had designed to print it, to show the experience of that holy man, of in-dwelling, &c. Mr. Hutton and I have forbid our son being concerned in handing such books into the world; but if your brother John, or Charles, think it will tend to promote God's glory, they will soon convince my son God's glory is to be preferred to his parents' commands: then you will see what I never expected, my son promoting rank fanaticism. If you can, dear sir, put a stop to such madness, which will be a work worthy of you, a singular charity, and very much oblige,

Your sincere and affectionate servant,

E. Hutton.[21]

It was in the midst of this controversy that John Wesley decided to go to see Zinzendorf in Germany. The meeting eventually took place in Marienborn and Wesley described his impressions in a number of letters and in a lengthy entry in his *Journals*. In each case his reaction to Zinzendorf seems entirely positive. To his mother he wrote on July 6, 1738, ". . . About one o'clock on Tuesday, we came safe to Marienborn, a small village seven hours from Frankfort, where Count Zinzendorf has hired for three years (till one is built a few miles off on his own land, which is already begun) a large house and tolerably convenient, which lodges the greater part of the small congregation here. The Count received us in a manner I was quite unacquainted with, and therefore know not how to express. I believe his behaviour was not unlike that of his Master (if we may compare human with divine) when he took the little children in his arms and blessed them.

---

21 *Memoirs of James Hutton*, p. 33 ff.

We should have been much amazed at him, but that we saw ourselves encom-
passed with a cloud of those who were all followers of him, as he is of
Christ. Eighty-eight of them praise God with one heart and one mouth
at Marienborn; another little company at Runnerburg [Ronneburg], an hour
off; another at Büdingen, an hour from thence; and yet another at Frankfort.
I now understand those words of poor Julian, 'See how these Christians
love one another.' Yea, how they love all who have the faintest desire to
love the Lord Jesus Christ in sincerity. Oh may He sanctify to use their
holy conversation, that we may be partakers of the spirit which is in them;
of their faith unfeigned, and meekness, wisdom, and love which never
faileth. . . ."[22] On July 7, 1738, he wrote to his brother Charles, "The
spirit of the Brethren is above our highest expectation. Young and old,
they breathe nothing but faith and love, at all times and in all places. I
do not therefore concern myself with the smaller points that touch not the
essence of Christianity, but endeavour (God being my helper) to grow up
in these after the glorious example set before me."[23] On July 12, he participated in one of the Moravian "Conferences" and heard Zinzendorf speak on
the question, "Can a man be justified, and not know it?" Wesley summarized
this address as follows: "1. Justification is the forgiveness of sins. 2. The
moment a man flies to Christ he is justified; 3. And has peace with God;
but not always joy. 4. Nor perhaps may he know he is justified, till long
after; 5. For the assurance of it is distinct from justification itself. 6. But
others may know he is justified by his power over sin, by his seriousness,
his love of the brethren, and his 'hunger and thirst after righteousness,'
which alone prove the spiritual life to be begun. 7. To be justified is the
same as to be born of God. 8. When a man is awakened, he is begotten
of God, and his fear and sorrow and sense of the wrath of God are the
pangs of the new birth."[24] In the first edition of the *Journal* these statements
were accepted without comment. In later editions, however, the words "Not
so," were added in parentheses after proposition No. 7.[25] By then his movement away from the Lutheran-Moravian interpretation had begun.

Immediately upon his return from Germany, on September 17, 1738,
however, he reported glowingly on his visits with Zinzendorf and his Moravians. At this time he was using the existing "Religious Societies" of the
Church of England as his base of operation. As Curnock describes it, "On
his return from Herrnhut Wesley attached himself closely to these societies,
and they, as a rule, welcomed his ministrations. He read prayers for them,
preached, expounded, read his 'Account of Herrnhut,' visited their sick

22 *Journal of John Wesley*, 2:8.
23 *Journal of John Wesley*, 2:13.
24 *Journal of John Wesley*, 2:13.
25 *Journal of John Wesley*, 2:13.

. . . ."[26] One of these societies was the one at Fetter Lane, where love feasts and prostrations before the Lord in the Moravian manner were practiced.[27] It was to this Fetter Lane Society and to James Hutton that Wesley sent detailed reports concerning his ministry in Bristol from March 29, 1739, to March 21, 1740. But in the same year, 1740, the break between the English followers of Zinzendorf and John Wesley and his followers occurred. At the time, the cause of the division was seen quite differently by James Hutton and the Moravians and by John Wesley and his followers. To the Moravians the split was the result of two things: Wesley's personality and Wesley's theology. We obtain Hutton's view from a letter which he wrote to Zinzendorf in English on March 14, 1740:

J. Wesley being resolved to do all things himself and having told many souls that they were justified, who have since discovered themselves to be otherwise; and having mixed the words of the law with the Gospel as means of grace, is at enmity against the Brethren. Envy is not extinct in him . . . I fear by and by he will be an open enemy of Christ and his Church. Charles Wesley is coming to London, and determined to oppose all such as shall not use the means of grace (after his sense of them) . . . J. W. and C. W., both of them are dangerous snares to many young women; several are in love with them. I wish they were once married to some good sisters, but I would not give them one of my sisters if I had many. . . .[28]

The open break in the Fetter Lane Society took place on July 20, 1740, and was reported by Hutton in these words:

John Wesley, displeased at not being thought so much of as formerly, and offended, as he said, with the easy way of salvation as taught by the Brethren, publicly spoke against our doctrine in his sermons, and his friends did the same. In June, 1740, he formed his 'Foundry Society,' in opposition to the one which met at Fetter Lane, and which had become a Moravian Society. Many of our usual hearers consequently left us, especially the females. We asked his forgiveness if in any thing we had aggrieved him, but he continued full of wrath, accusing the Brethren, that in following Luther without discrimination, they, by dwelling exclusively on the doctrine of faith, neglected the law and zeal for sanctification. In short, he became our declared opponent, and the two societies of the Brethren and the Methodists thenceforward were separated and became independent upon each other.[29]

Wesley's view of his break with the Moravians can be found in the fourth part of his *Journal* from November 1, 1739, to September 3, 1741, which was published in 1744.[30] He makes it quite clear that his objection to the Moravians was based on their alleged separatism, i.e., their intention to

---

26 *Journal of John Wesley*, 2:71 n. 1.
27 *Journal of John Wesley*, 2:122 n. 1.
28 *Memoirs of James Hutton*, p. 46 ff.
29 *Memoirs of James Hutton*, p. 54.
30 *Journal of John Wesley*, 2:307-500.

establish an independent Moravian Church, their neglect of the means of grace, in particular the Lord's Supper, and their "Lutheran" quietism. He described the official break with the Fetter Lane Society on July 20, 1740, as follows:

In the evening I went with Mr. Seward to the love feast in Fetter Lane; at the conclusion of which, having said nothing till then, I read a paper, the substance whereof was as follows: "About nine months ago certain of you began to speak contrary to the doctrine we had till then received. The sum of what you asserted is this: 1. That there is no such thing as *weak faith:* That there is no justifying faith where there is ever any doubt or fear, or where there is not, in the full sense, a new, a clean heart. 2. That a man ought not to use those ordinances of God which our Church terms 'means of grace,' before he has such· a faith as excludes all doubt and fear, and implies a new, a clean heart. You have often affirmed that to search the Scriptures, to pray, or to communicate before we have this faith is to seek salvation by works; and that till these works are laid aside no man can receive faith. I believe these assertions to be flatly contrary to the Word of God. I have warned you hereof again and again, and besought you to turn back to the Law and the Testimony. I have borne with you long, hoping you would turn. But as I find you more and more confirmed in the error of your ways, nothing now remains but that I should give you up to God. You that are of the same judgment, follow me." I then, without saying anything more, withdrew, as did eighteen or nineteen of the society.[31]

Wesley's entry in his *Journal* of June 15, 1741, a year later, contains a most significant observation, namely the claim that the errors of the Moravians could be attributed to Luther's influence upon them. He wrote:

I set out for London, and read over in the way that celebrated book, Martin Luther's *Comment on the Epistle to the Galatians.* I was utterly ashamed. How have I esteemed this book, only because I heard it so commended by others; or, at best, because I had read some excellent sentences occasionally quoted from it! But what shall I say, now I judge for myself, now I see with my own eyes? Why, not only that the author makes nothing out, clears up not one considerable difficulty; that he is quite shallow in his remarks on many passages, and muddy and confused almost, on all; but that he is deeply tinctured with mysticism throughout, and hence often fundamentally wrong. To instance only in one or two points: How does he (almost in the words of Tauler) decry reason, right or wrong, as an irreconcilable enemy to the gospel of Christ! Whereas, what is reason (the faculty so called) but the power of apprehending, judging, and discoursing? Which power is no more to be condemned in the gross than seeing, hearing or feeling. Again, how blasphemously does he speak of good works and of the law of God — constantly coupling the law with sin, death, hell, or the devil; and teaching that Christ delivers us from them all alike. Whereas it can no more be proved by Scripture that Christ delivers us from the law of God than that He delivers us from holiness or from heaven. Here (I apprehend) is the real spring of the grand error of the Moravians. They

---

31 *Journal of John Wesley,* 2:370.

follow Luther, for better, for worse. Hence their 'No works; no law; no command-ments.' But who art thou that 'speakest evil of the law, and judgest the law'? [32]

It was not much later during the same year that James Hutton made another effort to reconcile Moravians and Methodists by arranging a meeting between Zinzendorf and John Wesley, which the latter reported in Latin in his *Journal* of September 3, 1741, and introduced with the following statement: "James Hutton having sent me word that Count Zinzendorf would meet me at three o'clock in the afternoon, I went at that time to Gray's Inn Walks. The most material part of our conversation (which I dare not conceal) was as follows: [33]

Zinzendorf: Why have you changed your religion?
Wesley: I am not aware that I have changed my religion. Why do you think so? Who has told you this?
Z: Plainly, yourself. I see it from your letter to us. In that you have abandoned the religion which you professed among us, you profess a new one.
W: How so? I do not understand you.
Z: Yea, you say there that true Christians are not miserable sinners. This is most false. The best men are most miserable sinners, even unto death. If any say otherwise, they are either wholly impostors, or diabolically led astray. Our brethren, teachers of better things, you have opposed: and have refused peace to them desiring it.
W: I do not understand what you mean.
Z: When you wrote to me from Georgia, I loved you very much. I perceived that you were then simple in heart. You wrote again: I saw that you were still simple in heart, but disordered in your ideas. You came among us: your ideas were then still more disordered and confused. You returned to England. Some time after, I heard that our brethren were contending with you. I send Spangenberg to effect a reconciliation between you. He wrote to me, that the Brethren had injured you. I wrote back, that they should not only not persist, but even ask your pardon. Spangenberg wrote again, that they had asked it: but that you, boasting of these things, were unwilling to be at peace. Now being come, I hear the same.
W: The matter by no means turns on that point. Your Brethren (it is so far true) did treat me ill. Afterward, they asked my pardon. I answered, that that was superfluous; that I had never been angry with them: but was afraid, 1. That there was error in their doctrine. 2. That there was sin (allowed) in their practice. This was then, and is at this day, the only question between them and me.
Z: Speak more plainly.
W: I feared that there was error in their doctrine, — 1. Concerning the end of our faith in this life, to wit, Christian perfection. 2. Concerning the means of grace, so called by our Church.
Z: I acknowledge no inherent perfection in this life. This is the error of errors.

---

32 *Journal of John Wesley,* 2:467.
33 In later editions of the *Journal,* the following sentence is added: "To spare the dead, I do not translate." In fact, Wesley had left this conversation in Latin even in those editions which appeared before Zinzendorf's death in 1760. The translation here reproduced is from *Journals,* vol. 1, *The Works of the Rev. John Wesley, A.M.,* 3rd Am. & std. ed., 7 vols. (New York and Cincinnati: Methodist Book Concern, n.d.).

I pursue it through the world with fire and sword; — I trample it under foot; — I exterminate it. Christ is our only perfection. Whoever follows after inherent perfection, denies Christ.

W: But I believe, that the Spirit of Christ works perfection in true Christians.

Z: Not at all. All our perfection is in Christ. All Christian perfection is faith in the blood of Christ. The whole of Christian perfection is imputed, not inherent. We are perfect in Christ; — in ourselves, never.

W: We contend, I think, about words. Is not every true believer holy?

Z: Certainly. But he is holy in Christ, not in himself.

W: But does he not live holily?

Z: Yes, he lives holily in all things.

W: Has he not also a holy heart?

Z: Most certainly.

W: Is he not, consequently, holy in himself?

Z: No, no. In Christ only. He is not holy in himself. In himself he has no holiness at all.

W: Has he not the love of God and his neighbour in his heart? Yea, even the whole image of God?

Z: He has. But these constitute legal, not evangelical holiness. Evangelical holiness is, — faith.

W: The dispute is altogether about words. You grant that the whole heart and the whole life of a believer, are holy: that he loves God with all his heart, and serves him with all his strength. I ask nothing more. I mean nothing else by Christian perfection or holiness.

Z: But this is not his holiness. He is not more holy, if he loves more; nor less holy, if he loves less.

W: What? Does not a believer, while he increases in love, increase equally in holiness?

Z: By no means. The moment he is justified, he is sanctified wholly. From that time, even unto death, he is neither more nor less holy.

W: Is not then a father in Christ more holy than a new-born-babe (in Christ)?

Z: No. Entire sanctification and justification are in the same instant; and neither is increased or diminished.

W: But does not a believer grow daily in the love of God? Is he perfect in love as soon as he is justified?

Z: He is. He never increases in the love of God. He loves entirely in that moment, as he is entirely sanctified.

W: What then does the apostle Paul mean by, "We are renewed day by day?"

Z: I will tell you. Lead, if it be changed into gold, is gold the first day, and the second, and the third. And so it is renewed day by day. But it is never more gold than on the first day.

W: I thought we ought to grow in grace!

Z: Certainly. But not in holiness. As soon as any one is justified, the Father, the Son, and the Holy Spirit, dwell in his heart: and in that moment his heart is as pure as it ever will be. A babe in Christ is as pure in heart as a father in Christ. There is no difference.

W: Were not the Apostles justified before the death of Christ?

Z: They were.

W: But were they not more holy after the day of Pentecost, than before the death of Christ?

Z: Not in the least.

W: Were they not on that day filled with the Holy Ghost?

Z: They were. But that gift of the Spirit had no reference to their holiness. It was the gift of miracles only.

W: Perhaps I do not understand you. Do we not, while we deny ourselves, more and more die to the world and live to God?

Z: We spurn all (self) denial: we trample it under foot. Being believers, we do whatever we will, and nothing more. We ridicule all mortification. No purification precedes perfect love.

W: What you have said, God assisting me, I will thoroughly consider.[34]

The substantial accuracy of this report is supported by the fact that this conversation was reprinted in the so-called *Büdingische Sammlung*[35] published in Büdingen in 1745. This was a collection of letters and documents made generally available by the Moravians in order to clarify and support their position in various controversies. Thus Zinzendorf's recollection of this conversation must have coincided with Wesley's, and Zinzendorf was quite prepared to stand behind his expressed opposition to Wesley's teaching concerning sanctification.

For the history of theology in the English-speaking world, it is significant that Wesley's view of Luther was so largely dependent upon his feelings towards the Moravians. He had been led to Luther by the Moravians and his eventual break with Zinzendorf amounted to a break with Luther. This decisive influence of the Moravians and Zinzendorf on Wesley's attitude towards Luther and Lutheranism makes a better understanding of Zinzendorf essential for a better understanding of the history of Christian thought in the English-speaking world. But Zinzendorf had also a direct and indirect effect on the history of Christianity in North America. He was instrumental in the establishment of a Christian community still in existence today and known as the Moravian Church in America. Concerned about the future of his followers in Germany, remnants of the ancient unity of Czech Brethren and descendants of John Hus's reformation which he had invited to Berthelsdorf in Saxony and settled on his estates together with Lutheran and Reformed Christians who held views somewhat different from the official orthodoxies and who had joined them in building the community of Herrnhut, he sought to find permanent places of refuge in the new world in case of renewed persecution in Europe.

The Saxon government had proved unreliable as far as the toleration of deviant forms of Christianity was concerned when in 1733 it withdrew its protection from the Schwenkfelders, religious refugees from Silesia, then under Roman Catholic rule.

---

34 *Journals*, vol. 1, *The Works of the Rev. John Welsey*, pp. 220–22.
35 Nikolaus Ludwig von Zinzendorf, *Ergänzungsbände zu den Hauptschriften*, eds. Erich Beyreuther and Gerhard Meyer, 12 vols. (Hildesheim: Georg Olms, 1966) 9:1026–1030.

The possibility that a similar fate might await the refugees from Moravia and Bohemia, now settled on his estates, seemed very real.

Fear for the future safety of the Brethren was increased by the intrigues against Zinzendorf at the Saxon Court which led to his banishment from Saxony in 1736.

Thus various colonies of Brethren were established outside of Germany. The first settlement on the American continent was begun in 1735 in Georgia under the leadership of August Gottlieb Spangenberg. Because of political pressure on the Brethren and the unhealthy climate it was eventually abandoned (1740) and the settlers moved to Pennsylvania. George Whitefield, the Methodist Evangelist, had been instrumental in the relocating of the small colony and supplied the first land for this resettlement. It was Whitefield who in 1739 wrote to Zinzendorf to send German preachers to the forests of Pennsylvania, where so many Germans had found their homes. Zinzendorf not only sent a number of men but on September 28, 1741, set sail for America himself, accompanied by his sixteen-year-old daughter, Benigna, and a few other followers. He hoped that America would be the place where he could proclaim the Gospel without the interference from various established churches which had troubled him in Europe.[36] His mood at the time was expressed in a speech which he delivered on the way to England before the Congregation of Brethren in Herrendyk, Holland, on August 19, 1741:

> I am destined by the Lord to proclaim the message of the death and blood of Jesus, not with human ingenuity, but with divine power, unmindful of personal consequences to myself. And this was my vocation long before I knew anything of the Moravian Brethren. Though I am and shall remain connected with the Moravian Brethren, who have accepted and taken to heart the Gospel of Jesus Christ, and have called me and other brethren to the ministry in their congregations, still I do not on that account by any means separate myself from the Lutheran Church, for a witness of Jesus can well live and remain in this Church. Nevertheless I can not with my testimony confine myself to *one* denomination; for *the whole earth is the Lord's, and all souls are His; I am a debtor to all.* I know that I shall find opposition in future as well as hitherto; but the message of the crucified Jesus is divine power and divine wisdom, and whosoever opposes it, will be confounded.[37]

America and particularly Pennsylvania, appeared to Zinzendorf the ideal place to attempt his ecumenical ministry. But it was after his arrival in the "new world" on November 29, 1741, that he discovered that religious anarchy can be an equally destructive alternative to the rigidity of the established churches as he had observed it in Europe.

It was Zinzendorf's plan to foster unity by holding open conferences for

---

36   For the following see also Mary E. Forell, "Zinzendorf's Journey to America" (Senior thesis, Yale University, 1971).

37   Levin Theodore Reichel, *The Early History of the Church of the United Brethren, Commonly Called Moravians in North America, A.D. 1734-1748* (Nazareth, Penn.: 1888), chap. 2, pp. 93-94.

all who were willing to attend and thus to create not a united church organization but rather a united Christian people who would serve the Lord in harmony in Pennsylvania. In order to avoid offense, he relinquished his office as Bishop of the Moravian Church, as well as his rank and title as a count of the German Empire, and traveled as a simple Lutheran pastor under one of his lesser, but legitimate names, Herr von Thürnstein. Far from reducing suspicion, however, this procedure was seen by his opponents as further evidence of Zinzendorf's deviousness.

Upon his arrival in Pennsylvania, he preached in Reformed and Lutheran Churches and held services in a rented house in Philadelphia. He made contact with ecumenically minded individuals, especially Henry Antes, a Reformed lay-preacher who issued a circular letter calling for the first of these open conferences. The invitation read as follows:

In the Name of Jesus! Amen.

MY BELOVED FRIEND AND BROTHER, etc:

Inasmuch as a frightful evil is being wrought in the Church of Christ among the souls which have been called to the Lamb, mainly through distrust and suspicion toward one another, and that often without foundation, whereby the goal of anything good is constantly cut off; although love is commanded of us; therefore for two or more years we have had it under consideration, whether or not it might be possible to arrange a conference, not to wrangle with each other over opinions, but rather to treat in love concerning the most important articles of faith, in order to ascertain how nearly we can approach each other in the fundamentals, and in other matters of opinion which do not subvert the ground of salvation to bear with one another in love, that thereby all judging and criticizing might be diminished and done away (among) afore-mentioned souls, by which they now expose themselves before the world and give occasion to say: Those who preach peace and conversion are themselves at variance. Therefore this matter of such great importance has been under advisement again with many brethren and God-seeking souls and tried before the Lord, and it has been decided to meet on the coming New Year's Day in Germantown. Consequently you are cordially invited to attend, together with several more of your brethren who have a foundation for their faith and are able to state it, if the Lord permits you. It has been announced to almost all the others through similar letters. There will probably be a large gathering, but do not let this deter you, for everything will be arranged without great commotion. May the Lord Jesus grant us His blessing thereunto.

From your poor and unworthy yet cordial friend and brother.

Henry Antes

Frederick Township in Philadelphia Co.
December 15, 1741.[38]

---

[38] Richard C. Wolf, *Documents of Lutheran Unity in America* (Philadelphia: Fortress Press, 1966), pp. 10–11. By permission.

The first meeting took place at the vacant house of Theobald Endt in Germantown and was followed by six other conferences held in different places near Philadelphia during the first six months of 1742. They hardly produced the unitive results Zinzendorf had hoped for since the participation at the later conferences consisted mainly of Moravians and Lutheran and Reformed sympathizers with Zinzendorf and his followers.[39] But while the direct results were negligible, the indirect result of this activity was the denominational organization of Pennsylvanian Protestantism. Especially the Lutheran churches of America may be indebted to Zinzendorf for the prompt arrival of Henry Melchior Mühlenberg in Pennsylvania.

For years Lutheran congregations in and around Philadelphia had unsuccessfully requested a pastor from Halle. Only when it became apparent that Zinzendorf was going to Pennsylvania to attempt his ecumenical experiments did the hitherto slow-moving wheels at the Pietist headquarters in Halle begin to turn with greater speed and brought Mühlenberg to America by October 2, 1742.

Mühlenberg had gone to Halle in 1738, where he met Professor Gotthilf August Francke (1696–1769), son of the famous August Hermann Francke (1663–1727), founder of the Halle institutions where Zinzendorf had received much of his education. The younger Francke, only four years older than Zinzendorf, had known and apparently disliked the count since their school years in Halle. The tension between the two had increased as the result of Zinzendorf's support of August Gottlieb Spangenberg, dismissed as superintendent of the Halle orphanage in 1733 because of his association with the Moravians. It was Spangenberg who eventually became one of the most influential Moravian leaders in America and Europe and one of Zinzendorf's closest collaborators. By the time Mühlenberg arrived in Halle the animosity towards Zinzendorf and his work was firmly established. Mühlenberg spent a year as an instructor in various educational institutions in Halle.[40] He was then urged by Francke to accept a call to the diaconate and inspectorship of an orphanage in Grosshennersdorf in Upper Lusatia under the patronage of Henrietta Baroness von Gersdorf, the aunt of Count Zinzendorf (July 1739). He accepted this position reluctantly since he had hoped to go as a missionary to India. But Zinzendorf's aunt was also one of the count's severest critics and Mühlenberg must have received a somewhat biased view of Zinzendorf and his work in Grosshennersdorf.

It was while on a visit to Halle on September 6, 1741, that Francke offered Mühlenberg the call to the Lutheran people in the province of Pennsylvania. It was hardly coincidental that Zinzendorf had left Marienborn on

---

39   Cf. John R. Weinlick, *Count Zinzendorf* (New York: Abingdon, 1956), pp. 158 ff.
40   William J. Mann, *The Life and Times of Henry Melchior Mühlenberg* (Philadelphia: G. W. Frederick, 1887), pp. 14 ff.

August 7, 1741, to begin his journey to America. All this prepared the way for a confrontation between Zinzendorf and Mühlenberg shortly before the count's return to Europe, which the latter reported in detail in his *Journal*.[41] This is how Mühlenberg described the encounter:

December 30, [1742], Thursday.
After dinner the Count sent word to me, politely requesting that I should visit him. I went, expecting to speak to the Count alone. When I arrived, however, there was in the room a large gathering of his generals and corporals, the Count presiding at a small table. This was the first time I ever saw the Count face to face and I expected to hear something great from the *Reformator Ecclesiae*. The Count asked me first about a number of circumstances with regard to Grosshennersdorf in Upper Lusatia. What I knew I answered. Then the following ensued:

Count: On what conditions are you here?
Reply: I have been called and sent through the Rev. Court Preacher Zigenhagen, who had a commission from the congregation.
C: What sort of commission did Mr. Zigenhagen have?
R: The three Lutheran congregations in New Hannover, Providence, and Philadelphia had been urgently requesting a pastor for several years past. The copies are deposited in Providence and the letters in London, which can be published at any time, if necessary.
C: When did the congregation last petition for a pastor?
R: I do not know; I must look it up in the copies.
C: You must say at once when they wrote the last letter to Mr. Zigenhagen.
    The brewer and several others of his people chimed in and said that the last letter may have reached there about 1739. I did not know, because nothing had been said to me about it.
    I replied: I really cannot say just now, and besides, it is of no importance, for I have been called, sent, and accepted. The deacons and elders of the three congregations have signed an acceptance.
C: Here in Philadelphia no deacons of the Lutheran congregation gave their signatures, for the deacons of the Lutheran congregation are sitting here, and there is no other Lutheran congregation and church here other than the one we have. Haven't you seen the church yet, which was just recently built?
R: I know nothing about it, because I am convinced that I preached to Lutheran people and was accepted by them.
C: They are not Lutherans, but rebels, brawlers; and you have become the head of such people and preached to them in the house from which they expelled my adjunct, Pirlaeus. The rebels must first come to us and apologize.
R: My dear Count, your people must first come and apologize to our Lutherans because they broke the lock off our church and started the tumult.
C: That is not true!
R: It is true to the extent that they are still involved in a lawsuit over it.
C: I know of no lawsuit.
R: Well, everybody knows what happened last summer, July 18.

---

41   Henry Melchior Mühlenberg, *The Journals of Henry Melchior Mühlenberg*, translated by T. G. Tappert and J. W. Doberstein, 3 vols. (Philadelphia: Mühlenberg Press, 1942), 1:76–80. By permission.

C: Let us stick to the subject. The last time I asked Mr. Zigenhagen how things stood as far as Pennsylvania was concerned, he replied that he could send no preacher there because the congregations were not willing to stipulate the salary. Now, since Mr. Zigenhagen knew that I had come in here, why did he send you afterwards?

R: I was sent to investigate conditions here and to see whether order cannot be established.

C: Mr. Zigenhagen is an archliar and hypocrite! When I am in his presence, he is meek and humble and submissive; when I am away from him, he inveighs and slanders. This is another spiteful trick which he and Mr. Franke are playing off on me! I shall tell him of it to his face when I get to London.

R: My dear Count, it is a shame to speak that way. I have often heard in Germany that you, yourself, were a liar. Am I not forced to believe it?

C: I have heard that you have read all my writings; did you not read that I have established a Lutheran consistory here in Philadelphia?

R: I read in Charlestown the printed reports of seven conferences, and through them learned that a certain Mr. von Thürnstein had caused disturbances in various places, but I did not know that the Count had established a Lutheran consistory.

C: These are jesuitical tricks.

R: I once heard in Germany that you were appointed a Moravian bishop by a Reformed preacher. How does that jibe with your being able to establish a Lutheran consistory?

C: I am inspector of all Lutheran churches in Pennsylvania and Lutheran pastor in Philadelphia. I have held synods in the country and here, also installed pastors in several places and even deposed a pastor named Stöver.

R: Can a Reformed preacher give such authority to you?

C: Don't you understand canonical law? Don't you know that in Wittenberg the foremost Lutheran theologian was ordained by a Catholic?

R: But how is it that sometimes you can be a Moravian bishop and sometimes an inspector and a Lutheran pastor?

C: I publicly resigned my episcopal office in Holland in the presence of lords and princes.

R: You change frequently.

C: I have been called as pastor in writing by the Lutheran congregation here in Philadelphia, and likewise my adjunct, Pirlaeus.

R: Is your call signed by anybody?

C: It doesn't need it.

R: My call has been signed and I shall trouble myself no further, but just follow the instructions of my superiors in Europe. If this does not please you, you can settle it with them.

C: But is it not contrary to all fairness and courtesy that after I have been so long in this country you should not have come to visit me? If you have been sent to investigate matters here, why did you not inquire into our affairs? When a person learns that there is a consistory and an inspector in a place, even granting that it is illegal, does not one first make inquiries there?

R: Even if I had desired to call on you as a stranger, you would not have been there in any event, for it was said that you were among the Indians. There are all kinds of sects here, and how is it possible for me to run around to all of them? I have enough to do with the Lutherans who have been assigned to me.

C: I am the Lutheran pastor. Why did you not come to me?

R: I had no orders to do so and still have none.

C: Did Mr. Zigenhagen say that you should pass me by?

R: When I was called, I inquired as to how I should conduct myself with regard to the Count and the reply was made that I should have no fear of the Count.

C: Did Mr. Zigenhagen say that you should pass by the inspector and Lutheran pastor?
R: No.
C: Now just see, my brethren, how this man contradicts himself and lies, since he replies both yes and no to the same question.
R: Not so, Confrater. Mr. Zigenhagen knew well enough that Count Zinzendorf had gone to Pennsylvania, but he did not know that the Count wanted to be an inspector and Lutheran pastor.
C: Did you not know that I was inspector and pastor?
R: I already knew in Germany that you went to Pennsylvania and intended . . .
C: What did I intend?
R: Yes, you intended.
C: Just speak out: What did I intend?
R: I do not know. You yourself said at the conclusion of the reply to Adam Gross's publication, 'Brethren, I am now going to Pennsylvania; pray the Saviour to reveal to you what I intend!' So who knows what you intended?
C: As soon as I get to London, I will go to the archbishop and tell him that I established order among the Lutherans here, but that as soon as order was established, Mr. Zigenhagen sent a man who spoiled it all again and brought confusion.
R: You may say what you wish, I shall not concern myself with it. Now you have put everything in confusion and I hope, by God's grace, to establish some order.
C: Go ahead and do it. If you accomplish anything, it will only serve to increase my church. You have my good wishes. It cannot be denied that you were a Lutheran student in good standing, that you had a pastoral charge, as was reported to me nine months ago from Herrnhut. You have nothing more to do than apologize here, since you made an intrusion here and passed me by.
R: Count, the time will come when you will have to beg the pardon of the whole Lutheran Church.
C: What is he saying? He is a young parson, a village pastor!
R: You must not become excited, Count.
C: Make haste to consider and acknowledge that you have done wrong, otherwise I will make the whole thing *public* when I return to Germany.
R: When I do wrong before God I pray for forgiveness, but I owe you no apology in this affair. You may publish in Germany what you please; if you touch me, I shall answer you with the truth. Your affairs are well enough known in Germany.
C: The things published against me are nothing but pasquils to which no one will venture to put his name. I am willing to grant you time to reflect and beg my pardon; it merely comes down to a *point d'honneur* and you should not let that sway you.
R: You certainly are full of suggestions; in fact, you are just what your aunt told me you were.
C: Hold your tongue as far as my aunt is concerned, or I shall be compelled to expose her. I could speak quite differently to you if you want me to.
R: Go ahead, speak.
C: Were you not reared at Halle?
R: No, I was reared in the province of Hannover, completed my studies at Göttingen, and was also at Halle.
C: The Hallensians are Pietists; aren't you a Hallensian?
R: I am a Lutheran and shall remain so.
C: Are you such a Lutheran as Mr. Zigenhagen is?
R: I was with Mr. Zigenhagen for some time and learned to know his character.

I am and hope to become, more and more, such a Lutheran as Mr. Zigenhagen is.

C: Before the year is out, I shall bring forward more than a hundred witnesses to prove that Mr. Zigenhagen is not a genuine Lutheran.

R: Mr. Zigenhagen is certainly not afraid and is not likely to be. I am surprised, my dear Count, at the way you cavil at me with your questions and try to hook something on me!

C: Yes, I am casting a hook into his conscience.

R: Oh, no; you do not touch my conscience, but I gather enough from your questions to know that your heart is not right. If you had a heart or spirit without guile, you would not ask such questions.

C: You came here to speak to me about a church book and a cup?

R: Yes; I wanted to ask you whether you would return them or not.

C: What should we return? They belong to our Lutheran church and congregation. However, if you are so much in want that you need the book and the cup, we will present them to you, provided you sign a receipt which we will make out for you.

R: I desire no present from you. I only claim what belongs to us, since the cup and also the book were paid for out of our collections. (Here I stood up.)

C: Consider well the matter of apologizing; otherwise you will regret it.

R: I need no consideration, for I do not acknowledge you as a genuine Lutheran, much less as an inspector and Lutheran pastor.

C: Do you hear that? Now it is clear what the man has in his heart. (The brethren and toadies of the Count assented to everything by nodding their heads and marveled at the Count's ravings as though they were divinely inspired.)

R: It has also become quite apparent what you have in your heart. If you are such a genuine Lutheran, why would they not let you preach in the Swedish church?

C: That was prevented by only one man, the Swedish merchant, Koch.

R: Mr. Koch is a deacon of the Swedish church and he certainly would not have prevented you without the knowledge of the Swedish minister, Mr. Tranberg.

C: Can you say that Mr. Tranberg refused me?

R: I cannot say it positively. Enough, you were refused.

C: There you see, brethren, the man contradicts himself and lies. (Because of the noisy assent of the brethren I was unable to reply. The Count further asserted that I would not preach in the Swedish church more than two or three times before they threw me out just as they had thrown out his adjunct from the old church.)

R: I am willing to wait and see. I have nothing further to say except to wish you a happy voyage. Good-by!

While this account represents clearly Mühlenberg's point of view, the discussion also shows that Zinzendorf was convinced that his trip to Pennsylvania had forced Halle to send Mühlenberg. This is even more plausible in view of a letter which Francke had written to F. M. Zigenhagen, German court-preacher in London and an ardent supporter of the missionary efforts of Halle. Under the dateline March 14, 1736, he wrote:

As to the congregation at Philadelphia, I wish most sincerely that wholesome counsel may be given them; but as their condition has been represented to me,

I could not encourage and advise any good man to go and labor among them; for I cannot, at present, see how he could be sustained. . . . A short time ago Count Zinzendorf with his lady, his oldest son and several servants, went to Holland. Whether his purpose is to return hither or go to West India, remains to be seen.[42]

Francke apparently changed his mind when he learned that Zinzendorf was about to venture forth to Pennsylvania. Thus, paradoxically, the establishment of a Lutheran denominational organization under Mühlenberg's leadership in America, the Ministerium of Pennsylvania and Adjacent States, was indirectly the result of Zinzendorf's futile pan-denominational efforts.

A few days after the above described confrontation, which cast a shadow over his last days in America, Zinzendorf was ready to leave for Europe. He summarized his reactions to his American experience in a speech before the men and women he left behind in Pennsylvania.[43] He considered this address his "Last Will and Testament" for the people in America.[44] It does show the impressions that this journey had made on him and reveals a certain sense of frustration. Everything would have gone better, he says, if Spangenberg had been along to take care of the situation in Pennsylvania and thus left him free to concern himself with the American situation as a whole. He saw the failure of the European churches as well as those in America as being caused by their emphasis on the attainment of some human perfection rather than trust in God's grace and summarized: "Briefly, the Saviour has set my heart in such a way that I realized that I shall be and always remain a sinner. And when eternity dawns I know for sure I shall not be able to change this situation. I will have to come in the shape of a sinner, in the poverty of a sinner, in the shame of a sinner and shall never attain the status of those people who speak of the blessed eternity of perfection. . . . I am convinced, I shall live and die in this knowledge that in time and eternity our cause is nothing but grace."[45] He continued later, that two truths had become very clear to him on this journey. First, America had to be steeped in the blood of Jesus, just like Europe and, secondly, America must be dealt with differently than Europe. Indeed, those who want to treat the situations in these two worlds in an identical manner will spoil everything in the Saviour's cause.[46] "Therefore," he explained, "I was afraid that if I came to America as a Moravian bishop, then my brothers in America and many others might get the idea that it is the plan

---

42 C. W. Schaeffer, trans., *Reports of the United Evangelical Lutheran Congregation in North America, Specially in Pennsylvania*, preface by John Ludwig Schulze (Reading, Penn.: Pilger Book Store, 1882), 1:92 f.
43 Zinzendorf, *Ergänzungsbände zu den Hauptschriften*, 9:188 ff.
44 Zinzendorf, 9:189.
45 Zinzendorf, 9:198.
46 Zinzendorf, 9:200.

of the Saviour even here that His cause should be carried forth under the banner of the Moravian Church. But in America, and especially in Pennsylvania, freedom of conscience prevails, but if there is such freedom the Saviour does not need such a visible house. He can get through everywhere with the stone without hands. He can make room everywhere. Indeed, a witness of Jesus who belongs to none of your denominations is more apt to spread the kingdom of Jesus in this country than one who is associated with a denomination."[47] But why then did he come as a Lutheran pastor? Because he felt that the various Christian denominations had become idols (*Götzen*) in Europe but they were mud in the street (*Koth auf der Gassen*) in America.[48] Thus he felt, Zinzendorf continued, that it was his duty to demonstrate that one could be brought to the Lamb of God within the particular denomination to which one happened to belong. Since he was a Lutheran, and since the Lutherans needed help, he tried to demonstrate the possibility of working through existing denominations by concentrating his efforts on the Lutherans.[49] "If there are only faithful people in every denomination, doing their work honestly and without secret designs to overthrow or undermine religion, it is certain that it is the Saviour's plan to win many souls through the preaching along denominational lines [*Religions-Predigt*], which others might call sectarian."[50] Whether in the long run, the denominational pattern will prove appropriate to America, Zinzendorf concluded, time alone will tell.[51]

Thus it appears that Zinzendorf was willing to let the denominational approach of which Mühlenberg was an outstanding representative, have its day. His objection to Mühlenberg was more procedural than substantial. Indeed, he suggested to his followers that if the people from Halle should start institutions for the education of children, as he confidently expected, they should be encouraged and competition should be avoided. For, "When it comes to teaching, you can learn as much from the Halle people in eight weeks as from us in a year. I am myself a child of Halle."[52]

Zinzendorf's major contribution to religion in America was that he served as a catalyst. Opposition to him helped precipitate the culture-language denominationalism which dominated the American development for the next two centuries.

Quite apart from his importance in the history of religious thought, his influence on Schleiermacher and the resulting trend in theology, Zinzendorf's

---

47 Zinzendorf, 9:208, 209.
48 Zinzendorf, 9:210.
49 Zinzendorf, 9:213.
50 Zinzendorf, 9:215.
51 Zinzendorf, 9:216.
52 Zinzendorf, 9:241.

influence on Wesley and his importance for the developments in America are reasons enough why the English-speaking world should be given access to some of his writings. But in view of the vast amount of material available, the question arose which of his many works filling sixteen volumes in the Beyreuther-Meyer edition should be translated in order to introduce an English-speaking audience to Zinzendorf's thought. The so-called London Lectures which follow were in Zinzendorf's own judgment the way he wanted to present his theology to the people of London and the English-speaking world.

Zinzendorf had come to England in 1746 in order to clarify the position of the renewed Moravian Church in relation to the Church of England.[53] It is clear that he did not consider his Moravians a new denomination in addition to Anglicans, Lutherans, and Reformed Christians. He wanted them rather to be a leaven in the dough of the established churches. This had been his approach on the continent. He was convinced that a person did not have to cease being an Old Moravian, a Lutheran or a member of the Reformed Church, in order to be a member of the *Brüdergemeine*, the Community of Brethren. More correctly he was persuaded that participation in the new brotherhood would make one a better member of one's native or traditional denomination. In Germany he had appointed *Brüdergemeine* bishops for each of these traditional denominations. He himself had accepted this responsibility for the Lutherans (after the Reverend George John Conradi of Schleswig-Holstein had refused the honor). Now he hoped to proceed in the same manner in England and relate the Community of Brethren closely to the Church of England. He expected to find some Anglican bishop who would be willing to serve as superintendent of the Anglican version of the *Brüdergemeine*.

The recognition by the Church of England was especially important since the Moravian missionaries in the New World had been classified by the New York assembly in 1744 with "vagrant preachers" and "disguised Papists" who should not be allowed to work among the Indians unless they were prepared to swear an oath of allegiance and abjuration. It was the result of Zinzendorf's activities in England in 1746, of which the London Lectures are a significant part, that Parliament passed an act on December 27, 1747, amending the naturalization act of 1740 by extending to all foreign Protestants in the British colonies those exceptions granted earlier only to Quakers in Pennsylvania.

It is against this background that the London Lectures were presented at Fetter Lane Chapel between August 28 and October 16, 1746. August Gottlieb Spangenberg (1704–92) the distinguished bishop of the Moravian Church and biographer of Zinzendorf, commented somewhat opaquely on

---

53 To the following compare Weinlick, *Count Zinzendorf*, pp. 190–93.

these lectures when he wrote: "Some of his [Zinzendorf's] London sermons were printed with the title 'Nine Public Lectures on Important Subjects in Religion.' They are conspicuous because of paradox propositions and unfamiliar expressions, indeed, even through their content. For example, the claim that the Lord's Prayer should only be used by God's children and the assertion that it is a blessing and great fortune to be a human soul etc. Nevertheless one can find in these lectures much that is beautiful and edifying."[54] This observation indicates that even sympathetic contemporaries felt that these lectures deviated from the conventional theology and piety of the time. It is for this reason that they give us an insight into some of the original theological ideas of Zinzendorf as expressed during the most fertile period of his life, the so-called *Sichtungszeit* or "Sifting Period" (1743–50). This particular period has been generally embarrassing even to Zinzendorf's admirers[55] and the object of vicious attacks by his enemies who called him "the ape of Mohammed" and a veritable Anti-Christ. They claimed that "Mohammed in order to gain favor with the male sex permitted polygamy. Zinzendorf in order to obligate not only men but also women permitted every form of lewdness especially to the brothers and sisters closest to him and used such lascivious words in his hymns that they may not be read or quoted here without giving offense."[56] The London Lectures fall into the middle of this period which to both friend and foe was the most controversial of Zinzendorf's life.

The translation which follows is based on the text in Volume VI of the Olms edition of the *Hauptschriften* edited by Erich Beyreuther and Gerhard Meyer (pp. 1–186). Biblical references in parentheses in the text are mine. (RSV-Revised Standard Edition; LT-Luther Translation.) The scripture quotations were generally identified by the editor, since Zinzendorf usually quoted from memory. In the preparation of these pages, I have been helped by many people. Special thanks are due to Dr. Elizabeth Bettenhausen who helped in preparing the translation, to Carol Hines who typed the manuscript, and to Mary Forell Davis who encouraged me by sharing my fascination with Nicholaus Ludwig Count von Zinzendorf, the noble "Jesus freak."

George Wolfgang Forell
Iowa City, Iowa

---

54 A. G. Spangenberg, *Leben des Herrn, Ludwig Grafen und Herrn von Zinzendorf und Pottendorf*, 8 vols. (Barby: Herrnhut, Verlag der Brüdergemeine, 1772–74), 6:1672 ff. (1774).
55 Cf. "Costly Enthusiasm" chapter in Weinlick, *Count Zinzendorf*, pp. 198–206.
56 Johann Leonhard Fröreisen, *Vergleichung des Graf Zinzendorfs mit dem Mahomet* (Frankfurt and Leipzig, 1748), p. 15.

Author's Preface

I KNOW the spirit of our present era of the Church. The Word of the Cross has become for many the power of God, and the agonies of God their Mediator are for the brothers and sisters of the English nation a blessing which completely enraptures their hearts. And in view of certain extravagances with respect to religion, these agonies become a blessed preservation or a thorough cure. This I can testify of them.

Recently, more than fifty of the brethren, clergy and laymen, took the trouble to travel to Germany in the middle of winter, and after residing with us for three months they returned with hearts blessedly happy and united.[1] They have convinced me.

I think as a result they will now read these lectures much more easily than when they heard them before. May He, of Whom they speak, bless the English readers as well as my own countrymen.

In the first lecture I have told them that, according to my study of the Scriptures, much nonsense troubles religion. The seemingly trifling matter of battology[2] in the holy prayer-form, which is on everybody's lips,[3] is a clear proof that the advantage of the pardoned children of God over the wholly natural and dead people must still not be understood at all (even though all the creeds of the so-called Christians[4] are full of it). I have pointed out who those people are who can say, "Abba, Father," those namely, whom the Holy Spirit Himself led in praying the seven petitions.

In the second lecture, I have explained the basic meaning and purpose of this prayer and what a treasure of material these few lines contain. The English have a special interest in the text of the Lord's Prayer, for a Pope

---

1   In A. G. Spangenberg's *Leben des Herrn Ludwig Grafen und Herrn von Zinzendorf und Pottendorf*, 8 vols. (Barby: Herrnhut, Verlag der Brüdergemeine, 1772–74), 6:1663 (1774), we read "some Englishmen decided to visit the German *Brüdergemeinen* and actually accomplished this purpose." Earlier (p. 1661 f.) Spangenberg had claimed: "Many Englishmen had learned the German language for the reason given was to understand better the Count's lectures and writings." For John Wesley's earlier journey see the Introduction to this translation.
2   Battology: Excessive and wearisome repetition of words in speaking or writing.
3   The Lord's Prayer.
4   Zinzendorf uses the term *Christianer* for Christians in name only.

of their own nation once sent them the finest version of this prayer ever seen.

In the third lecture, I have said that the preaching of the Gospel is not necessary, properly speaking, for the sake of the elect bride of Jesus Christ and of those who belong to her. Rather, the preaching is necessary for those whom we are to regard as guests and who, without such a call, either would not think of any marriage of the Lamb or would certainly not guess by themselves that they were also invited to it as guests. And this is an idea which brings to its full light the difference (looked upon as essential by Dr. Luther[5]) between the homilies addressed to a church of Jesus and the sermons to the multitude in general.

In the fourth, I have described the saving faith of the human soul and that this may certainly be understood under the general heading of love, may even be perceived as a property of a heart in love with the object of faith.

In the fifth, I have spoken of the main point which makes a believer blessedly happy [selig].

In the sixth it is clearly proved that being a human soul is in and of itself a blessing for which one can never thank his Creator enough.

The seventh gives the essentials of a Christian inwardly and outwardly.

The eighth, that it is true *in sano sensu* that from the human side nothing more is required for salvation than an upright heart.

The ninth concludes with a frank confession that the object of their faith, although invisible, is nevertheless, in the most real sense, nearer to Christians than the shirt on their backs.

If one or another reader should wonder at the newness of the expressions and at the candid utterance of such paradoxes (as a certain eminent prelate said concerning one such production of our church, that he did not find an error anywhere, but he did find nothing but new and unexpected things and a series of truths which he had never come across before in any book in his whole life), then I would not have much really to suggest in return and would only have to be sorry that I cannot send such a person my glasses, through which I see when I speak. But the Holy Spirit sells the same thing free of charge, and because I can guarantee this to every well-meaning reader, I will exempt him only from the preparation necessary for it, which is God's work alone, and with that heartily recommend my readers to my and their Saviour.

---

5 Zinzendorf refers to Luther as Dr. Luther Sel. ("blessed Dr. Luther"), a manner of speaking made popular by orthodoxy.

Lecture I

That the Prayer to the Father of Jesus Christ can be Prayed by No One but Children of God

Preached in the Brethren's Chapel in London, August 28, 1746

TEXT: John 17:25. *"O righteous Father, the world has not known thee, but I have known thee; and these know that thou hast sent me."* (RSV)

WHAT INFLUENCE toleration of various religious denominations has on political government and the degree to which all sorts of opinions can, according to this idea, be permitted is a matter completely foreign to what I have to say now and one which I do not fully understand. But whoever is not tolerant in his heart, whoever is fond of forcing other people to accept his own notions and modes of worship, whoever is eager only to bring other people over to his manner of worship if it does not cost much — this person thereby shows that he is not a wise child of God and does not possess the right spiritual understanding.

So long as they stay away from Him and have nothing to do with Him respecting spiritual matters, the freedom which God allows mankind is great. Not only in former times did He allow many nations to go their own ways and overlooked them with inexpressible patience. Our own days teach us, the example of the times in which we live shows us, that the object of His judgments is really not at all the actions and demeanour of men in themselves and in so far as they affect their own persons. No one is more tolerant, more patient with the whole world, its ideas and their execution, than the Creator Himself, who made it. Any man who has learned to know

Him will show that the more closely he knows Him, the more tolerant will be his disposition.

But as soon as someone starts to have something to do with God, comes near to Him in any way, performs divine worship to Him or someone else, so that He becomes necessarily involved, then it puts matters immediately upon quite another footing; then God immediately proceeds in a different manner: then He begins to be serious.

Not to know Him is a misfortune; but to make use of His name and yet not know Him is forbidden as it is said in the Second Commandment:[1] "You shall not take the name of the Lord your God in vain; for the Lord will not hold him guiltless who takes his name in vain" (Exod. 20:7). The man who does this appeals to Him without having the right to do it. Death was incurred by a prophet of the Old Testament who passed himself off falsely for a servant of God. For as long and as far as a person pretends to have to do with God (under ordinary circumstances, for there are occasions when one is in great affliction, and then God does not deny Himself to His creature), and is in the constant habit of dealing with Him, appeals to Him, yet does not know Him, such a person becomes guilty in the sight of God and has reason to fear the judgment of the Law, the divine regulation which is provided against such an illegal worship, which is nothing but impudence and insolence.

Now I gladly admit that, on the one hand, I believe that a person who forces and compels, or even thoughtlessly persuades other people to his own [religious] ideas is not an intelligent child of God; for this is putting one out of the state of innocence, where he is tolerated, and bringing him into the danger of a divine judgment. But, on the other hand, I believe that the procedure which obliges people for political reasons to serve God in this or the other way and which prevails in most countries of the world (excepting only a few happy ones where it is different)[2] causes many people to find mercy with God. It is the law that compels people in many places to go to the Lord's Supper, if they want to remain in the republic, or to join in this or that ceremony of divine worship, if they want to keep their privileges as citizens. This situation extenuates their guilt considerably in the faithful and merciful heart of God. He knows that it is not a matter of their choice or election. Perhaps they would not of themselves be so presumptuous. They probably would have been afraid or would have waited until they themselves had had feeling and insight. But they are compelled to such worship. Indeed, they lack strength, grace and courage to admit

---

1 Zinzendorf uses the division of the Ten Commandments customary among Roman Catholics and Lutherans.
2 Zinzendorf has been impressed by the religious tolerance which he first observed while traveling as a law student in Holland in 1719 and later in Pennsylvania.

their error and inability, to expose themselves to worldly danger out of honesty in divine things; but God does not really demand this of them.

This, my dear friends, is the reason why the judgment of God, before which unbelief (that is, when people refuse and oppose themselves to that which comes before the heart) actually is condemned, is not extended over the whole world. God knows best in what an astounding confusion the state of religion is in the whole world; He knows that a heathen, when he is convinced of everything else, must still be convinced that he will be considered an honest man among his own people when he adheres to the one true God, whose so-called people by their behaviour make themselves intolerable even to the savages. Not only in Christendom is this the case, but throughout the world. Religion is made a point of honor; for people must always first look around to see what their neighbors have to say concerning that which their heart and mind and their own corruption put in the way of salvation. Though no one gladly puts his worldly affairs into strange hands, people seem under a compulsion to give their spiritual affairs into the hands of their neighbors, even if the state gave them the freedom to act as they think.

A person who is concerned with the salvation of his fellowmen must sweeten for them, as much as he can, the universal misery, the universal bitterness. He must be concerned not to become another tyrant of the human race. For the mind of Christ, who came not to condemn but to redeem and save, ought to show itself in all his words and actions.

This gives a certain society[3] in the Protestant[4] religion (which has been known for some years and need not be named, for more than too much has been spoken about it) occasion to be more sparing in certain religious usages, indeed sometimes not to use them at all, not because they reject these religious acts in themselves, but rather because their use would not be fitting for everybody.

To this belongs the scrupulosity with which I have long been burdened, namely, why I seldom pray the Lord's Prayer in public gatherings. I do use it in those places where I know that the omission would do more harm to the minds of men and when I do not know how to explain myself to them; but I omit it in all those places where it is up to me. The reason is this: the listeners are so apt to join in the prayer, and at the same time they all have the idea that the prayer is directed to the first person in the Godhead; and yet the Saviour has declared in the most positive and preemptory manner that no one can invoke His Father but the children of God. Thus, whoever prays the Lord's Prayer and is not a child of God, takes

---

3 *Societät:* The reference appears to be to his own "Society of Brethren," which he conceived as an *ecclesiola in ecclesia*, a little church within the Church.

4 Zinzendorf speaks of the *Evangelische Religion*.

the name of the Lord his God in vain and incurs the judgment of the Second Commandment. The Saviour has declared that He did not disclose His Father's name to anyone but His brethren, who have first been begotten by His Father, born of the Holy Spirit, and afterwards consigned to Him as first fruits. To them He spoke privately about it. For when the disciples came and said, "Lord, teach us to pray" (Luke 11:1), then He answered, in opposition to John's disciples, "You shall say, 'Our Father who art in heaven, Hallowed be thy name. Thy kingdom come,' " etc. (Matt. 6:9–10).

This makes the Lord's Prayer one of the most serious parts of religion, a strict *common-prayer*,[5] a true church-prayer. To be permitted to pray it is one of the greatest gifts of grace, a privilege which one first obtains through the deep fundamental solidity of his own salvation, through one's everlasting pardoning, through the eternal absolution of all sins. The first thing that a person who knows that from the moment he leaves time he goes up to heaven, who knows that his soul goes directly into the Saviour's arms — the first thing that such a person can then do to evidence his joy and thankfulness and his claim is to pray the prayer to the Father which Jesus taught His disciples.

These are indeed things which we must consider awhile before we speak of them. We hesitate before saying things which everyone should have known. At the same time we fear that the general notions which have been instilled from infancy may often so obstruct the minds and understandings of men that they still do not comprehend their truth, simplicity, and infallibility. Now it is undeniable that when a person comes to hear the Gospel, the Word of God, he is never to be excluded. Everyone may come; for either he will hear nothing, or, if he does hear, then there is certainly a call of the Lord in his heart, and a beginning of salvation is already present. He cannot from his heart say yes to what he hears without being saved. But to use a liturgy, to use a *common-prayer*,[6] to join together in prayer, to praise and adore Him whom we regard as our common Lord and God — this is a matter which neither the hearers, if they have no right to it, dare presume to do, nor which teachers, if they have the power to act according to their knowledge, ought to encourage.

It is true that we are all brothers; one God made us all, and we all have one plan, one purpose. This is the meaning and purpose of creation, for we all have one Creator who acknowledges that He is the rightful Husband of the most miserable and pitiful creature, of even the most detestible prostitute.[7] This is an astonishing, incomprehensible, and heart-stirring truth: He makes no distinctions; all souls are His. But as, on the one hand, He

---

5 Zinzendorf uses the English word here.
6 Zinzendorf uses the English word again, referring to the Anglican liturgy.
7 Zinzendorf uses the term *Lazareth-Hure*, a prostitute who plied her trade in a hospital.

acknowledges all souls, so that the most miserable sinner may think, my Saviour is, in spite of everything, my Husband; He is, in spite of everything my Creator; "your Maker is your Husband" (Isa. 54:5); so again, on the other hand, it is a horrible impudence to go farther than the bounds that are set us.

Is it not enough for us to call Him our Creator and Husband? Is it not enough that a soul in the most perplexed and intricate circumstances, most entangled in the snares of Satan, can think in a happy hour, I am, however, created for Him; I am a soul, a creature; therefore I belong to the Creator; He is my husband; is not this enough? Must we enter into the deep mysteries of God and venture to utter mysteries with an unwashed mouth, to think mysteries with a mind not sprinkled with blood, to demonstrate mysteries with a raw, unprepared head? And yet this is the common practice.

Where is there more prating about the mystery of the Trinity than in the schools, by men who do not love their Saviour? Where is the Father of our Lord Jesus Christ spoken of more than among dead people who have no sense of feeling in their hearts for the blood of Jesus? This is 'as clear as day.' Who gave them the commission to talk at random among the so-called Christians concerning the Trinity, concerning the Father, concerning the Holy Spirit, etc.? For they have not yet experienced the Saviour and His blood, the guarantee of their inheritance, the point of their redemption, the substance and means of their reconciliation with God. Yet we cannot have the joyful confidence, the courage to cry, "Abba! Father!" (Gal. 4:6) until the Holy Spirit has cried it in our hearts. The cantor in the church cannot make us sing it, nor the minister in the pulpit make us pray it; rather, it is the Holy Spirit. The Bible assures us that He must do it; He cries in the heart, "Abba! dear Father!" then it will do. "Because you are children, God has sent the Spirit of His Son into your hearts" (Gal. 4:6, LT).

Thus we seek to point all those persons without distinction who dare not freely confess that they have experienced the power of the death of Jesus in their hearts, that they are cleansed from all sins through the merit of His blood, that they stand before Him bathed clean in the bloody grace and go their entire course with the seal of grace upon their foreheads — these people, I say, we seek to point to the one God, the Creator of all the world, who is God over all, praised for evermore, concerning whom John says, "Little children, keep yourselves from idols (I John 5:21); the Son who was sent in the flesh, He is the true God" (I John 5:21, alt.). On the other hand, the Saviour says, "Father, whoever has happiness to know Thy Son, to know that man whom Thou hast yielded up to the world, that person can say to Jesus, 'My bone! I am flesh of His flesh and bone of His bone; I am called Christian because I am taken out of Christ, because I belong to Christ, because I am one spirit with Him'; afterwards he can also say,

'You are my God, Father! You are my God! God of the Communion of Saints,[8] You are my God.' " And when one can do this, he is a blessedly happy man; he lives already in heaven, and his happiness is eternal, for he need no longer be anxious; he need not think of death any longer for he can die no more; but he passes out of temporal death into the living land of eternity, directly into his Husband's heart, towards that sign which on the last day will be the sign of the Man who created, lost and won the world again with His blood.

My friends, how gladly one would wish this for all, how earnestly one would wish that all might learn to honor the Son, that the Father might be honored in the Son:

> The Father on the Father's throne;
> His true Son, His very own;
> Glad Comforter, the Spirit alone:
> Honor to the Lamb to all is shown.

This is the *Enchiridion*, this is the little catechism, the short compendium of theology of which Paul writes in his Letters to the Ephesians and Colossians. Thus the ancients said, *Si Christum discis, nihil est, si cetera nescis;* i.e., if you know the Saviour, if you study Him, it does not matter if you are ignorant of all other things. This is an old saying; we have not invented it in our time, but rather the ancients said it. Why? They had read John: "He who has the Son of God has life; he who does not have the Son does not have life, but the wrath of God rests upon him" (John 3:36, alt); and Paul: "As long as we had no Saviour, we were atheists in this world" (Eph. 2:12, alt.), as John in his first letter also says, "He who does not have the Son has no God" (I John 5:12, alt.).

Therefore, my friends, let all other things be set aside; let us push the whole body of theology into a drawer to be taken out again at the proper time, until we have learned

> The blest Creator of all creation
> Assumed a servant's low condition,
> To win the flesh and blood again,
> He employs human flesh and blood, so men,
> His creatures, not bring all to ruin.

This is an old Catholic hymn, which Dr. Luther has translated into German because it is such a dear truth and because he believed from his heart that Jesus Christ is His Creator.

---

8 The word is *Gemeine*.

> In a manger He was laid,
> Into a manger He was placed,
> He for whom the world was too small
> Lies in a crib not noticed at all.
> O Lord! You Creator of earth and space,
> How have You come to be born so base
> That you lie there on withered grass.
> You came to me, into suffering here:
> How can I thank you for something so dear?

Thus it is. The Creator of the world Himself, the inventor of creation, of the whole universe, He has invented an eternal redemption; for so it is said in express words. It is commonly represented as if the Father had invented the work of redemption and then ordered His Son to go into the world to ransom it; but this is not scriptural. Jesus Christ invented eternal redemption; He is the inventor of it (Heb. 9:14). "No one," He says, "takes my life from me, but that is in my power to do as I will (John 10:18, alt.). If I even now while I stand here and they are going to apprehend me and put me in chains, wanted to say, as in Genesis 6, 'I repent this'; I will let mankind perish; they will not thank me for it: I will not atone for them — what do you think would be the issue of this? Twelve legions of angels, who would turn everything in Jerusalem upside down and accompany me to heaven. Do you think that if I even now chose not to suffer and rather resolved to let the world go to ruin, that my Father would not immediately second me? But I know what I want."

And thus it was. The Saviour never prayed that the cross and suffering might be dispensed with; He never said, "Father! If you will, do not let me suffer"; but rather, "Father! If you will, put an end to this present penance-agony on the Mount of Olives; let these pains of hell which force bloody sweat out of my body cease; it is an insufferable thing.

> How greatly man incenses
> The Lord with his offenses,
> How red His anger glows.
> How rigorous He chastises,
> When He with wrath baptizes,
> Our Saviour's suffering fully shows.

But that was only one hour, a heavy and sorrowful hour, an hour full of anguish, a power of darkness, a penitential conflict and agony for the world which ended with the eternal and plenary absolution for all human creatures; for He was absolved through the Spirit (I Tim. 3:16).

Thus the grievous suffering and death of Jesus Christ are an invention of Jesus Christ. "I will die; I will gain my creature again; that which I have created for the joy of my Father, which I have made for my Father, which I have produced by the breath of my mouth: that I will rescue and restore; I will draw out its poison and bring it out of the abyss of its corruption; and though it were cast out to the ends of the universe, yet I will bring it into the arms of my Father again and say, 'Here am I and my child, that which I have made, my creature.' Just as a prince marches at the head of the victorious army with his spontoon and salutes his father, so the Creator, together with His saved creature, will greet His Father, and all the world will be obliged to confess that He has conquered." When John proceeds to weep over the confusion of the world and complains and laments in a deep melancholy, a messenger of God says to him, "Do not weep; your Lord will be victorious; He will have the last word; He will carry out what He has begun; He will not make much ado about it, but He will gain His cause" (expansion on Rev. 5:5).

These are all biblical words, truths of Scripture, things which we experience as true as soon as we become sinners, as soon as we throw ourselves at the pierced feet of our Creator and beg for grace. For the first thing is that the Lord Jesus becomes for us God, Creator, Redeemer, Sanctifier, and every good thing that can be expected in time and eternity. Later, He says, "I will reveal also this to you, that I have a Father, and my Father is your Father, that my spirit is your spirit, that my angels are your angels, that all that is mine is yours; for I am glorified in you; I have made you as majestic, as glorious, as divine as I am; I have made you a partaker of my nature" (based on John 14).

Therefore the purpose of this sermon and my request is that the Lord's Prayer may not be thoughtlessly babbled, lest the name of God be taken in vain and men fall under the penalty of the law. Rather let us fall at the feet of the God whom I preach, Jesus Christ, who has delivered us from the wrath to come, and to take this invaluable grace in the right order, to be permitted to say, "Abba!" with Jesus Christ, and, when Jesus Christ accosts His own Father as His God (that in all things He may be like His brethren, His flesh and bone), then with Him to join in chorus and say, "Eli! Eli!" — what a salutation this is! This is eternal life.

PRAYER

Faithful and gracious Father! True Father of your children, true God of your hearts, who are one spirit and one body with Jesus your Son, who lie with Him in His human nature at your feet, for you are His God with us! Be pleased to take into your care His congregation, the souls upon the whole face of the earth whom your child Jesus shall deliver to you; bless them and bring them through the many heavy circumstances which they experience throughout all the world, to your praise. But be pleased also to place a special blessing upon those under whom your people lead a peaceful and quiet life; and thus especially, as the God of blessing, keep your hand over King George the Second, our dear King, and over all who are in office under him and are preservers of the happy constitution of this realm. Let him feel that he has children of God in his realm and that he allows them to live peacefully under him. Let this land, whose laws tolerate your people, experience that its laws are wise laws in regard to the best part. Let the victory, protection, and assistance which your servants have in you come over them too.

Among us keep all hearts in respect, veneration, moderation, and childlike love to this present government, that it may be felt on which side your divine will is.

You, who make kings and hold the regents of the world in your hand, You, before whom all nations are as a drop in the bucket, be gracious to us and our fellow citizens in these lands. May there still be thousands of them who, in the plan and way assigned them and in the orders into which you have called them, without leaving their way of worship and forming a new church for themselves, prove their identity as inward men of God, as members of your invisible and true body before all people, for your own sake. Amen.

Lecture II

Concerning the Simple Meaning and the Great Idea of the Lord's Prayer

Preached in the Brethren's Chapel in London, September 4, 1746

TEXT: Matthew 6:9–13. *"You shall pray like this: Our Father, which art in heaven! Oh, that your name might be reverenced. Oh, that your kingdom were here. Oh, that your will were done on earth as it is done in heaven. Give us today also our essential bread. And remit our debts, as we remit those of our debtors. And do not allow us to fall into temptation; but deliver us from evil."* (ALTERED)

DEAR HEARTS! To join together in one form and liturgy, to say the same words with two different hearts, to profess something of which one has no inner conviction, or to hear various truths which one has not yet attained — this is not a matter of small consequence.

It is sometimes the practice to proclaim truths because we know that they of themselves awake a yearning, a longing, an eager desire in the soul to partake of them and their blessedness; and, for this reason, when the Saviour told things to the disciples which concerned no one but them, He very often allowed all men to listen.

I do not need to prove this with many arguments; I would point out only the 5th, 6th, and 7th chapters of Matthew, which are, according to all men's ideas, a sermon full of paradoxes from the first line to the last. In it there are things which are so impracticable in a well-ordered commonwealth that even true children of God, as things now stand, cannot be governed by them.

II

I will only cite the sentence, "You shall not resist one that is evil" (Matt. 5:39). Were this to be generally accepted and introduced into political life, then one would have to expect a general overthrow of the entire human race; no order in the world, no government, etc., could last any longer, and no man would be secure in the possession of his property. This is the reason why well-disposed minds who do not have their thoughts particularly ordered, do not have a whole heart, yet want to meddle with the Saviour's matters, have hit upon such extremes that they have rejected all kinds of defense of a country, all legal procedures, and other systems of government. They speak from the 5th and 6th chapters of Matthew, but they speak with a lack of understanding.

It is indeed certain, and the Saviour himself would not deny it, that His sermon did not refer to all those who were present; for to prevent such a thought, he made use of the discreet caution, "For whom it is good to hear this, let him listen" (Matt. 11:15, alt.). Likewise, when at one time a general rule dropped in among special ones, He said, "What I say to you I say to all: Watch" (Mark 13:37). By this He shows at the same time that the foregoing matters were not said to all; but watching, giving attention to the mind, to the thoughts, to the work of the Spirit in the heart — this He recommended to all.

But what then is the paradox in doctrine? A paradox must not be confused with an error, for it can be a divine and dear truth. But either it is not a timely [oeconomische] truth which fits the present period, or it is a truth which is not for everybody, which fits only certain subjects, which is for those persons only who have experienced its reality and practice it from their hearts.

Therefore a deep wisdom of God lies in the development of teaching, in such a way that truths appear as paradox to people as long as these truths are not for their heart. They seem strange to them, and they do not know what to make of them. Thus, from this it follows that when they nevertheless do listen to these truths, these truths awaken in them either a shame in their heart that they do not yet understand them or a longing that they also might understand them. This is also the reason why the Saviour, under the name of the Lord's Prayer, repeated the known core of all prayer to His disciples in the presence of the entire people: He said, "Pray then like this" (Matt. 6:9). This is the reason why it is so beautiful and edifying for people who are called to the eternal kingdom of our Lord and Saviour Jesus Christ, that they beforehand, in this time, learn to understand and comprehend the Lord's Prayer and what an important, blessed plan, what a system of theology lies in it.

In order to begin the explication of it in a natural way, one cannot look at this form of prayer as it might be applied to our circumstances today for the sake of edification. Rather, we must see what the Saviour meant and intended to show His disciples at that time and what He wanted to recommend to them as the subject matter of prayer. Then, as I have just said, the entire theology of that period, the fullness of time, will come forth.

It referred to the order[1] of the New Testament which was about to come into existence, and if we explain it in this way and seek the closest literal sense, then we find it in harmony with all the rest of the Saviour's teaching.

"When you pray, my disciples, my people whom I have sought for myself from out of the world, my people which serve me, which shall see my glory, which shall know my suffering, and which shall bring my faith among men, when you pray, then say, 'Our Father, which art above in heaven.' " For it is well known that there were many fathers at that time — many people were called fathers; as many people of high rank were called gods in the political sense, so many esteemed men were called fathers in the theological sense. This was so prevalent that the Saviour had to forbid His disciples to call anyone father and made it a mark of the New Testament order that no man be called father; for the souls at that time had gained a new father, with whom the world was utterly unacquainted. So: You our Father, who are above in heaven, you are the one with whom we speak. We are yours; your children have something to tell you: their heart has something to bring before you which they would so gladly like to have happen at this time.

The first concern is this: "May your name be hallowed." I do not know whether this expression is taken in its natural and simple sense. Dr. Luther explained it admirably: What is this? Answer: God's name is indeed holy in itself; but we ask in this prayer that it also be hallowed through us.[2]

This is exactly what it says; it does have to come to this, that one divine worship prevail in the world, that divine honor be rendered to the Father in heaven, that He be acknowledged as the God of the Communion of Saints, that liturgy also be directed to Him, that not only "Jehovah Elohim" be said, but also "God, You the Father, Jehovah!" For that had, up to that time, not happened; as yet no one had worshipped God the Father, and in the entire Bible there is found either nothing at all or obscure expressions about Him as Father. Thus the Saviour explains Himself; the Bible treats properly of Him himself. And Peter says that by all that was spoken by the prophets the Holy Spirit pointed to the sufferings of Jesus and the glorious things which were to follow them. This is the plan of the entire Bible. The God of Abraham, Isaac, and Jacob, the God who led the people of Israel out of Egypt, the God of all flesh, the God of all gods, the God by whom alone one was to swear, who made us and is our Husband — the

---

1 Zinzendorf writes *oeconomische Verfassung*.
2 A reference to Luther's *Small Catechism*.

Saviour was all of this, who once in human form told His enemies, "You are wondering that I am so old: I was before Abraham was thought of. If Abraham had once had opportunity to see me in this way, he would have left the body for joy; and when I once appeared to him only incognito, that day remained a day of blessing to him which he never forgot" (expansion on John 8:56–58). And in another place He says, "When the great kings and prophets wanted to enjoy something extraordinary, then they imagined such a day as you always have. Meanwhile their business was to walk with God, to have a feeling of Him, to be near His Spirit. When something like this came over them, when they even once felt something like this in the spirit which you have every day in the body (but which they could not have, because I was not yet in the tabernacle, because I was not yet clothed in a human body, and no one could see me), how happy they were! You have this advantage, that you have me here."

In a word, the whole order up to that time was purely the order of the Saviour, the Creator, who intended yet to redeem the world and had out of grace preserved and secured His creature until His appearing, that all might not perish; who invented the Law and the whole order of the Old Testament, the covenant period of the patriarchs, as well as the theocracy of the people of Israel, so that some of His creatures might be saved and kept from wrath until His appearance in the flesh. At that point a new period, a new worship began; now His pre-elected little band, His chosen household, was also to worship God the Original Being,[3] who was still hidden, the Father of Jesus Christ, who, as the Saviour says, is in secret. For this is His phrase which He uses more than once in the Sermon on the Mountain: "My Father who is in secret (Matt. 6:6, 18), who dwells in darkness, or indeed in a light which no one can approach, of whom no one knows anything: He shall now begin to receive divine worship, have a religion in the world." This then is the first petition: "Hallowed be your name," dear Father! If only the time would once come that you would be preached; that there would be people to whom you could be proclaimed, who would all worship you; that even if not all knees which are in heaven and on earth and under the earth, yet at least the chosen people of your Son might, at the command of their Lord, cast themselves down before you and worship you. Therefore we sing, "God, in whom the Church believes, for the sake of Jesus."

The second petition is the means to attain to the first: "Your kingdom come!" If only your order [oeconomie] would commence. This refers to the words of the Saviour: "You people, you must conceive new thoughts, and I will make them for you; I will propound matters to you which correct and supplement your entire former theology, things which you have never

---

3. Zinzendorf's term is *Urwesen*.

heard of before: but first you must have become other men. A new order will begin, the order of my Father." But in what does that order consist which began at that time and endures to the present day? It consists in this, that He makes a marriage for His Son, and enters in a special manner into the affairs of grace; He begets, according to His will through the word of truth, men whom the man Jesus Christ obtains as His inalienable portion, His property, His *peripoiesis*,[4] His own personal people, His particular people, and — as John in particular so often expresses it — His bride-people, souls predestined for His eternal marriage.

This is the order which has now lasted for seventeen hundred years and concerning which the Saviour says, "This is the Father's business, to make you believe in the Son of Man." And no one can, in the ordinary way, become acquainted with the humanity of Jesus, if the Father has not first begun this demonstration with them: "He draws the souls to me. Now, whomever my Father presents unto me, he comes to me gladly; and whoever comes, him I will receive and promise him, by my honor and faithfulness, that on my day I will present and set him before my Father again and will openly acknowledge him" (based on John 6:44–47). This is the meaning of "Your kingdom come." Indeed let the time soon commence when it pleases God to reveal His Son as man, as Reconciler, as sacrifice for sin — all of which is implied in the expression, "His Proclamation." The Father works upon souls and carries on the great business of drawing all elect souls to their Creator as man (not excluding those that the Saviour obtains otherwise and Himself fetches). "When I shall be lifted up upon the cross" (John 12:32, alt.), the Saviour says, "then I will not be satisfied that I have a little chosen flock, that I have a bride; rather, I will draw all souls without distinction to me. When I shall come to the cross, then it shall begin. For all souls are mine, all who are called men are mine." "Show my children and the work of my hands to me" (Isa. 45:11, LT).

This is the mystery through which the heart learns to judge in the important matter of predestination. This is the reason why Dr. Luther says that the old Adam must truly be dead first, if one wants to speak of predestination, and then the new man must speak of it. It is indeed a predestination in the order of the Father, who draws the souls to the Son, who has selected souls before the foundation of the world was laid. Thus they are holy and irreproachable in the eyes of Him who acts towards them in love, in condescension, in affection as the exposed ones of His Son. This is true and eternally true, and it is confirmed in the New Testament with hundreds of arguments; many instances prove that there are souls who must be saved because the Father has drawn them; they can do nothing towards their election. But, on the other hand, the Son, as sovereign Lord of all souls,

---

4 Ephesians 1:14; purchased possession.

does have power to save whom He will. He is not tied to this election, and we are not to think that no more men will be saved than the first-born, or, as they are frequently called in the Revelation of John, first-fruits. He lives forever and is able to save evermore, and the people whom He saves do not so much come to Him through the Father as through Him to God: He carries them home upon His shoulders.

When one has no heart, this is a source of confusion. Sometimes it is said in the Bible that the Father draws the souls to the Son: "No one can come to me, except the Father draw him" (John 6:44); and again at another time, "No one comes to the Father, but by me" (John 14:6). Someone without a heart cannot tell what to make of this; but he who has in his heart the divine order which rules in the world and who has a share in it — he understands this. There are not two kinds of men, two kinds of souls; we are all brothers and sisters. Therefore, we can regard all the sinners in an entire city, in half a world of men in this way; and there is not a single soul who cannot be looked at with brotherly eyes. For even if their looks and their whole manner show that they are not people whom the Father has given to His Son as first fruits, nevertheless we are so certain that we could stake our lives on it; no human creature walks the streets, there exists no human creature, be he whoring, drinking, and living as he ever lives in all sins, who cannot, through the sovereign power of Jesus Christ, the Creator of the world, be delivered from his sins, be snatched out of his misery, be turned around, and be freed from the power of Satan. And as soon as a yearning, a longing in wretchedness with themselves has begun in them, they will be grasped and carried home in the arms of the God and Creator of the universe. The Saviour forgets, as it were, for a moment in His pasture the sheep of His hands (whom He has made, and not they themselves), His entire first-born, His dear hearts, His bride, and occupies Himself with the miserable man, with that sinner there, with the harlot who had seven devils and carries them home on His shoulders. And He requires that all His dear hearts should rejoice over the soul who does not belong to the election of grace but whom He has saved through His sovereign power, because it wanted to be saved, because it was in fear about itself, because its sins rose higher than its head and became for it like a burden weighing tons.

This is the reason why we love our enemies, why we bless those who curse us and pray for those who wrong us and persecute us; for it can help. It is not possible that a heart elected beforehand can curse the Saviour, that it can persecute anyone on His account, that it can be designedly hostile to the Saviour, for this is contrary to its nature. But as soon as a veritable enemy of God, a servant of Satan, a spoil of hell and death — and not only a spoil, a captive, but rather up to that time a volunteer of sin and death — wants to be saved, then he can be saved, then he can become a brother; indeed, it may go so far that all the elect of the Saviour are shamed by his blessedness.

It is no doubt certain that the life of the robber on the cross was not the life of an elect person; for the Father does not so prostitute His gracious election that He should allow His Son's *peripoiesis*[5] to spend its life in murder and robbery. But thus the saviour conquers, thus He gains His case, thus He shows His creative power, that without ceremony, without order, without system, He can say to every rogue of the devil, "You would really rather be mine; you would rather come with me." "O yes, Lord! Do remember me and do not forget me; and when you have finished meditating on all your blessedness and glory, then let even the robber also come into your thoughts." "Amen!" says the Saviour, "come with me this very day; I will take you with me. Then I will not delay calling you to mind, for I will take you with me right now" (based on Luke 23:42 f.).

Observe, this is the meaning of "Your Kingdom come." My Father, let things come to pass in the world, so that a church becomes visible, so that a people becomes visible which acts in your name and appeals to the marriage celebration of the Father of Jesus Christ, which He makes for His Son. The King was sent out to create wedding guests for His Son and has commanded it to be declared throughout all the world: "Come, for everything is ready" (Matt. 22:4).

The third petition is "Your will be done, on earth as it is in heaven." This is a profound saying of the Saviour's and signifies that hitherto people had had little conception of the will of the Father upon earth. The Son has indeed done everything according to the Father's will, for He and the Father are one, and He always rejoiced at that which the Son did. The Son would do nothing but what He had seen the Father do. But the Father had not ruled immediately; He had not acted in such a way that men thus knew that this is the Father's will, the Father will have it this way, which phrase the Saviour used all the time. "This is the will of him who sent me" (John 4:34), etc. "This is the will of the Father" (Matt. 7:21; 12:50; 18:14). Thus the meaning here is as if we had said this: In heaven we knew it very well; there it was our life, there it was my meat and drink to do what pleased my Father, to play before you, O Father! and act according to your heart. You yourself have indeed given me the testimony that you have delighted in me. The angels, who see your face, have also stood before you, ready to execute in the regions of heaven what was your will. But, dear Father, if it were only this way in the world too, if there were only people who joyfully took pleasure in knowing and doing the will of the Father of Jesus Christ, who would be ready in everything for the Father,

---

5 See footnote 4.

to go to Him and say, "Father, do listen. This is your Son's concern; do help us in it. You must give us the strength and wisdom and success in this; it affects your Son's interest." If only the whole world were indeed to be filled with people, heroes, who would want to accomplish nothing else but this loving will of the Father. This is the third petition.

Now follows the fourth petition, concerning which there is so much quarreling in Christendom, and which Dr. Luther, in accordance with his happy custom, explained in a sermon on this text according to the pure truth.

Now according to the truth and the entire context, it means nothing other than "Give us our supernatural bread." For the simple meaning of *epiesios* is supernatural, all other meanings are forced and affected. Thus, according to the etymology, it means "Give us every day our supernatural bread." And now we will also add to this what the context involves: in John 6 the Saviour says, "Moses did not give you bread from heaven, but rather my Father; That is the true bread which comes from heaven and gives life to the world (John 6:32–33, alt.). And he who will eat this bread can be reckoned among the living" (John 6:51, alt.). This is, therefore, the simple meaning everywhere, and the words have never had any other meaning, although it is no sin to ask for one's daily bread, and if one does so and believes, God certainly hears him too. This, however, was not the Saviour's meaning for His disciples. For He had expressly forbidden them to ask for bodily bread and told them that it is a totally useless thing, because their heavenly Father knows what they needed without that, and if they concerned themselves with heavenly things, He would supply their bodily needs as a matter of course.

The Saviour was at a loss because the apostles so often understood Him bodily when He spoke of bread: "I know what you do when I speak to you of the leaven of the Pharisees; right away you think it is because you have forgotten to take bread along; but I do not mean it that way (Matt. 16:6–8, alt.). Rather I mean the supernatural bread, which men do not understand and for which they leave me and go from me, my flesh and my blood which are the true meat and drink; ask the Father for this. O dear Father!" There is indeed a bread, a supernatural bread, which no man understands and which is such a paradox to all men's ears that they do not want to hear such teaching. Now give us this bread every day and let it revive and support our spiritual life; for our Lord has said, "If you do not have this, if you do not eat my flesh and drink my blood, then you have no life in you; but he who eats it, who has eaten it temporally and taken the nourishment of immortality, him will I raise up again on the last day and present with body and soul to my Father" (John 6:53–54, alt.). This is the ingenuous and simple meaning of the fourth petition.

The fifth petition is "Remit our debts, as we remit those of our debtors."

This treats precisely of the sins of omission, which gave the last Archbishop of Armagh, James Usher,[6] who wrote so many important books, so much concern at the end of his days when he was about to leave time: *Domine remitte mihi peccata mea omissionis!* O dear God! Forgive me the sin of having left so much good undone; this sin is meant in the fifth petition. Remit everything that we owe to you; we also will gladly forgive those people who are indebted to us and of whom we might justly have expected more faithfulness and integrity; we too want to be good-natured people and not take things too strictly. Only do forgive us; we have neglected much and still do neglect much in your matters, in your Son's matters, every day. We make many blunders, many mistakes, and often miss the mark; and if you would be strict, we could not answer you one time in a thousand. Do let it pass.

This is the language of a child of God, a servant of Jesus Christ, who has surrendered his life to the service of his Lord but freely confesses every day that he does too little for Him: for "whoever knows what is right to do and fails to do it, for him it is sin" (James 4:17, RSV). It is also wrong, it is in fact sin, that we do not do all that we can and know; thus one has to ask daily, forgive me the sin that I have known just what to do and yet have not done it at all. And this makes us gladly forgive our neighbor where he remains indebted to us. But if we treat our neighbor with severity and are rigorous towards our brethren, then we shall be dealt with again in exactly the same way.

The sixth petition is "And lead us not into temptation." By this the Saviour meant precisely the hour of temptation which afterwards came over His disciples; for in the midst of His distress He admonished them, "Watch and pray that you may not enter into temptation" (Mark 14:38, RSV). With this petition He wanted to tell Peter beforehand that he would draw his sword at the wrong time, that he would go needlessly into the palace of the high-priest and undertake all sorts of other things which no one required of him, if he did not avert it by prayer. With this He told Judas that he should pray, that his great rashness and greediness might not lead him into the temptation to take money from enemies, as once the prophet's servant did from friends. For Judas undoubtedly believed that they could not apprehend the Saviour, but that He would elude them as usual. For this reason he gave them the ironical advice, "When I have brought you to the place where he is, then be sure to hold him fast." But this very thing was a temptation, and here Judas yielded, and Peter was delivered; Judas's body thereby became a spoil of Satan, and Peter's body and soul were

---

6 James Usher (1580–1656), important church historian, who attracted Zinzendorf's attention because of his irenic spirit.

preserved. "Simon, Simon, behold, Satan demanded to have you, that he might sift you like wheat, but I have prayed for you (Luke 22:31 f.), that your heart may remain with me, that your faith may not cease, that your warm feeling for me may not grow cold, and therefore you will come through." This is the meaning of "Lead us not into temptation"; do not let us get so far into it that we remain stuck fast.

The seventh petition is "Deliver us from the wicked one." *Ho poneros*, the wicked one, the evil, the dangerous spirit — this is the usual title which the Saviour gives to Satan. Thus the children of grace then pray: O dear Father! Do not let us come into those circumstances, or at least not so far where there is no turning back. Your Son experienced it in the wilderness, and He did master the wicked one; but keep us rather out of his way; let us keep alert, do not let us fly higher than our wings will carry us, do not let us become meteors, do not let us float about in the air. Keep us from pride, from presumption, and from heroic deeds that are not required of us. And if it does happen that we come into such circumstances through our own fault, then deliver us from the wicked one, then snatch us out of his teeth and allow him in the end to maintain no power over your children. This is the plain and simple meaning of that which the Saviour recommended to His disciples in the Lord's Prayer.

Properly speaking, this prayer was given for a certain time. He gave it to His disciples for that specific hour, just as that prayer which forms John 17 was a prayer for a certain time. But the divine truths continue quite naturally, and, as it is said in one place that "whatever was written for our instruction, that through patience and comfort of Scripture we may have hope" (Romans 15:4, alt.), so is it the case here too.

This prayer thus concerns us too. It is of importance to us that there be a church on earth which can say to the Father, "Eli!" and to the Creator, "My bone, my flesh and blood." It matters to us that the Kingdom of God, the Kingdom of the Father, should flourish — the spiritual kingdom which the kingdoms of this world do not obstruct, which puts nothing in the way of the potentates of the world, which actually has nothing to do with the world, except when the world interferes in matters of the soul. For when that happens, then it also happens (but *per accidens*) that the Kingdom of the Father becomes a dangerous kingdom for them, and not only by accident, but rather contrary to its proper purpose. For the children of God are commanded to keep within a narrow compass, to take a narrow path, not to spread out, not to exalt themselves, to have no part in the kingdoms of this world; this is laid down clearly for them. They dare not come too close to these kingdoms; they are made to be subjects and not lords of the world. Those children of God who are at the same time disciples who have to do with matters of the soul, who are to deal with the Saviour's people in the name of the Father — these are exempt from the duty incumbent on the office of lords they are *Liturgi*. This is thus, to this day, the idea of a spiritual kingdom, for which we pray.

The business of our whole life is that (as in heaven, so also on earth) the will of the Father may be done, and that the Saviour may see His first-born already in such order here that the entire world has to say: it really is true; God indeed has His work with these people; it is the finger of God. Thus a veneration, a reverence may arise in the hearts of all men. We would like that the thousands which are saved through the sovereign power of Jesus Christ, even though they are not among the first-born, would yet feel a brotherly love in their hearts towards the first-born. The sayings manifest this when the Saviour says, "He who receives a prophet because he is a prophet; he who receives a disciple because he is a disciple; he who does the slightest service to one of my Father's children because he is such — he shall experience that it will not remain unrewarded; he shall be well paid for it (Matt. 10:41 f., alt.). These words would have no real sense and meaning, if they did not characterize people who are not themselves those in whom the Saviour takes an interest and whom on the day of judgment He calls His brethren. Among these are included many good people who, properly speaking, do not have a complete understanding of our matter, who have all sorts of scruples about our language and think that it is a new theology, and who, nevertheless, love and help us according to their understanding. They have the hope of being temporally and eternally rewarded for it. "As you did it to one of the least of these my brethren, you did it to me" (Matt. 25:40). This will be what the Saviour will say to those on His right hand, to the people whom He has saved by His sovereignty. And it is this for which we pray.

Now with regard to our petition for the Lord's Supper, you know that for us this is a real truth and no poetical figure:

> I wish forever that my Bone
> Through God unite me with God alone.

We know what happens to us when this takes place; it is a profound mystery to go to the Lord's Supper. It is a sacramental reality and a heavenly diet at the *opus operatum* of the children of God, when we believe it. *Crede* and *manducasti;* we go there and present ourselves, that our minds may be made like the mind of the Lamb and our bodies like His corpse. Then we experience that through the tormented body of Christ we are united with the divine nature and come into a condition which foreshadows something of the resurrection, being even in this life as if we were already risen again; and thus the *omnium terribilium terribilissimum*, death, becomes a delicacy for our heart. We consider how this frail tabernacle will be mortified, transformed, and distilled into a new being and nature; our souls rejoice and delight in thinking of it. If only it might begin this very day!

This is the communion's Lord's Supper, the sacramental meal which at certain times the whole body and all members have together, when He takes the children to the breast and recognizes the mature ones. Beyond this there is still a daily Lord's Supper, a spiritual one, a Lord's Supper for each individual, for each heart.

Now He who will give this to us, who will favor us with it, will also provide us with the morsel of bread which natural life requires and indeed so abundantly that we will be able to supply others with it in turn. For it is not enough for a child of God to have enough for himself; he must be able to make others rich too. Yet we know how poorly we fare with our wisdom and power in everything that is to be executed quickly and wisely in the Father's business; here is reason enough to beg forgiveness. Thus whoever is a true disciple, whoever is a child of God, he is kind and obliging; he is a comfort to all men and burdensome to none; he never asks much of anyone, but he rejoices when he can do much for another. He easily finds an excuse for his neighbor, should he make a mistake; and if someone begins a dispute with him concerning temporal and spiritual matters, then he always supposes the other to be right. If he is wronged, then he always thinks, haven't I also done something which makes it my fault? And instead of thinking how he can get the better of him, his first and last thought is whether he should not rather attempt to bring about mutual understanding or, in any event, to be able to serve his enemy.

One is removed from all vainglory, from exalting one's self above others, from insisting on being in the right. If one is spoken or written against or opposed, then one is the first among the readers and hearers to help the slanderers and persecutors to the point by which they appear more innocent and equitable, thinking that the accusations were perhaps not without foundation. Indeed, one thinks before another thought arises, by what means did I give occasion for that? "Dear Father, do forgive the fault that is mine in that book, in that slander, in that persecution." This is always the first thought of a heart which has received grace.

The Saviour says, "Father, forgive them" (Luke 23:34). But we have still another prayer previous to this, before we too can speak in this way. We must usually first say, "Forgive me the responsibility I have in my neighbor's offence, my hidden fault." For to be persecuted purely for righteousness' sake, solely for the sake of the grace in which we stand, is something which does not easily happen with us. *Datur tertium*, there is a third factor, arising from misunderstanding, and to this we too could well have given so many opportunities that we have even yet suffered too little and might very well say to the slanderer, "Do forgive me my fault." This is how the fifth petition hangs together.

But at the time of the apostles it was a distressing fact that there were temptations which simply could not be avoided. The Saviour could only be implored, to keep them from falling too deeply. "Do not allow us to fall into temptation."

Here we have a great advantage over the first disciples, since He has shed His blood for us, since we are healed by His wounds, and since His passion reigns among us; now we have another consolation. He to whom Jesus' passion is everything; he who honors the torments of God; he who desires to know, hear, or understand nothing, to have his salvation no other way, to have no wisdom, no theology, except that alone which arises from the Saviour's suffering and death and is founded only on His merit and blood — he who is thus minded, him will He preserve from coming into any temptation. And when everything succumbs to temptation, when all others can hardly escape so as to be saved, like brands coming out of the fire, then the relatives of His suffering and passion, the lovers of His merit, the adherents of His corpse, of His bleeding form in which He delivered their souls, the hearts who are in love with this, who concentrate all their thoughts on it and thus walk and stand, sleep and wake, eat and drink, work and rest, and leave this time as men who crave the sign of the Son of Man in hands and feet and in the side — these shall have the privilege that the devil will not come near them; the devil will be obliged to remain a certain distance from them: as John says, "The evil one dare not touch them" (I John 5:18, alt.).

This is the great blessedness of the merit of our Lord, and a blessedness of the Gospel, to which we can invite all souls with all our hearts, if they only take notice of this one thing:

> How greatly man incenses
> The Lord with his offenses;
> How hot His anger glows,
> How fiercely He chastises
> When He with wrath baptizes:
> Our Saviour's suffering fully shows.

Then they will be ashamed of themselves; their sins will become as the fire of hell to them; they will judge themselves; they will condemn themselves. And then they will come with the explication of the second article: "I wretched, condemned, and lost sinner";[7] or with the first part of the church's confession: "I poor, wretched, sinful man." And when they are so minded, which of itself, without them having first to resolve on it, embitters the world to them, lying with this upon their beds and walking with this in

---

7   A reference to Luther's explanation of the Second Article of the Apostle's Creed.

the streets, eating without appetite and speaking without knowing what they say — in a word, when they come into total and persistent perplexity concerning their misery, immediately the Prince with the bleeding side stands before them, and they sense how He twists to embrace their souls.

Then there is no need for an examination, no question whether one is elected. Rather, as soon as one feels this, as soon as one is so oppressed in his spirit, stands there as a confused sinner, and is grieved in his heart at the cause he has given to the suffering of Jesus, then the kingdom of Christ belongs to him with all its blessedness. Then one may expect entrance into the Father's order, into the religion in which the Father of Jesus Christ is honored as God. One may also expect to become Christ's flesh and bone; and the first spiritual joy is a look, a feeling, a thought which has no parallel; transcending everything which a person can encounter in the rest of life; it is a felt salvation.[8]

PRAYER

O God of all the world! Be pleased to let your grace and faithfulness, your omnipotence and sovereignty over all souls, who are indeed your creatures, and your ordered thoughts of the Gospel which you command to be preached now to all creatures — let this be approved and made clear also in this place in the hearts of still more men and be made so present to them that they may discern it with complete blessing and with their eternal happiness. Let all external circumstances also serve men to this end; bless them in their situation, and let everything that is a hindrance to others be for them an occasion to know themselves and thereby to come to the sense of a misery from which no one but you can deliver them.

Let this your grace be experienced by the whole human race, and let the orders of the world, the constitutions, the managements of your servants the magistrates, and in particular the government of King George the Second, our sovereign, and of all his officers concur to promote that quiet and blessed state in which your Gospel may find more faithful ears, more willing hearts among men who have the time and opportunity, the liberty and courage to concern themselves with heavenly things.

Therefore let the difficulties of the human life which do indeed weigh minds down, but also make them hostile, malignant, and unhappy, become fewer and fewer among the people of these realms. And, on the other hand, let a blessed, happy, peaceful, and moderate condition prevail among men, in which your Gospel always gains the most among ready and willing minds. Do this for the sake of your faithfulness and your Creator-love. Amen.

---

8 *Eine Empfindliche Seeligkeit.*

Lecture III

Concerning the Proper Purpose of the Preaching of the Gospel

Preached on the same day, September 4, 1746

TEXT: Matthew 22:2, and Luke 14:17. *"The kingdom of heaven may be compared to a king who gave a marriage feast for his son;" "and at supper-time he sent his servants to say to those who had been invited, 'Come; everything is ready.'"* (LT)[1]

THE WORDS which I have just read fall of their own accord into a division which is quite natural. A marriage requires a bridegroom, a bride, and guests. The servants who are sent out to call the guests give us less cause for concern, since they, in the spiritual marriage, must necessarily belong either to the bride or to the guests.

This passage does not say how the bride is called, how the souls are called who are looked upon as members of the bride. For everyone who has read the Bible knows that the bride is not just one soul. It is said often enough that it is not one person, but rather whole multitudes which constitute the wife of the Lamb, the bride of the Lamb.

Here there is no description of how the bride, how the members of the bride are now brought together; and if we look through the whole Bible, we will hardly come across one syllable in any one of the evangelists or

---

1 Zinzendorf gives Matthew 22:1 ff. as the text. But the verse from Luke, which is cited later in the lecture, matches the German exactly. Matthew 22:1 has relevance only as an introduction, and Matthew 22:2 takes care of only the first half of the cited text.

in any one of the letters of the apostles concerning the nature and the circumstances of the call through which the members of the bride of Jesus are brought together. On the other hand, however, we find throughout the entire Holy Scripture of the Old and New Testaments many places indicating the bridal state and its nature and also how the Saviour busies Himself with such hearts once He has them. But how He obtains them in the first place is still a mystery between them both. The whole Bible, and especially the New Testament, is full of descriptions of the calling of the guests. It is the subject which Paul treats so extensively in the Epistle to the Romans. When he comes to the preaching of the Gospel, he calls himself a herald, and says, "The people must have a preacher. How can they hear without a preacher?" (Rom. 10:14, alt.).

It is, therefore, worthwhile to speak among men concerning the subject of the bride and bridegroom, of the invitation to the marriage, and of the guests who are invited. And because the last concerns us above all else, since we have to deal with the preaching of the Gospel, I shall deal with it first.

"He sent his servants out to say to those who had been invited, 'Come, for everything is ready'" (Luke 14:17). From another evangelist I have added the construction, "He sent out at supper-time" (Luke 14:17).

It is an important matter that the Gospel may not be preached whenever it enters a person's head to do so; rather, it too has its appropriate time. "When the time had fully come" (Gal. 4:4), is a biblical expression. The Saviour makes use of these words several times, "The time is fulfilled" (e.g., Mark 1:15); thus He says, as He weeps over Jerusalem, "at this your time" (Luke 19:42, LT). This agrees with the words of the text which stand in another evangelist: "at suppertime."

My friends! We must establish this principle, that the blessed, fruitful, and almost irresistible[2] "calling in" of many thousands of souls presupposes a little flock in the house which cleaves to the Saviour with body and soul, souls which are already there, united with the Saviour, so that one may point to these very people with the finger when one wants to invite others. It is an advantage, a blessing, a sound preaching of the Gospel, when one can say, "Come, everything is ready. I can show you the people who are already there; just come and see." This is the suppertime, when bride and bridegroom are already prepared, have already spoken with each other, have already completed their blessed engagement, and now, in order to solemnize it still more, make their appearance at a place. One perceives a people of God with whom the bridegroom concerns himself, people who glory in him, as he does in them. Thus it has come so far that the city on the hill can no longer be hidden, and it is a light which one does not put under

---

2 Zinzendorf uses the English word.

a bushel but sets upon a candlestick. Thus a preaching of the Gospel must come out of this little flock: "Come, everything is ready; the time to come is here. Whoever comes now, comes at the right time." This is very simply that which is called preaching the Gospel. This is nothing other than the general and earnest call to all creatures: "Come, for everything is ready."

But in order that it be even less possible to imagine that this call is not serious, (which would anyway be inappropriate to think of God), the Saviour says expressly of the kind of people who did not partake of this supper, who did not attain to salvation in this time, "They would not come" (Matt. 22:3). This cannot reasonably be said of people who were not able to come and who were not meant by the call but were called only in jest. Rather, the call must have been in earnest, if it can be said, "They would not come." "Jerusalem, Jerusalem," said the Saviour, "how often would I have gathered your children together as a hen gathers her chicks under her wings; but you would not" (Luke 13:34).

Now it is true that sometimes this is the fault of the messengers. It is the servants' failure if they do not take great care in calling the people. They selected people who did appear to them to be worthy to come to the marriage; they selected without doubt, the most distinguished, the most clever, learned, and wealthy, thinking that these are honorable and good people; as things stand in the world these days, we must call these above all. If a poor man can be saved with a fifteen-minute exhortation, the person of distinction must certainly have several weeks, and they are gladly invested in him. It is indeed a great weakness to imagine that it is of greater importance that the soul of such a person of rank is saved than that of a common and poor person. As if there were a difference among souls. The Holy Scripture has always sought to take away such distinctions from the minds of men and has shown that it is a false idea as far as the preaching of the Gospel is concerned. Therefore, Paul, in the first letter to the Corinthians, treats this topic so extensively and says finally, "I entreat you, simply look into your congregation: Where are the wise? Where are the eminent? Where are the rich?" (I Cor. 1:20, 26, alt.). Thus he demonstrates to them how to proceed in preaching the Gospel, to avoid fruitless work and threshing empty straw. The rich and the eminent are not excluded; but they do not have the least prerogative. They have no privilege before others with respect to salvation but rather a hundred difficulties which others do not have, and therefore one must not stay too long with them; one must not go to them first. And what is true about people respected for natural reasons, is equally true of those who are respected for spiritual reasons, the devout and religious men. If one would think in this case, "That is a man who serves God," (ten or twelve years ago the phrase was "a pious man"), "one whom I must indeed seek to bring to the Saviour," it could result in a great loss of time. The Saviour showed by means of a parable how the matter stands. He says to His servants, "Go out to the highways and hedges, and compel people to come in, that my house may be filled (Luke 14:23). See where you can get them, the poor, the common men who have absolutely nowhere to go; those to whom it could never occur that a lot of care be devoted to them — call them; they will come; to them you will be welcome." This being done, they brought a great number of people together, and among them there was only one who was thrown out, and this single one was without any doubt the most highly regarded person among them. For the fact that he did not want to accept a wedding garment clearly shows that he was not one of the beggars, not one of the ragged loiterers, but rather that he was well dressed. It was an old custom to give people marriage garments; also the richest and most eminent people received a festival garment when they came to a marriage. It is not possible that one of the beggar-people would have rejected the garment and would not rather have rejoiced over it. If he came half naked and a garment was given to him, he would have thanked God that he received a garment.

But one, either a naturally respected or virtuous person, full of spiritual gifts, full of aptitudes and merits, did not find it necessary to accept a garment, because he thought perhaps that his own clothes were better than those which he was to have received, and he was expelled in disgrace. And this is certainly remarkable, that among the entire great multitude of invited people only a single one was expelled, and precisely because of his unsociableness, because he did not want to look like the rest, because he would not accept the festival garment that every one of the marriage guests had received. I do not really need to explain what kind of a garment that is:

> Christ's own blood and righteousness
> Is the well-known wedding dress,
> So that we can before God stand,
> When we shall enter that joyful land.

Now concerning the preaching of the Gospel, it is clearly and fully described to us in so many places in the Bible. It treats of none other than Jesus and consists in this, that the Bridegroom be distinctly set forth to the souls.

Now what is the Bridegroom's beauty? What is His principal quality? What should be said to those who are invited? Should His glory and power and majesty be expounded to them? This is not worthwhile; they know all this already from the fact that He is the king's son.

Therefore what really matters is that His beautiful form and inner qualities be described to them. And since at all solemnities in general people have a desire to see the principal person, we must know how to identify Him so clearly that as soon as they come they can see that "this is the Bridegroom."

This happens when He is described the way He really looks. For this purpose, fathers devised very nice parables for themselves, and if they are taken as parables, they are edifying. Among others, one relates that there was a bishop named Martin who, among many other singular occurrences that happened to him, also had this experience, that Satan appeared to him in the likeness of the Saviour, but in the form of a majestic king, surrounded with heavenly glory. He said to him, "Martin, you see how I love you and what an important servant I consider you, for I personally appear to you rather than other men." Martin is said to have answered, "If you are Christ, where are your wounds?" The reply was that he did not come to him as one wounded, as one from the cross, but rather he came from heaven; he wanted to show himself to him in his glory, as he sits at the right of his Father. To this Martin answered, "You are the devil; a Saviour who is without wounds, who does not have the mark of his sufferings, I do not acknowledge." This is a fine parable and a charming example, and if the story were true, it ought to have been handled just that way. For the Saviour is never in all eternity without His sign, without His wounds: the public showing which He makes has His holy wounds as its ground. After His resurrection, when He did go through doors without a key, when He did go through the walls, "then He showed them His hands and His side. Then the disciples were glad when they saw the Lord" (John 20:20).

If we, therefore, want to invite people to the marriage, if we want to describe the Bridegroom, it must be said like this: "I decided to know nothing among you except Jesus, as He hung upon the cross (I Cor. 2:2, alt.), as He was wounded. I point you to His nail prints, to the side, to the hole which the spear pierced open in His side. Do not be unbelieving; let it be as present to you as if He had been crucified before your eyes, as if He stood there before your eyes and showed you His hands and His side. As soon as this look strikes your heart, you run to the marriage feast and then no house nor property, no husband, no wife, no child, nor anything else can keep you back anymore. You will not rest until you get to see this man. 'Such a one,' you say to all your neighbors, 'such a one is my friend. My friend looks like this.'" And this happens whenever there is preaching.

But how does it go when there is no preaching, when men have no need to preach because the Holy Spirit Himself is working? That there can be such a method cannot be doubted by any man who has read the Bible and who listens to Paul, "It pleased God to reveal His Son in Me" (Gal. 1:15 and 16), and who calls John 3 to mind, where the Saviour says, "Do listen. When a man is begotten again, it is just as if a wind should come; you do perceive that the wind is there and you hear its sound; you go out to see where the wind is coming from, and then it is already gone" (John 3:7 f., alt.). The immediate begetting of God is such a secret, sudden, unknown reality, hidden from the eyes of all mankind, that it can never be described.

Therefore, my friends, Methodism,[3] which tells people how a man is begotten again, is in danger of becoming absurd. And for this reason a man's own endeavor to explain to people how he was begotten again is also totally futile, because the man himself does not know, nor can he know, how he was begotten again. One man is begotten again in his cradle; another in the mother's womb; the third in the midst of his dead, natural condition, in his ignorance; the fourth on the occasion of great good fortune; the fifth on the occasion of a misfortune: one young, the other old; one in his last hour, the other near the very first beginning of his life. In a word, the new begetting, when the Spirit from God comes into our heart, when Jesus Christ with His five wounds is formed in us, when we are allotted to Him in heaven above — this is a divine moment.

We see this in John, who in his mother's womb was filled with the Holy Spirit; the child Jesus, who was Himself hidden in His mother's womb, formed Himself in his soul and came into such a relationship with his soul, into such a harmony, that when Mary visited Elizabeth, one fellow brother leaped to meet the other. The expression which King David, the great theologian of his time, once used — "My body and soul sing for joy to the living God (Ps. 84:2, alt.); my body and soul throb for the living God" — showed itself here already in the unborn child; John's body and soul throbbed for Him. "Why is this granted me," said Elizabeth, "that the mother of my Lord should come to me? No sooner did I see you, no sooner did I greet you, than behold, my babe leaped to greet you. And oh, blessed are you who have believed all the promises; for all will come to pass as it is promised you" (Luke 1:43 ff., alt.).

This is one instance, and there are many of the same kind. The Saviour is tied to absolutely nothing. He will not be dictated to. Each instance takes its course. The Holy Spirit portrays Jesus to souls; He preaches His wounds. To one this happens distinctly, to another indistinctly. To Saul, the persecutor, who went around and massacred people who adhered to Jesus, who for this purpose had passports and mandates with him from the high priests, to him He appeared so distinctly, to him it was so clear in his soul that the crucified Jesus of Nazareth was the Saviour that he needed no further explanation, but laid hold of it immediately. Queen Candace's treasurer was reading about a slaughtered lamb that was so happy, hearty, and willing, etc. to go to the slaughter. "Tell me," he said (it was an obscure description, a picture which required sharp eyes), "tell me, about whom does the prophet say this? About himself or about someone else?" Philip answered immediately, "I will indeed tell you about it." And he

---

3 Zinzendorf uses this term in the specific sense. See Introduction, pp. xvii–xix.

made it clear to him and explained to him with human words the language of the Holy Spirit in the heart; he spoke to him the *arrheta rhemata*, the unspeakable words (II Cor. 12:4), the words in the heart. And he catches on immediately: "Baptize me into His death and into His wounds; here I am; what is to prevent it?" (Acts 8:36, alt.).

And just for this reason we are not to be very concerned about the bride which the Holy Spirit courts in this world for Jesus Christ; the proxy-marriage in the name of Jesus Christ takes its course, and no devil can obstruct it, let him do what he will. No worldly circumstance, no absolute prohibition of the Gospel in any country, no drought and famine of the divine Word can thwart it. He is sure of His souls; they are souls which live and move and have their being in Him. They live no longer, but rather He lives in them. At that moment they die to corruption and sinning, and continue dying, as long as man is in the body,[4] so that the spirit is rightly set free and is not connected by the slightest filament when it is called out of the body.

And the blessed work goes on forever and remains in the Spirit's hand, in His disposition. We have no need to be anxious about it. We need not be worried how the Saviour obtains His bride. He is sure of her; He keeps her eternally, and no one will snatch her from His hand; no one dare waken nor rouse her if it does not please her. "I have promised you this, that you should be mine" (Ezek. 16:8, alt.).

But what do those people experience? Though they cannot tell the moment of their begetting, though they cannot specify the hour, how do they feel? For so many movements of grace take place which resemble each other that one would have to become converted ten times, if at every great and exceptional grace one would think, this was my conversion. Each grace, each breath of grace that comes over us is blessed and highly blessed, and the more often it comes, the more we have to thank and praise Him and the more whole we become.

But all the less can the days and hours be given. For as the wind is there one moment and then gone again, so it is too with everyone who is begotten of the Spirit. But if one asks, "How are you now?" — if one asks a person begotten of God, a person begotten of the Father of Jesus Christ, a man begotten for the bride of Jesus Christ, "How are you now? What is before your eyes? What do you see?" — the answer is, "The slaughtered sheep, Jesus Christ." He sees just this; he lives in that very thing in which all the marriage people and all the guests must live who go to the marriage feast.

The bride and those invited have one object, one beauty, one virtuousness of the Bridegroom to admire. They admire that this man, the Son of God,

---

4 Zinzendorf uses *Hütte* — tabernacle.

the Creator of the world, should have wanted to die on the cross for His poor human beings, that He obtained His bride with His blood, that He brought back His fallen bride, His fallen wife, His adulteress and on the cross saved this His property, His possession, His creature as a spoil. This is also the impression which the bride-hearts have, which the souls have who throughout their whole life know nothing and want to know nothing other than their Bridegroom.

Therefore it would be a great mistake for anyone to suppose that the bride-hearts who day and night live, eat, drink, sleep, and get up with the Saviour would probably want to have something else; that they would not be taken up with His cross and suffering, torment and merit, and similar catechism concerns; rather that they would maintain such a familiarity with the angels and cherubim, with heaven and the heavenly Jerusalem, associate with them, and have visions of spirits or deep insights into the Revelation of John. But no, this is not at all the case. An invited guest may be more learned, wiser, and more experienced and have a deeper insight into all truths than many a heart that is bound to the Saviour in the closest manner. A soul most tenderly in love with the Saviour may be ignorant of a hundred truths and only concentrate most simply on Jesus' wounds and death. Oh, how ardently this soul meditates on this part of the body, which on the day of His coming will be the sign of the Son of Man, the hole in His side, His heart, out of which flowed blood and water. This is its wisdom, its knowledge, which reflects the soul like a mirror:

> O sacred head, now wounded,
> With grief and shame weighed down,
> Now scornfully surrounded
> With thorns thine only crown!
> O sacred head what glory,
> What bliss 'til now was thine.
> Yet though despised and gory,
> I joy to call thee mine.

This is the Bridegroom's form which so captivates the soul's heart that it has no time left to think of anything else; and the more the soul falls in love with this and becomes involved, the blinder it becomes to other things, to the glories of the world. It does not become hostile to them, nor does it censure them much; but rather it does not have very much to do with them. It does not think about this miserable life, because God delights its heart.

Therefore there is no known difference, according to Scripture, between the bride and those who are invited, neither in object nor feeling nor in the kind of conversation. The only difference is that the call to be the bride of Jesus Christ, to be the first-born, one engaged to the Lamb, one who knows nothing but Him and has not climbed higher than into the wounds and must first be led by the hand to everything else that he should or should not think (as Paul says, "When you should think this way or that, then God will certainly reveal it to you" [Phil. 3:15, alt.]) — the only difference is that this call happens immediately and with less observance than does the ordinary conversion. The structuring, creation and preservation of such simple hearts of the Saviour is the immediate work of the Holy Spirit and indeed His alone.

But there are still millions of souls who come to participation in this salvation who are at the marriage and are also joyful, who draw a conclusion about the future from the present blessedness, and who join the supper as invited guests; and they are always called through the preaching of the Gospel.

Therefore there is no ground to debate whether God performs the work of conversion in a soul Himself or whether He makes use of men to this end. Certainly He is in need of no one, for He Himself can draw, can beget, can bring forth, through His Spirit all the souls whom He wants to give to His Son, whom He will marry to Him at the time when He will be the Consecrator, when the creature shall marry the Creator. And this He actually does. But these are not enough; they do not make a *numerus clausus*, a number which may not be exceeded. Rather, the number is innumerable; the multitudes who through the Gospel of the merits and death of Jesus receive the invitation to go to the marriage will exceed all thought. "Compel people to come in, that my house may be filled" (Luke 14:23), that innumerable more may share my salvation; "Come, O blessed of my Father, inherit the kingdom prepared for you," etc. (Matt. 25:34).

This is an admirable thing, to know that our Lord, as rich and great and generous as He is, nevertheless is not satisfied that He has His assured reward, the souls of whom He is sure; but, having already been crucified and dead, He wants to be looked at and to manifest Himself as the Saviour of all men. "Go into all the world and preach the gospel to the whole creation" (Mark 16:15); whoever will now believe you, whoever will hold to me, whomever I will please, whoever will come to love me, he shall be saved; he shall be delivered from this present evil world and from the wrath to come and shall enter into my rest.

This then is the ground and purpose of the preaching of the Gospel plain and clear.

Now when the souls who love the Lamb as the bride loves the Bridegroom hear that there is preaching (although they do not need to be called, to have the Lamb painted before them, for they live and move in Him; they always have Him before their eyes, as David says, "I keep the Lord always before me" [Ps. 16:8]), then they rejoice with all their hearts when the Gospel is preached; they look forward to the guests, and they are as embarrassed as the Bridegroom if there might be only a few, for they want the house to be full.

And this is a blessed combination to see in one gathering such a crowd of souls in love with the Saviour, together with a number of guests, who will have supper together and together will greet the holy wounds. And may the Saviour also in this place present more living examples of this, as time passes, for His wounds' sake!

Lecture IV

Concerning Saving Faith

Preached in the Brethren's Chapel in London, September 6, 1746

TEXT: I Peter 1:7–8. *"At the revelation of Jesus Christ. Without having seen him you love him; though you do not now see him you believe him."* (RSV)

THE SPECIAL connection, "You love and believe now in Him," compels me to make a very necessary observation, namely, that in many places in the Holy Scriptures faith is called love; and this is so not only in the New Testament, but rather this occurs already in the Old Testament. For when God wants to praise Abraham for following and believing Him through thick and thin (for Paul says this, "Abraham believed God, and it was reckoned to him as righteousness" [Gal. 3:6]), then God says to him, "Now I know that you love God" (Gen. 22:12, alt.). It is necessary that we mark this well, for otherwise the whole thirteenth chapter of the First Letter to the Corinthians would be an unintelligible chapter, since Paul explicitly says, "Even if one believes, yet he will not be saved, if he does not love" (I Cor. 13:2, alt.).

Now the Saviour states positively that he who believes shall be saved (Mark 16:16); and Paul says, nevertheless, that even though one believes, he will not be saved, if he does not love.

Hence it is quite clear that the Holy Scripture wants to point out to us that there is no saving faith which is not simultaneously love for Him who laid down His life for us, for Him who has created us, without whom we cannot live and exist for one moment.

In order to make myself clear on this subject, I must now treat faith, and, out of necessity, I must divide my lecture.

I will call faith *fiducia implicita* and *explicita.* Faith as it is in our own selves shall be called *fiducia implicita*, and faith which is manifested to others, which unfolds itself, shall be called *fiducia explicita.*

Now both of them, when they are together, are such that they make the man who has them unspeakably happy and even here manifest eternal life.

But in any event, if they cannot be together, then it is sufficient if only the first is there, the *fiducia implicita*, the undisclosed but affective [1] believing within the heart. And this faith within the heart which one has within himself I also view from two perspectives: the first is "faith-in-distress" [2] and the second "faith-in-love." [3]

No man can create faith in himself. Something must happen to him which Luther calls "the divine work in us," which changes us, gives us new birth, and makes us completely different people in heart, spirit, mind, and all our powers. This is *fides*, faith, properly speaking. If this is to begin in us, then it must be preceded by distress, without which men have no ears for faith and trust.

The distress which we feel is the distress of our soul when we become poor, when we see we have no Saviour, when we become palpably aware of our misery. We see our corruption on all sides and are really anxious because of it. Then afterwards it happens as with patients who have reached the point of crisis; they watch for help, for someone who can help them out of their distress, and accept the first offer of aid without making an exact examination or investigation of the person who helps them. That is the way it went once with the woman whom the Saviour healed. For twelve years she had gone to see all kinds of physicians and had endured much from them. And finally she came upon Him too and said, "If only I would touch that man's clothes, it would help me; even if I could not get to the man himself, if I could only get hold of a bit of his garment, then I would be helped" (Matt. 9:21, alt.).

This is faith-in-distress. And here I can never wonder enough at the blindness and ignorance of those people who are supposed to handle the divine word and convert men, for example the Jews and heathen, those abortive "so-called Christians" [4] (who are indeed as blind as Jews and heathen) who think that if they have them memorize the catechism or get a book of sermons into their heads or, at the most, present all sorts of well-reasoned demonstrations concerning the divine being and attributes, thus funneling the truths and knowledge into their heads, that this is the sovereign means to their conversion. But this is such a preposterous method, that if one

---

1 Zinzendorf's word is *gefühlige*.
2 *Der Glaube in der Noth.*
3 *Der verliebte Glaube.*
4 Zinzendorf calls them *Die Ungerathenen Christianer.*

wanted to convert people that way, reciting demonstrations to them, then it is just as if one wanted to go against wind and current with full sails, or as if one, on the contrary, would run one's boat into an inlet so that one could not find one's way out again.

For that same knowledge of divine things which is taken to be faith, although it appears only, other things being equal, as an adjunct of faith, puffs up and nothing comes of it. And if one has all of that together, says Paul, and does not also have love, and even if one can preach about it to others, still it is nothing more than if a bell in the church rings. As little as the bell gets out of it, as little as it is benefited by the fact that it hangs there and rings, just so little does the fact that a teacher makes the most cogent demonstrations benefit him as far as his own salvation is concerned.

But what results from this faith-in-distress, from this blind faith which one has out of love for one's own salvation? What comes of a bold trust in the physician that he can and shall help, without knowing what his name is and who he is, without having known and seen him before, without having clearly sensed what sort and nature of man he is? Thankful love results from it, as long ago with Manoah and his wife, who so loved the man who came to them; they did not know him, though, for they said, "What is your name? We do not know you, but we love you. We should like to know who you are, that we may praise you when what you have said to us comes true" (Judg. 13:17, alt.). So it is exactly with the faith-in-distress: it has to do completely with an unknown man, yet with a man of whom one's heart says, "He likes to help, he likes to comfort, and he can and will help." My heart tells me that it is he of whom I have heard in my youth, of whom I have heard on this or that occasion. They called him the Saviour, the Son of God, the Lord Jesus, or however else one has heard him named and however anyone in anxiety and distress thinks of him. In short: "He must help me; oh, if he would only come to my aid! If he would only take my soul into his care, so that it would not perish! *Kyrie Eleison!* Lord have mercy!"

Now faith-in-distress has the infallible promise that one shall be helped; the man having faith-in-distress shall obtain grace. No one shall come in vain, no one ask in vain. This was the faith-in-distress of the thief on the cross: "Lord, remember me when you come into your kingdom (Luke 23:42). I love you as an unknown Lord, of whom I know nothing, whom I have never known. But I hear now that you have a kingdom and that you are hanging here because you have said that you are a king. It may indeed be true; I believe you. Now when you come to the place where your kingdom is, do think of me, do remember me then!" The Lord instantly agreed: "Today you will be with me in paradise" (Luke 23:43). Had the thief been so inclined in prison, then one doubt or another would probably still have developed in the meantime; but because the thief had no time, it went very well. With people who are healthy and prosperous, who can be distracted or deliberate in the interim, who can eat, drink, sleep and go to work in the meantime, they will probably have second thoughts which will disturb their faith. Such disruptions do not consist in doubts whether there is a Saviour, or whether this man could help, or whether the invisible Jesus of whom one has heard could rescue souls from their destruction. Rather, the question will really be whether He wants to help such a sinner, who is such a thoroughly miserable and wretched creature. Sin begins to dawn on one only after faith, after trust, after the yearning and longing for help, for rescue, when one has time for reflection, when the distress is not too pressing. When distress and aid do not succeed each other so quickly that one cannot think of anything in between, then doubt comes, saying, "I am too great a sinner." But doubt is no sooner there, it is no sooner arisen, than it is really refuted by the actual forgiveness of sins: "Take heart, my son; your sins are forgiven" (Matt. 9:2).

At the same time we must note that all this is God's work in us, *fides implicita*, which has to do with the heart alone. It is within the heart, regarding which one has nothing to demonstrate to anyone else. Here one has to do with God alone and with His work in the heart; and here, at the very moment when one knows and feels himself to be so wretched, grace and forgiveness of sins is preached into his heart. This happens with infallible certainty and without anxiety that it could come to nothing. Man emerges at once out of the deepest sorrow and dismay over himself into blessed rest and contentment and, at the same time, into love and thankfulness and attachment to Him who died for his soul, who gained eternal life for him with His blood (whether he had thought more about the matter or less, knew more or less, does not matter). From that very hour he loves Him as his highest good, and the Saviour can say to him, "You do indeed truly love me, and I have also forgiven you a great many sins; I have rescued you from genuine misery, it is true; now you stand there and feel ashamed for all eternity and can hardly get over your astonishment at how much I have forgiven you."

> Were the patience of them all,
> In every heavenly hall,
> In nations all around,
> And in God's people true,
> In one heart to be found —
> Good friends, I say to you,
> His patient gentleness
> Surpasses even this.

Peter experienced something of this. In the Saviour's affairs he was not just a natural, unconverted, unfamiliar man (which indeed is in itself sin enough), but rather he was a deliberate denier, what today is called a renegade. He would rather not know his Lord; he was ashamed of his Lord; he abjured his Lord three times. And a few days later his Lord came up and rose from the dead and was loved by those people who had followed Him to death itself, by the women who had helped to place Him into the grave and who came back at early dawn and looked for Him out of love. "Ah," says the Saviour to them, "You dear children, I absolutely beg of you not to delay here with me, but go and tell my Peter that I am here again" (Mark 16:7, alt.).

This must have been an astonishing message to Peter. Was this all his punishment, to be notified that his Lord is risen again? And if so, should he have been the very first who was comforted, whose heart was revived? Thus, when the Saviour said to him afterwards, "Do you love me more than these do?" he said, "You know all things; you know how much I love you" (John 21:15 ff., alt.). And at that time he really did love Him more than all the others. Before he had loved Him in his imagination; he had honored Him and out of esteem for Him had rashly claimed to be ready to suffer death for Him rather than forsake Him. He did make a bold beginning, but he got stuck, because his love was dry and intellectual. But when the Saviour forgave him everything, when He acquitted him of his sins, when He declared a renegade to be His apostle, then Peter could hold back no longer. If anyone said anything about his Lord to him, tears filled his eyes, and his body and soul were humbled. Already in the high priest's palace the bare presentiment of the character of his Lord had made his eyes fountains of tears.

All this is still *fides implicita*, the faith which is God's work in the heart in the middle of our stillness, where we and He have to do with each other alone, where nothing comes between us and Him — no man, no book, no knowledge, no learning, not even the most necessary truths — but only the distress, the sinner's shame, and the faithfulness of the Shepherd.

Now I come to the other faith, which I have called *fides explicita*, the faith which unfolds and manifests itself. And this faith is also of two kinds: faith while one is still learning about the Saviour, and faith when one expounds and teaches the Saviour to others.

Not seeing and yet loving makes one ask afterwards, "Who is that? What is that which I love this way?" And then one soon enough gets information for one's heart.

The people who had seen the risen Lord, who had loved Him so tenderly, went away with fear and joy and told no one anything. They knew now that He was not a mere man; they knew that something more profound, indeed something inexpressible lay behind the man; but they lacked the words, the fitting expressions. They felt it sufficiently[5] that their Creator was their Saviour. Thomas, when he had to do only with the eleven and the Saviour, could cry out without reflection, "My Lord and my God!" (John 20:28). But if they would have had to go and tell the people that the Saviour was God, that He had redeemed the whole world, then they would not have had words for it. This they could not yet explain, for this was for them not unraveled for speaking. They could not bring it into a discourse nor make it plain. It did indeed shine through all their expressions, but not in any orderly fashion.

One has only to compare the first sermons of the apostles with the subsequent ones; one has only to read Paul's epistles which he wrote at the beginning and to contrast them with the others which came out later. One has only to read John's letters and after that his Gospel, with which he concludes. Then one will see how the apostles' faith itself evolved, how the solid ideas of God the Creator as a human being successively develop. They obtained one important grace and power of demonstration after the other in their addresses. They had grace not only for confessing in the face of all the world, but also for learning to prove what they preached and for finding words to make themselves clear on these subjects.

It is one of the greatest pleasures to read the Bible according to the epochs, according to the periods, according to the stages by which the preaching of the Gospel has from time to time been growing and ascending. If one starts with the thirties, after the Saviour's birth, down to the nineties, and keeps this development in sight and meditates upon it in a simple and childlike way, then one sees what Paul means by saying, "That your love may abound more and more, with knowledge and all discernment (Phil. 1:9), that thereafter you may make such progress that you will measure the length, the breadth, depth and height of things" (Eph. 3:18, alt.). You will also be able to speak as plainly of the profoundest mysteries of God your Lord as if they were catechism questions. Then you will have to stand and say at last, "It is good that Jesus is my Creator and my God, that He is the God over everything." But what an observation this is, that my Creator has laid down His life for me! All your theology, all your theosophy, insight and knowledge will be caught up in this as the central point; all of this will run together into the wounded heart of Jesus, it will disappear and be lost in love. Nothing greater, nothing higher can be thought of. John, full of the eternal power and majesty of his God, full of the *causa causarum*, full of the *logos* of the Godhead who was in the beginning and was with God and was Himself God; "all things were made through Him, and without Him was not anything made that was made" (John 1:3); full of these stupendous ideas, says, "Jesus Christ has loved us and washed us of our sins with His blood" (Rev. 1:5).

---

5 Zinzendorf says: *Es war ihnen gefühlig genug.*

And when he portrays the majestic hours in heaven, the great disclosures of the heavenly revelations; when he describes the temple of God open in heaven and the ark of the covenant; when thunder and lightning and trumpets of angels are heard, and hosts which no one can number are seen: then their song is, "You have bought us with Your blood!" (Rev. 5:9, alt.).

This is the great subject matter; this is the chief object of faith. I know nothing but that You have died for me out of love; You have laid down Your life for me. I know that if You had not died for me, I should have been lost; I should have sunk into the bottom of hell, had You not extinguished hell for me, had You not (as Dr. Luther says) drunk up death.[6]

This is the first part of *fides explicita*. One knows in his inmost person[7] with whom he deals. One knows Him from head to foot, in heart and body. One knows Him in His most profound nature as it is now and was then. And when one has thought and felt this long enough and has arranged it in all possible drawers of the mind[8] and has become a scribe instructed for the kingdom of heaven, then one takes out one truth after the other, presents it and demonstrates it with reasons grounded deep within oneself, which grasp the hearers' hearts. For if one would speak to those who know and love the Saviour about His glory and majesty, then they say, "There is no doubt about that; that is clear enough to me, and I have no hesitation here. But the trembling of God shakes my soul. His suffering, His death, His anxiety,[9] His atoning-battle which He endured for me, the fact that He had to be absolved through the Holy Spirit for my sake, that with Him all my sin is forgiven, that with Him I have leave to be eternally blessed — this is the reality for which no word, no expression is adequate." One's feeling of this cannot be made plain to someone who does not have it himself. It all gets stuck or comes out only half and half. These are the *arrheta rhemata*, the unspeakable things.

> When that Heart confronts my eye
> In all His godly greatness,
> Then I think, "I die!"
> To gauge again that greatness,
> According to His humanity,
> No heart can be so small,
> So weak no other ever can be,
> As this Heart at all.
> Then I think: Good-bye,
> You self-empowered repenting.

---

6 Zinzendorf quotes Luther: *"Den Tod ausgesoffen."*
7 *Gemüth.*
8 *Gemüth.*
9 *Angst.*

Like wax before the fire, I
Want to melt in Jesus' suffering.
My heart shall see the wrath
In this suffering, pain,
And see the cleansing bath
For all my transgressions' stain.

When a person has this faith, this faith-in-distress, this faith made doubtful by reason of great unworthiness, this faith which has fallen in love through the real help, through the blessed happiness and grace which the heart has obtained, is that not beautiful? When a person has within himself the meditations of faith and the lasting feeling, the searching in Jesus even up to His eternal Godhead, finding His Father and His spirit, and all this coming from His side, out of His heart, is that not beautiful? And when he at last has, experiences, and obtains as a gift the learned faith which preaches from the wounds of Jesus to His Creator's power and from His Creator's power into the side of Jesus, into His wounded heart, and which makes everybody convinced and wise and brings them to an evident and demonstrative certainty, is that not beautiful? Is that not a great blessedness? Does that not make a blessed man, who, as Paul says, believes all this from his heart (Rom. 10:9) and can say and confess it with a *plerophory*.[10] His faith so flows from his heart that he can thus pour himself out before mankind.

But what grace, what patience and condescension it is, that the Creator, who knows His poor creature better than it knows itself, requires of it no other faith for being saved than the faith-in-distress, the first faith. When my anxiety, my sin, my corruption makes me believe, then I think, "He who appears before my heart, who has such a bloody appearance, who is said to have died for me, certainly it will be He. Yes! Yes! It is He! That makes me blessedly happy; that helps me into the eternal kingdom." Whoever does not learn to believe this way, that is, whoever does not have so much misery, so much distress that he must believe, how can that person be helped? He is already judged for this very reason, because he does not feel misery enough to cause him gladly to believe.

Faith is no great art; rather, the first beginning of faith, the very first faith is an effect of misery. No man except one who has the spirit of Lucifer, who has a satanical pride and blindness so that he does not want to see his physical and spiritual distress, who has been brought to insensibility because he will not feel his daily plague (and that is a Satan's spirit, a Satan's pride), none but such a person is in danger of missing the faith-in-distress. For even though a man is proud and egotistic in a merely human way and finally nevertheless does find in himself the fibres of his utter

---

10 Subjective complete assurance.

corruption and distress, his excuses cease, he begins to inveigh against himself, to condemn himself. And as soon as he does this, as soon as he discovers himself lost, then he is so full of anxiety that he does not have to create any for himself; he does not have to imagine any misery. And if this anxiety remains in him and increases and pushes its way into all his business, into his well-being, and he is forced to cry out for help, then he is in faith, in the faith-in-distress, in the midst of saving faith, and does not know himself how he got into it: "I believe it gladly because I delight in it."

So easy is it to be saved; so completely without excuse remain those who perish through unbelief.

Lecture V

That Aspect of Faith Which Actually Makes One So Blessedly Happy

Preached in the Brethren's Chapel in London, September 11, 1746

TEXT: I Corinthians 13:2 alt. [Last phrase is end of 3rd verse.] *"And if I have prophetic powers, and understand all mysteries and all knowledge, and if I have all faith, so as to remove mountains, but have not love, I gain nothing."* (RSV)

IF TERMINOLOGY, that is, the science of conveying the truth in apt expressions which conform to the subject and bring it closest to the mind, were really employed to that purpose, it would have been a noble science. But since the men who have so diligently concerned themselves with it have been deficient in the main point, they have been intent on hunting for expressions outside of Scripture in order to expound (with some degree of plausibility to mankind) those passages of Scripture which they found obscure. As a result they have made that which was before obscure so pitch dark that, if earlier, before hearing it explained one did understand a little bit, now after the explication one no longer has the slightest idea what to make of it.

This is the usual effect of all commentaries, of all explications, but particularly of the greatest part of theological terminology in which those people are trained who are to teach in the future. From this situation among others has arisen the confusion which makes no distinction between faith in miracles[1]

---

1 Zinzendorf's term is *Wunderglaube*.

and saving faith. For not long ago people did not hesitate to affirm all over Christendom that a person who performs miracles has reached the highest degree of a disciple of Christ.

There were at one time people in this country who claimed to raise the dead; and if they had only done it, no man would have doubted that they were servants of God, the kind, indeed, whose words lead right to heaven, who excelled in eminence among all other Christian people.

On account of this erroneous basic principle the philosophers, on the other hand, have made an astounding blunder and shown that their sophistry is also impracticable. For when they were opposed to the Christian religion, then they used to attack miracles and diligently set them forth as the workings of nature. And when they wanted to help the Christian religion, then their chief concern was to demonstrate that miracles had really happened. Now if this is viewed in the right light, then the whole quarrel is *de lana caprina*: [2] for no matter how it turned out, nothing would have been proved.

Doing miracles does not belong at all to the essence of a Christian; it does not belong at all to the Gospel. It is a gift which is usually bestowed either in condescension to this or that person or from the nature of the matter, because a miracle is necessary just at that point. If a servant of God intended to perform a miracle, in condescension to a heathen, barbarian people, the Saviour would certainly not disappoint him; or if someone in ordinary life needed a miracle in some circumstance or other and could not attain his goal without it, the Saviour would certainly help him so that he could perform one. And when it was done and the matter thereby set in motion, no great to-do ought to be made about it later, because it would prove nothing about the heart of the matter.

Thus, when the disciples returned home and told the Saviour that even the devils were subject to them, the Saviour gave them to understand that it was natural, that it indeed had to be thus for that time, that it was a part of their message. Yet He hoped that this would not be the reason for their satisfaction and happiness. They had something completely different about which they should rejoice: they were children of God and belonged to heaven; their names were already entered in the Book of Life. This would really be reason to rejoice; this would be glorying in Christ (cf. Luke 10:17–20).

I continue. Had care been taken to retain this from the beginning of the preaching of the Gospel, the unfortunate situations would not have arisen in which good rulers and zealous teachers made an error in some point or another the mark of a damned person or, on the other hand, the confession of this or that truth the mark of a child of God. Yet this precisely was the object of all the councils without distinction. Their truth is not called into question, but their conclusions are: the one is that whoever does not

---

2 Beside the point.

comprehend a matter in a certain way cannot be saved; the other is that whoever has mastered this or that concept will be saved.

We, according to our understanding in our communion,[3] know how to manage this issue. We can help the councils out, because we hold that one has ordinarily no knowledge in the matter of salvation without being at the same time saved. We differ only on this point, that we do not believe that when someone does not know this or that, that he is therefore damned. For knowledge has degrees, and knowledge of important things does not come all at once. But since there are, nevertheless, still certain people who have insights into truths and yet are not saved, it cannot be made a universal principle that knowledge saves. But it is an exception to the rule if at some time knowledge does not save a person. I mean that which can be called true knowledge, the central knowledge that really matters, the point into which everything runs together: the *cardo*, the hinge of knowledge, does save; that is certain.

Therefore, the Apostle does not say simply, "If I had all knowledge, it would profit me nothing"; but rather, "If I were a prophet and that way had all knowledge," etc. (I Cor. 13:2, alt.). This points out the connection. There have always been extraordinary men in the world who have been called prophets and who have had the purpose of setting up and establishing certain orders[4] in the church in this or that manner. Because of their office various things were communicated to these people which other people did not know. They also saw further than other people and for this reason were called "seers." These seers expounded stupendous matters and spoke of things in such a penetrating manner and with such simplicity that people supposed that a seer and a saved man are one and the same. Therefore Paul found it necessary to instruct the congregation that this was false. A man may be a seer, an extraordinary servant of God, who serves this or that order,[5] to whose words one must listen, to whose words attention must be paid, whose lectures are solid, and who nevertheless is himself not saved. If his prophetic office and gift lead him into pride, and he uses them to make himself shine out among mankind, in order to be honored by people and to be preferred to the rest of his fellow creatures, and if he likes this, then he may go away empty handed regarding the main point. Even if he spoke with the tongues of angels, yet he would be nothing more than a ringing bell, impelled by a spirit foreign and unknown to himself, but not full of the spirit inwardly in the heart.

I have stated this here in advance, because everybody who is acquainted with my principles knows that I do not believe that someone can recite

---

3 *Gemeine*.
4 *Oeconomien*.
5 *Oeconomie*.

the explanation of the second article by heart and with understanding, if he is not a child of God. And this is as much as saying that there is no devil's faith among men. Rather, among men whoever believes, he is saved; among men whoever gets so far as to believe, he is saved. For no man can do this, believe in Jesus and His wounds, without being immediately set free from the guilt and punishment of his sins. This is evident from Acts 2, "They that gladly received the word" (Acts 2:41, alt.); they that had a liking for the word, the word pleased them; they that took pleasure in it and believed it gladly — these were immediately baptized and were received as members of the communion[6] that very day. Here Peter did not say first, "You still have all these debts to pay; you have murdered; you have committed adultery; you still live in hatred against your neighbor; you still are involved in this or that lawsuit and dispute: first go and settle your affair with your neighbor and then come back." Rather, whoever gladly received the word (whatever situation he might be in as far as everything else is concerned, be he in confused or clear circumstances), he was immediately baptized and became a member of the communion. Afterwards, the other things, too, had to be put in order. First a person was saved, and then he manifested his blessedness by straightening out his entangled affairs so that new fruits appeared. In short, he conducted himself in such a way that grace, that the new Spirit which he received from God, was honored by it.

Thus, I stand by the proposition that on this account Paul says, "If I were a prophet and had all knowledge, I gain nothing" (I Cor. 13:2 , alt.), because, except for the extraordinary case of the prophetic office, he acknowledges no knowledge without faith.

It is an extraordinary case, when people can speak of heavenly and divine things without having experienced them in their hearts. It is something exorbitant rather than ordinary. As a rule, if a minister preaches and has nothing in his heart, then it is neither fish nor fowl; it lacks the *exousia*.[7] The man does not speak as one who understands what he is talking about, as one who is at home there, as one who is steeped in the subject; rather, if I may put it this way and use a comparison drawn from nature, he describes the four square corners of a round tower and a thing which lies to the west as lying to the east. He betrays by his description that he has not been at the place about which he is speaking. But if someone does speak distinctly, convincingly, solidly and truly of something which he has not experienced, he is a prophet. He is to be looked upon either as in an extraordinary state for this specific occasion or as an extraordinary person for all time, as a special servant used by God in an extraordinary way in His

---

6 Zinzendorf's term is again *Gemeine*.
7 Authority.

order for a specific purpose. For this reason he is to be venerated, which does not depend on his inner condition. But what is that of which the apostle says, one has to have it? It is the *ikker*,[8] as the Hebrews say; it is what really matters, *hoc si dixeris, omnia dixeris:* if that is in order, the rest will turn out all right. What is that thing called? For the Apostle Paul speaks of some such thing incessantly in this thirteenth chapter. He repeats it so often that one sees that it is very important to him; he would like everybody to know it inside and out. "This is love," he says, "Love." Now were this expounded according to the terminology which is customary in Christendom, then it would turn out as it has with most people so far. When they speak of love, they mean by it a goodness which is well-meaning toward the neighbor, serves him gladly and helps him out of distress. I have seen in the commentaries of most theologians that, when they come to this text, "If I give away all I have to the poor, and if I deliver my body to be burned, but have not love, I gain nothing" (I Cor. 13:3, LT), they explain it this way and say, "If someone did this and yet did not do it out of heartfelt love toward his neighbor, but rather out of pride, out of vanity of mind, in order to be seen, he would gain nothing by it." From this it can be clearly seen that they understand the entire chapter to be about that virtue which in everyday life is called love. It means to be loving and kind-hearted, to have a good disposition, to wish one's neighbor nothing bad, but rather to be helpful to him and work for his advantage, to have a sympathetic heart toward him. In this manner they expound it without much ado; and it was a great moment for me when I saw that one single commentator among all the rest thought of bringing that place in the Song of Songs to bear on I Corinthians 13: "You have ravished my heart with a glance of your eyes" (Song 4:9b); also "O that he would kiss me with the kisses of his mouth (Song 1:2a); your name is oil poured out; therefore the souls[9] love you" (Song 1:3, alt.). Such little crumbs are like balsam when, among such a multitude of men who err regarding such a divinely cherished truth and in addition teach all other men erroneously, one discovers a person whose eyes are beginning to open and who, though rather indistinctly, rather shyly, so that he will not become entangled in vexations and a theological brawl, comes out with a reference and cites a text which the reader himself may trace afterwards. This is, indeed, a real joy.

But I am not afraid to maintain publicly and candidly that the apostle, in this thirteenth chapter of the first letter to the Corinthians, means nothing the least bit different in his entire discourse from what we call saving faith.[10]

---

8 Zinzendorf uses this term repeatedly for "main point." The reference is to the Hebrew word *aqar*=Root which Zinzendorf transcribes in the Yiddish pronunciation as *ikker*.
9 The text reads "maidens." Zinzendorf writes *Seelen*.
10 *Seeligmachenden Glauben*.

This he calls love and distinguishes it in the last verse of the chapter from faith purely for the reason that as soon as one has a faithful heart toward the Saviour, one must trust in certain things and promises which one sees neither now nor then but must expect and which, when they are fulfilled, take away that part of saving faith which consists in hoping and expecting and leave nothing behind except that part which consists in love and faithfulness.

The two parts, the apostle says, will cease in time. Then nothing more will have to be believed, for it will be seen. Nothing more will have to be hoped, for it will actually be enjoyed. And therefore everything which is now distinguished from love under the names of faith and hope will converge in love. But in the time in which we live, in the time of faith and hope, all the rest is still included under the word *love*. In the word *love* faith is understood; in the word *love* hope is understood.

Thus the apostle explained once in another place what he meant. After making an extensive comment on how blessed, how experienced and strong believers ought to be, he then says finally, "And all this in love" (I Cor. 16:14). "Let us love Him," says John, "for He has first loved us" (I John 4:19, LT). And in a certain place the Saviour says of the woman, "Her sins, which are many, are forgiven" (Luke 7:14); therefore she loves so much. And when Peter had denied Him three times and had bound himself to it with an oath, the Saviour did not then say to him, "Do you now believe in me?" Rather he only asked him, "Do you love me?" (John 21:16). With this He included everything; for otherwise he would have had to ask three times, "Do you believe in me? Do you love me? Do you hope for salvation?" But the Saviour included everything in the word love: "Do you love me?" Peter did not explain himself further regarding anything else. He did not say, "Dear Lord! I believe"; but rather he said, "Lord! You know everything; you know that I love you" (John 21:17). And the Saviour, well-satisfied with the quality, this qualification, immediately invested Peter as the shepherd of His people. That was enough for Him. "Only love, only continue to love me. He who loves me will be loved by my Father, and I will love him and manifest myself to him" (John 14:21). Therefore Paul says that the highest perfection of a Christian is to know Him as one is known by Him (I Cor. 13:12, LT).

O dear friends, do not imagine that we know the Saviour; we begin to know Him only when we have loved Him very tenderly, when we have loved Him first above all things, when for us nothing more in the world is in competition with Him, when we have forgotten ourselves on account of Him, our health, our life, our possessions and goods, our enjoyment (for reputation in the world is indeed not the prime point at issue). When we have forgotten ourselves with body and life out of love toward Him and can at certain times out of love toward Him be angry with ourselves, then, I say, a small beginning of the knowledge of Him is responsible. It comes because we recognize that He has laid down His life for us. And our whole life consists in the increasing and growing in this knowledge, so that we know Him better today than yesterday and in a year know Him a year better, in twenty years twenty years better, and in eternity an eternity better than now. This is the great science; this is the great knowledge, without limit and end, the inexhaustible knowledge. In Him and His person lies hidden a treasure of wisdom and knowledge which cannot be fathomed or exhausted.

But what is this matter? What is the main point in the process of being saved? What is sufficient for the eternal kingdom? When can I say to Him, "My bone!" When He can say in all truth, "This is indeed bone of my bone and flesh of my flesh!" and vice versa: "Every spirit which confesses that Jesus has come in the flesh is of God" (I John 4:2), as John says positively. It is impossible, he says, that a person can look upon the most dear Saviour as his fellow man, as his flesh and bone, without being born of God. Paul says that nobody can call Jehovah Jesus unless he has been inspired by the Holy Spirit (I Cor. 12:3). It is not possible, he says, that someone can say that his Creator is his Saviour unless the idea originates with the Holy Spirit. Whoever can say "Jehovah Elohim, who has created mankind and all things, whose handiwork we are, who is exalted above all heavens, is my Saviour, is my infant Jesus in the womb, in the cradle and in the temple, is the carpenter from Nazareth who spent His life in sweat and labour at His handicraft until He was thirty years old; the teacher come from God whom the devil plagued for forty days in the wilderness, who began to establish His little church with twelve, with seventy, and with five hundred and upon the cross selected the first two elders of His church, His mother and His beloved John; this is the very Creator, the architect of the universe, of the sun and the moon and all the stars, and of all conceivable worlds" — whoever can take all this into consideration and bring it into a round proposition, whoever can declare this with feeling and understanding,

> I believe a point in time will be
> When Christ my Creator will come to me
> To wed me body and soul,

such a person is an angelic, heavenly and divine man (this is Paul and John's expression). This cannot happen without the Holy Spirit. This no one can do who is not filled with the Holy Spirit.

Now consider, what is more common in the world, what is more customary in the Christian world, what is more on men's lips than this? The Catholic and the Lutheran churches make up the majority of European Christians; and although in other denominations [11] the Saviour is handled in another way and things are moving toward a purely philosophical conception (and although even some Lutherans, who want to give themselves airs, are beginning to choose this dry way which will in the end make the Saviour into a Confucius), nevertheless this is certain, that the greatest number of our denominations still have the Creator as Saviour on their lips; they still sing:

> The blest Creator of all creation
> Assumed a servant's low condition,
> To win the flesh, He flesh employs,
> So that His creature not all destroys.

This is at the same time a Catholic and a Lutheran verse; this the two denominations have in common. Are therefore all these people men of God? Are all of these men saved? Do all of these people therefore go right to heaven on their words? One party in our denomination imagines this; it is not far from their thoughts. I do not want to oppose them on it, if only they have read correctly. The texts are clear, but it depends upon a phrase or two, upon a little point to which one must pay attention and which deprives them again of their whole hope. This is the little word *confess:* "Every spirit which confesses that JESUS has come in the flesh" (I John 4:2). But what does that mean? What kind of a change does that make in the idea? Answer: An astonishing one. Simply consider, who in the world can confess something without having experienced it? If someone is called to be a witness, and he is supposed to confess something, to declare something, and he has neither seen nor heard the thing, then he is not competent to do it. For what I am to confess I must have seen and heard; otherwise I can indeed say I believe it, I can take the *juramentum credulitatis,* an oath that one really thinks a matter is a certain way, that one's heart agrees with the testimony of others, that one believes that these people will speak the truth, because they are honest people. But this cannot be called a confession, but rather an attestation, a consent, a conformation with the thoughts and ideas of other people, believing the word of others. But this is no confession *au pied de la lettre.* [12] On the contrary, a confession always comes out of my own heart, out of my own knowledge of the matter. It presupposes that I myself have done something, that I myself have been somewhere, that I myself have seen or heard something which other people would like to know from me. Therefore whoever wants to be a confessor (but a confessor is a saved man, and this is something important; "Whoever confesses," says

---

11 Zinzendorf uses the term *Religionen* for denominations or churches.
12 In the strict sense of the term.

Paul, "will be saved" [Rom. 10:9, alt.]), he must himself have had, seen, felt, experienced and enjoyed the matter. Then he can say, "Good people, believe me, believe an expert; I was present." That settles the matter. The mouth and the tongue speak nothing but what lies in the heart; that which is uttered arises from the feeling of the heart: "I believe, therefore I speak" (II Cor. 4:13, LT). One is driven from within and could restrain a matter only intentionally and intentionally not want to admit that which one had nevertheless experienced in reality and in truth. If someone comes and says, "How can that be? How is that possible?" then one can answer with reason, "I know it; I was present; I saw it with my eyes, and I heard it with my ears." Do you belong to Jesus? Yes. Is He your Creator? Yes. Do you believe that you are and will remain His to eternity? Yes. How so? Has someone told you so? No, nobody at all told me so, but I believe it. I believe it not because of any speech or writing, but rather because I have it, because that is the way it is for me, because that which no eye has seen or heard and which has not come into the heart of any man (I Cor. 2:9a) has been revealed to me, according to the spiritual, invisible order.

But there is still something else which is also important to remember — indeed it is of the greatest importance — namely, that one is never converted by a preacher, never leaves a sermon in a blessed state, if one did not come into the church already awakened. And even though it happens *illo ipso momento*, [13] it is nevertheless never the responsibility of the preacher that one is awakened, but rather the Holy Spirit acted at least a minute, an instant, before a word touched me, before words fall into my heart, before a sentence, a paragraph, a conclusion, a proposition becomes my text, my principle, upon which I can rely. Here the Holy Spirit has done everything beforehand; everything invisible, everything inexpressible, everything that happens in the spirit of the mind, everything that takes place in the soul, out of which faith may arise — the Holy Spirit has inspired all of this. The word falls into prepared soil, into a cultivated field, and is nothing other than the explanation of the truth which already lies in the heart. It is not the conception; it is not the birth; rather, it is the first food of the living heart. The Word of God is the food. The eternal Word is Christ, the essential, the autonomous Word, the Cause of all things, the Creator of all things. He has gained a true, essential, bloody form in the heart. And then His word is our food, our refreshment, our nourishment, a part of our sustenance, one of our cordials; for He Himself is the main food and drink:

> If on Him I feed,
> It is for me most healthy,

---

13 In that very moment.

> When my dear husband indeed
> Lets His cordial steep within me.

This is the *ikker;*[14] this is promised us too. His flesh is true food, and His blood is true drink. His holy corpse and its real mixture with our spirit, body, and soul must constitute the truth of the matter. But His word is a cordial for us. To hear of Him, to hear His covenant-blood, His eternal atonement, the invention of our redemption discussed — this is afterwards to an awakened soul nothing other than as if balsam were poured all over it, as if scented oil were poured forth and perfumed a whole church, a hall, a house, filling everything with its pleasantness. It is as if one went into a garden in the evening, where all the flowers are in bloom, to refresh and revive. Thus it is afterwards, when the Lamb is mentioned to someone by name, whom the Holy Spirit has written in the heart with His stylus, when one hears the Saviour mentioned:

> The heart does rejoice
> When His name is professed.
> His all-powerful humanness also confessed.

Now there are many thousands of people in the world who, when they hear the Saviour proclaimed pay attention just as if they were reading a newspaper, where the people in the report are five hundred or a thousand miles away from them, do not concern them, and among whom they do not have a single acquaintance; in a few days they have forgotten what it was. Why? It was not important to them; to them it was a foreign matter. But he with whom the Holy Spirit has had to do, whose heart the Holy Spirit has reached, whose heart the Holy Spirit has unlocked, from whose heart He has rolled away the stone and has brought into that heart the bloody grace and the feeling of the atonement — when such a heart hears of the Saviour, of the Reconciler, when it hears that his Creator is his Saviour, when it hears a brother say,

> I believe a point in time will be
> When Christ my Creator will come to me
> To wed me body and soul,

it is indeed for such a soul as if someone received news of his son, of his father, of his brother; it is as if a wife received news of her husband; and they have reason to believe that it is true. As in such circumstances a person's frame of mind is made joyful or miserable, depending upon the news, and

---

14   See footnote 8.

as the confirmation of the news doubles the joy or misery, so is it afterwards with all that one hears about the Saviour, about the Lamb, about his Creator. It may have to do with His actions, or His words, or His merit; one finds everything coming alive. And this is the consequence not of the dignity of the person who is speaking, not of the words which are spoken, not of the moving presentation, not of the arguments produced, or of the charm of his person, but rather it is the consequence of the love which is in the heart toward the matter.

But how does one become involved in this love? "It is poured into our hearts through the Holy Spirit which has been given to us" (Rom. 5:5). When the Holy Spirit comes into the heart, he melts the heart; then the eyes fill with tears, then body and soul rejoice. As the occasion requires, the heart is grieved at its misery and rejoices at the grace, at the peace, at the blessedness which it feels, not knowing how it came about. This happened to Cornelius; this happened to Queen Candace's treasurer. They felt this joy, and they tasted this blessedness; but they did not know what name to give it. Then it was said to Cornelius, "Now send for Simon; he will explain it to you (Acts 10:32, alt.). He will tell you what has been done in your heart; he will name the man for you to whom you are to attribute all of this." And to Queen Candace's treasurer the Saviour Himself sent Philip. As soon as he wanted to know it, Philip had to climb up into the chariot to him and only name the Lamb for him which had taken hold of his soul, which had already seized his bones, and say, "This is His name; it is He." And then there was no question about baptism; it was immediately ready. It did not take several weeks of preparation first; there was no need to memorize a book; there was no need for answering twenty-four or thirty questions. Rather, "Who will prevent you from being baptized? Do you believe? Is that man important to you? Do you believe all the good said about Him, and believe it gladly?" "Oh yes, with all my heart." Then everything was well, and the blood of the covenant was poured over him. Then that grace was made known to him which so many thousands of souls have in common with him, who also gladly receive the word, are baptized and received into the community at the hour of awakening.

I would like this love to be the only pleasant and blessed reality, the pearl toward which all souls extend their desires, so that they might win it and forget everything else, so that each soul would ask itself honestly and candidly, "Do you have this love?" Can you feel it? Can you say, as you are going to a church, a meeting, are you going here and there, can you believe that you love something? Is your heart so disposed? Do you like that which has been explained to you, and do you care about it? Do you feel a condition which you have not had before? Has something happened to you which you need explained, if you cannot explain it yourself? Do you have a little verse in the Bible, a stanza from a hymn, something for which you need a good friend who can say to you, "The same thing happened to me; I am familiar with it."

Certainly, dear friends, such a person is a blessed listener. He really comes away from the sermon or conversation more learned. He comes away from his Bible more learned, as often as he looks into it. Or he may read a hymn, and it will be sheer life and spirit to him; it solves all of his difficulties for him; it sheds light on everything that was obscure to him before. And with this *Shekinah*,[15] with this light and privilege, with this divine diadem on the forehead, the poorest peasant and beggar, the most common man is on a par with the most wise and learned. Here is the greatest equality, the purest parity: what I am, my brother, that you also have become.

Thus Jude says, "Our common salvation (Jude 3), our common blessedness." As a republic says, "Our plantation, our commerce," etc., so a believer says, "Our heaven, our Saviour, our Jesus, our Father, our grace, our absolution, our blessedness." Here no one can usurp something from the others; everything is equal; everything is allotted equally; each one has what the other has. Then each one goes into his corner, and the one advances in his knowledge, the other remains behind; the one has the office of speaking much, the other of thinking much, of entertaining many ideas. Accordingly this makes a difference in talent, but it is of no consequence, for love, as the point on which everything depends, is the same in all. They all love unutterably; they are all deeply in love with Him. His soul has risen up in all their minds in full, sweet love; the bones of all of them are united with God through Him. Thus a Christian, a child of God, the very least beginner, cannot be venerated enough.

If natural men knew in what clarity of faith, in what priestly holiness a child of God stands and walks, sits and lies, acts and lives, they would have a deep respect for him. It happens sometimes that particular communities appear which have the advantage of inspiring that kind of respect in others, sometimes even against the will of the latter. Individuals reveal now and then so much ineptitude, so many human frailties, that they obscure the brightness of that light, the bloody light in the heart to natural eyes. It makes them ashamed of themselves because of their incompetence and unworthiness. This is a wise providence; it is an aspect of the present time in which we live, and it continues on to the grave, until the tabernacle is folded up and put into its crucible. Imperfection, the *tempus vicissitudinum*, the alternation of light and darkness continue until then, so that the honor and the glory and the majesty are not always recognized. This must wait until "our life with Christ will be revealed" (Col. 3:4, alt.). But this is certain; we have enough for present needs and it suffices for salvation. Satan feels

---

15 The presence of God among men. Cf. Exodus 24:16: "The glory of the Lord settled on Mount Sinai, and the cloud covered it six days; and on the seventh day he called to Moses out of the midst of the cloud."

it more than enough; it is more dreadful and terrible than he would like, and he does not come too close to any child of God. John says, "He dares not approach; he dares not touch you" (I John 5:18, alt.).

A poor sick woman, a woman who was debarred from the community because of her hemorrhage, was allowed to come near to the Saviour, was allowed to touch Him, was allowed to violate the law. This she did as a person in misery. All poor sinners still have this right today. But the devil, the prince of this world, does not have the power even to come near a child of God, a loving soul, one engaged to the Lamb. In this consists our safety, our rest, and blessedness:

> Gather in your little bird;
> If Satan would devour it,
> Let angels' singing then be heard:
> "This child shall be unhurt."

The ancients have had such fine ideas:

> You spirits of hell, get away!
> Here's nothing for you to do;
> This house belongs in Jesus' sway:
> Let it safely sleep without you,

and more of such expressions, which were given to them as the occasion demanded. They are prophecies concerning the communion of Jesus, concerning the souls of the Saviour, and they are true; they have their foundation in eternal election.

The devil does not dare to come near a child of God. I am indeed convinced that when one says that he is tempted by God, he is very much in the wrong; he sins against God. James had expressed this very aptly (James 1:13). But even the devil should not be blamed for too much. Man himself is a poor creature. Man himself is made up of so many contradictions as long as he is in the body that he can easily become nasty. Man has all kinds of rudeness in himself, gets himself into all sorts of strange circumstances without any help from the devil. Therefore man can unhesitatingly lay all the blame on himself. For from the moment that a soul has passed over into the pierced hand and is recognized as the Saviour's, the devil is turned back and banished. There is no more mention of him at all, and he is heard no more. "I do not pray that thou shouldst take them out of the world"; but this I say, "They must concur with the devil no more (John 17:15, alt.). He must not be allowed to come near them; he must leave them in peace. This I require; for they have no business with him, and the prince of this world has nothing on them."

This indeed is a great blessedness. Paul's armour shows clearly that the devil shoots darts at us (Eph. 6:16). What does that mean? Answer: If he could collar us and trample us under his feet, as David says, "The enemy pursues my soul and crushes my life to the ground and lays me in the darkness like the dead" (Ps. 143:3, LT) — if he could do this, he would not have to shoot at us. But because he does not dare to come near, he shoots fiery darts at us, and even these do not hit us but fall short. And if they do not fall short, then the shield against them is there, that is faith, which overcomes the world and its prince, so that a person can say, "I know in whom I believe" (II Tim. 1:12, LT). I know that my Creator is my Saviour. I believe that there is a point in time when God my Creator Jesus Christ will marry me in body and soul, this poor creature, His poor human creature, His little worm, His poor little soul, and fetch me home. Faith's courage is the shield which lets in none of the darts which are shot at us from a distance by Satan's malice, because he does not dare to come near us. For we are in a fortress, and if we do not let ourselves be decoyed out of our fortress (as the apostle warns, that no one go out of his fortress [Eph. 6:14]), then he really cannot lay hands on us.

We wish all mankind this great blessedness: "O that the whole human race would surrender itself to Jesus," etc. Then a blessedness would come upon all souls, if they would only gladly embrace it. If it thus were only their pleasure, if they thought from their hearts, "O who will carry me there, who will carry me into my Shepherd's arms! Who will deliver me there! If He would just take me, if He would only fetch me! I am still so far from Him; I am so tangled up in sin, in passions and in external things; I am such a foolish person and spoiled with so many philosophical fads; I am so crammed with false principles that I cannot find my way into order and simplicity; I am preoccupied in opposition to the Saviour! O if He would only take me! After all, His people sing:

> Had I not been pursued
> by you alone,
> I would never have gone looking
> for you on my own.

If He would just do this with me too, and take me, and all at once pull me out of all my misery, out of all the contradictory circumstances, out of all that which opposes Him, from my own mind, from my own obstinacy.

> If only the power of his blood
> Would master my hard heart,
> Push into every part!"

Whoever can think this way, whoever can be this way, already has the Holy Spirit actually standing before his heart. For no natural man can think like this unless the Saviour has really been at work on him already. The Holy Spirit has already begun to turn the key; He has already begun to make the heart open up. Already there is work; grace is there; the Spirit's business is there as soon as a man can think this way. But the people who cannot yet think like this can nevertheless do something else: they can experience consternation and perplexity. And here they ought to show faithfulness toward themselves and not drive away their consternation, their perplexity, their restlessness with something else or escape by some strange means. Rather, they must hold still for the Holy Spirit, who always keeps His eye on them until He can note His time, when He can come to their hearts and find a way into their hearts through all difficulties and impossibilities. In the meantime consternation, perplexity and restlessness must remain. Whoever gets rid of them on his own, be it through a spiritual or a temporal or any other circumstance, through a spiritual hymn or book, and although it were the Bible itself, for this man at this time it is poison. If something brings a man out of consternation and restlessness into freedom, into contentment, and the Saviour does not come into the heart at the same time, the Crucified One does not move into the mind at the same time, He does not stand with the opened side before the heart, and this peace and reassurance do not arise from a view of the wounds, from touching the marks of the nails, from the pierced side, but rather from some other, even the best quarter, then it is a perdition and misfortune for the poor human creature.

These are things which we must wish and hope and implore for each other and always testify what we have experienced of them, and what we believe — sometimes more distinctly, sometimes more blessedly, sometimes more strikingly, sometimes drier and weaker than at other times: but always from the heart, always according to the same true plan, "I believe; therefore I say it" (II Cor. 4:13, LT, alt.).

PRAYER

God our Creator! Who has so highly loved His poor human creature and has so truly laid down His life for him! Have patience with Your human creature, though he does not believe all things of You, though he cannot comprehend everything, for it is too great.

For, dear Saviour, how little compassion, how little sympathy for the miserable is there in the world! Who thinks of the miserable, of the afflicted, of the souls confused about themselves? Who goes about and looks out for the distressed, in order to help them? For how can poor men with their dead, hard, uncompassionate hearts now imagine a God, imagine the Creator of the world as passing into a miserable human tabernacle for the sake of their death, because they deserved hell. And yet this is the first point which they must imagine. Here is where everybody must begin. They must, notwithstanding the infinity of Your Godhead, worship You in a human person, in Your manger, in Your despised and base form, in the most miserable one that could ever be conceived and devised, wandering and vagabond, not having a place where You could safely lay Your head without having to worry about being ordered away, because even that place was not Your own.

In this way, dear Heart, You must come before our eyes. Thus we must see You fighting in our stead; thus we must see You in Your penance-agony, lying covered with bloody sweat, being ready to dig Yourself into the earth for the hellish anguish of Your soul. Thus we must see You hanging naked and bare before the eyes of the whole world, and the Creator of the whole world, the unfathomable Being of all beings, must occur to our minds in Your person. Then we are theologians; then we understand something.

Now You know, dear Heart, how childlike, how difficult, how great this theology is, which is looked upon as mere catechism teaching, and how foreign and remote a thing it is from human understanding. Therefore come rather directly to our heart; let us rather feel Your wounds and Your merits before we are able to name You; before we know Your name, before we understand anything of Your greatness and divinity. Let us become aware of that only when we are already reconciled, when we are already within the Shepherd's arms and embrace You with a heart in love. It is always seasonable for us to hear, "Behold, the man!" This is your God, your Creator; this is the God of the whole world, the God of the spirits of all flesh. O how gladly will we do You homage, how gladly will we fall at Your feet, how willing will be our worship in holy adornment. Begin in the hearts, grasp the souls, convince them through Your Spirit of their misery, let them be drawn to You by an invincible drawing, through the drawing of the Father, Who delights in delivering millions of souls, millions of unnamed and unknown souls into Your arms, in addition to the first fruits who are the reward of Your pains, the promised premium of Your cross. In this great city, in this little world, be not satisfied with such a few souls, with such a disproportionate number, whom You call forth; but let there also be at times multitudes brought to You through the savour of Your death, through the savour of Your tortured corpse, which nothing can resist, which nothing can refuse. This will be the joy of Your little hearts,[16] of Your People, the children of Your heavenly Father, to Whom it is pleasing when Your house is full. To this end let Your Gospel have

---

16 Zinzendorf uses the diminutive *Herzel*.

time in this land, under the happy and blessed government of our dear King George the Second and of those who honestly preside over his realm and this city. You well know what a blessed happiness it is when Your people can have a quiet life under Your servants, when their way of life is guided skillfully, properly, and respectably in the eyes of men. Grant us this in this city and in this country more and more, that in days and years to come we may here also see the blessedness which we have already seen in so many countries, that innumerable multitudes will be gathered at the feet of their Creator, because He is their Saviour, because He is their Shepherd. Amen.

Lecture VI

That it is Blessedness and Happiness to be a Human Soul

Preached in the Brethren's Chapel in London, September 18, 1746

TEXT: John 1:11–12. *"He came to his own home, and his own people received him not. But to all who received him, who believed in his name, he gave power to become children of God."* (RSV)

BEFORE I BRING this important and blessed text closer to our hearts, I will advance two observations, which will at the same time furnish us a key to the text.

The first is this, that there is a profound and sufficient fundamental reason why the consciences of men, and of teachers most of all, ought not to be forced; why it is almost impossible directly to hinder a person who entertains a false doctrine from propagating it, when he does it occasionally and without creating disorder; and why, in the end, no arguments other than spiritual ones can avail in Christendom against such men. That fundamental reason is this, that it is impossible for a man who does not come to the Holy Scriptures with a central knowledge, with an insight converging at one point, to extricate himself from the seemingly contradictory phrases and expressions.

In our text for this day we shall find two fundamental positions, through which the two denominations[1] of the Protestant Church are divided from each other. We shall find that they oppose each other with a great semblance

---

1 Zinzendorf's word is *Religionen*.

of reason based on this text of ours. If we act fairly, we shall also find that the party whose doctrine we do not hold has words in the text which are as plain and clear for their position as we have for ours — before one gets involved in explications.

But if we comprehend the matter with the heart, we shall find that both positions are true, and that the lack of moderation from which the separation has arisen on both sides, is always with those men only who have no heart. Thus, as soon as people of the two different denominations come together and have one heart, nothing can keep them from agreeing, except perhaps the prejudice resulting from their education. Afterwards they oppose each other in a kind of confusion and no longer even know why. For the heart unites in the moment of grace, and experience unites their ideas; they feel, as a necessary result, an inclination to join together, and feel also that if each would persist in his extreme, neither of them would have the whole truth. This is the first important observation.

The second comes nearer still to the point: if only we look at the matter quite simply as it presents itself to us, partly as it expresses itself in human idea, partly as it shows itself in daily practice, the scales will be balanced in today's text: "as many as received Him." This is the great and indeed the only complete argument for those who maintain freedom of the will. "To those He gave power"; that is the most important and real argument for those who deny at least the effect of the freedom of man's will, for those who maintain that even though a person wanted to obey, yet perhaps he could not; and even if he did not want to obey, he would have to.

There are two extremes. One is the thoughtlessness [2] in the so-called Lutheran denomination, as if the thing did turn simply upon our wanting to be saved and that such a wish were almost a favor to our Saviour. It might be put off as long as we pleased, possibly until the final hour, and then we could go directly to heaven anyhow. Sovereigns of the most ancient times already had such notions, reserving their baptism until the last breath, that in the meantime they might do as they pleased: all is well that ends well. This extreme brought sober-minded, reflective, serious people to attempt a palliative cure in the other extreme and to call this freedom into question. And that this is not merely Calvinian or Zwinglian may be seen from the fact that our Dr. Luther was for several years on the side which absolutely denies the freedom of man's will, and that he wrote a book in which he, disputing on the subject, maintains that man has no free will. [3] It is true that he did alter his opinion and altered it auspiciously. I bring this up only as an argument that the opposition of those who deny the freedom of the will does not proceed so much from any narrowness of

---

2 *Leichtsinnigkeit*.
3 Zinzendorf is thinking of Martin Luther's *On the Bondage of the Will*, published in 1525.

spirit, as from a certain devotion, from a kind of respect, from a veneration for God; it does not proceed from any enmity towards God, as those on the other side imagine, but out of a fear, lest salvation might be treated as a game and people in the end might find themselves wretchedly deceived. Thus they wanted to remove this abuse by means of a sovereign resignation to grace — so sovereign that it rendered men very little different from statues and stupid brute beings.

I have no occasion to consider these extremes, for I do not believe that there are many present here who have to contend with the one or the other. Therefore, I will take the text itself into consideration and from this, as may easily be imagined, especially recommend this momentous point to the hearts of all my dear friends, "that it is blessedness and happiness to be a human soul."

The text itself leads us to two propositions: first, that all human souls, actually and universally considered, are designed for salvation; secondly, that all souls, not one excepted, are, however, not saved, except upon a certain supposition. I will call it neither order nor rule; I will call it neither discipline nor form, but rather a supposition: something is presupposed, without which nobody is saved.

I have said that to be a man is to be a blessed creature; "one is created to have eternal life."[4] Such a frank sentence is in the Bible; it is indeed in a disputed book,[5] but it is still a true proposition. Yet at the same time we must necessarily suppose that a soul can perish if it will; it can put salvation aside. This John has positively said, concerning the Saviour, "He came unto His own, and His own received Him not" (John 1:11). This actually means that He came to His own home, and His countrymen would not have anything to do with Him.

You know what an effect nationalism has the world over; you know that there is hardly any nation but the German that likes to have anything to do with foreigners. In Germany a person has simply to come from England or France or Spain, and he will be preferred to all the natives. Why? Precisely because he is a foreigner. I will not say that this is such a very great honor to our nation, in so far as their ideas in this regard are completely unregulated; there is a touch of curiosity and flightiness in it, but yet it betrays a nobleness of mind, too. On the other hand, most of the other nations of the world hold the principle that it is preferable to be a native. From this preference are derived all those laws favorable to the citizens, and upon this foundation people so readily appeal to their indigenous situation: I am a native. From this principle comes Paul's frequent declaration, I am Roman born [6] (in contrast to those who might perhaps have been naturalized), as he once explained

---

4 Wisdom of Solomon 2:23: "For God created man for immortality."
5 The Wisdom of Solomon is part of the Apocrypha of the Old Testament.
6 Acts 22:28.

himself in plain terms to the chief captain. Now in order to show mankind so obviously that it does not want to be saved, the Saviour also had to be a native among the people who crucified Him and, as far as in them lay, destroyed Him from the face of the earth. Not only was He to come to His own home, but He was also to be of royal descent and of a family which had the right of inheritance to the crown. This was in a country where all depended upon such a right; where the people were uneasy with all foreigners; where almost anyone who came from the outside was at best only unwillingly tolerated; and where the people desired least of all to be in subjection to someone who was not of the house and lineage of David. This was to be so; He was to be a native citizen of the country in which all those prophets had been teaching who prophesied of the grace that was to come, who pointed toward the sufferings of Jesus Christ and waited for His majestic glory. Thus, the following exception was removed: 'we do not know where he came from, and we do not know who he is; he has brought strangers into our church' — as they once said of Paul, that he brought Greeks into it; or as the chief captain said, "Aren't you the Egyptian who brought the foreign bandits into the country?" (Acts 21:38, alt.). They could not accuse the Saviour of this, but rather, when the wise men out of the East inquired where the newborn king was, the Saviour's countrymen replied, "In Bethlehem, for so it is written" (Matt. 2:5); this is true.

But now what conclusions did His countrymen draw from their own confession? Perhaps that of the Chinese, who paid divine honor to Confucius for so many centuries, because they had the favor and honor of having such a great philosopher in their nation? Did their own testimony influence them to be as concerned about Him as they were about Elijah, after he was taken up into heaven, or about Moses? Oh no: they rejected Him; they did not receive Him; they would not have anything to do with Him.

That once cogent argument, indigenous birth, which had deified all the philosophers in their own nation and recommended all the prophets to their own people, must now be the argument against the Saviour. "We know this man; is not Mary, the last remaining virgin of the lineage of David, his mother? Therefore he is a false prophet."[7] This is a conclusion so absurd that it could not possibly have come from their heads: it must have proceeded from their ill-disposed hearts. Their enmity towards the Saviour and their friendship with Belial dictated to them such animosity against their countryman; we will not have him; away with him — "they received Him not." This is indisputable proof that they could have received Him, as it is here expressed: "I have set before you life and death, blessing and curse; therefore choose life" (Deut. 30:19) and (Ps. 109:17) "He did not like blessing."

---

7 Cf. Mark 6:3.

Will anybody object? But why then does the Saviour not make use of His power? It would not be the first time that He forced the people. Did He not force them to the law on Sinai? Whoever would want to deny that would have to deny the daylight. Did He not force them for forty years in the wilderness? He does not deny it Himself: "I will make a covenant with the house of Israel and with the house of Judah, not like the covenant which I made with their fathers, when I was obliged to take them by the arms and force[8] them. But this shall be the covenant: I will put my law within them, and I will write it in their hearts (Jer. 31:31–33a, alt.); their natural disposition may be what it will — they may be adept or quite stupid people; it shall be no hindrance. I will convey it into their hearts; I will appear before the heart with my truth which they shall have within. They shall not give themselves the least trouble about it; they shall not take a single step for it; they shall have no occasion to expend the merest trifle upon it. Before they are aware of it, they shall have it in their hearts, as the wind turns into a corner and cannot find its way out again. It shall come close to them in their hearts, and thus shall they know me: without having to be taught, they shall acquire a love and affection for me, small and great, children and old people; and I will draw no distinctions."

Here, at the same time, the alternative is implied: "If they will not be acquainted with me in this way, and if they are not inclined to love me in this manner, they may leave it alone; I shall force them no more — I do not want to have forced people. I do not want a seraglio of souls; I want free souls. I want to have bride-hearts; I will voluntarily be their bridegroom, and they will voluntarily be my bride." "Send my children and the work of my hands to me" (Isa. 45:11); say, as once the king of Israel said to a poor woman, "If the Lord does not help you, I cannot help you" (2 Kings 6:27). In a legalistic and hostile disposition he said, "If I could snatch Elisha's head from his shoulders, things would go better in this land (2 Kings 6:31, alt.). But by reason of that man I can do nothing; I can help no one; I have to let all people go away from me helpless."

In a Gospel sense we say this: dear hearts, we cannot help you; you will get little comfort from us. But there is someone: may He kiss you with the kiss of His mouth; may He let you experience His grace; may He let you share in His bloody atonement; may He let that blessing come upon you which He has pronounced over the whole world; may He let His penance for all the world bless you with grace and pardon of sins; may our Lord God bless you with all His merits. This is the case, when it is said, "Send them to me." When people ask you, "How shall I be saved?" then answer, "Believe in the Lord Jesus, and you are saved" (Acts 16:31, alt.).

---

8 "force" (*zwingen*) is from Luther's translation.

Now this is a peculiar circumstance: "as many as received Him." But how does this come about? How is this made to happen in our hearts, in the present circumstances and in this great city on this very day? How is it done? It is done this way: He comes.

> In a moment stands before us
> The Prince with His opened side.

We will leave out His own home, for in this context it is irrelevant; His own people are also irrelevant here though it is important when we have to do with Jews. I will not pursue now the subject that we also belong to Him; this is clear in all the scriptures of the New Testament, and it is not a matter to be settled now. Immediately after our text, the Saviour said, "not of blood" (John 1:13). It does not depend upon blood, nor upon the will of a teacher, nor upon the head of a party, nor upon the will of any man; the privilege is fetched from quite another quarter. Therefore the matter is like this: first, He comes; secondly, He is or is not received.

Theologians today disagree very much on the subject of eschatology;[9] one explains His advent in one way, the other in another way. I do not now want to speak at all of those lazy people who defer everything to the future for judgment or of those who defer everything until that coming which they imagine they find in the Book of Revelation. But rather I am speaking of those who are at present in earnest about souls, inasmuch as such people think that this or the other manner of His spiritual coming is the best and most convenient. That it may accidentally happen as they predict is certain; but they think that they can put His manner of coming into a predictable system. And here some think that He shall come with all sorts of judgments and calamities; with hunger and pestilence; when the outward affairs of a city, country or private family are in confusion; or when a poor man is personally oppressed and visited by affliction, sickness, poverty and the like; this they claim is a sign that the Lord is coming and will have his soul.

Another thinks that the advent of the Saviour consists in this, that a person begins to entertain more honest, civilized and serious thoughts than are usual in wild youth. And because this is taken to be a sign of the arrival of the Saviour and is so considered in a great, no, in the greatest part of Christendom, all people who by the constitution of their body are restrained from lusts and the commission of sin, who either by their poverty, their respectable poverty, or by other external, difficult circumstances, or by a certain misfortune, or by chronic illness are kept from the use or misuse of their senses — these people have the notion that they are now visited

---

9 Zinzendorf calls it "the article concerning His coming."

by God, that now He has come to them. When they have had this notion for a few years and have maintained their melancholy for a long time, then they hit upon the further idea that they are now children of God. Why? Because having been melancholy for quite awhile, having no longer committed the evil in which they were so merry before, and having through the passage of time almost forgotten certain customary sins, they are thus brought to moralizing. And the moralizing comes finally to this, that other people are sharply criticized who still commit this or that sin. And for this reason, because the person can no longer commit them himself, and because they have become spoiled and embittered for him, it comes finally to saying in a pharisaical spirit, "God, I thank Thee that I am not like other men" (Luke 18:11). This is the end of the morality song; nothing further comes of it.

The fewest are of the third sort, and they are, moreover, persons who find opposition everywhere. They maintain that the coming of Jesus Christ into the heart consists simply in nothing else than that the Restorer of our nature, who is at the same time the Creator of its being, begins to become important in one's heart, be it from necessity or through a special dispensation, so that one is really concerned to become acquainted with Him.

Dear hearts! If you with a single, serious thought think upon your Creator and Saviour, and no outward distress, no poverty, no worldly discontent, no particular or special vexation with your neighbor, no law suit, no troubles of war nor national calamities are responsible for it, but rather the free grace, which you yourselves do not yet know, brings the first serious thought which is directed toward the Saviour — if this happens, then conclude from these thoughts, unhesitatingly dismissing all doubt, that the bleeding Saviour stands before your hearts, that He is there in person, that He longs to have you glance at His wounds, that He would like you to "look to Him" (Heb. 12:2)[10] and your hearts to be so affected as if the bleeding Prince stood there with his opened side, ready to embrace your souls, or, as Augustine states it, as if He were crucified before your very eyes. Whether this experience afterwards turns first in a joy of your heart, into a surprising joy such as you have never felt before in your whole life, or into a dreadful shame or profound sorrow, it is all the same, for this depends on the circumstances. If He first appears to you in His beauty, in His bridegroom's beauty, then afterwards you will have sorrow as a remedy against frivolity. Here it begins with joy, and when you have rejoiced a long while, then only afterwards comes the contemplation of your misery, of your unworthiness, and the holy shame.

If at the first sight of the Saviour your sins come to mind, or if your sins, your corruption and spiritual poverty were the immediate occasion

---

10   Zinzendorf erroneously quotes Hebrews 12:1.

of your thinking of a saviour, then you begin with sorrow and with sadness, and at the first sight of the Saviour, the bleeding Saviour, your Creator, you get not any further than the comfort: "Surely He will be gracious to me; He will at last receive me after all; He will give me peace, with peace He will provide me nevertheless." The main point depends on this, that no doubt remains between you and Him: you want each other.

That is the first part of my discourse — namely, that every human soul, be it where it will (in whatever part of the world and in whichever religion it is born), is blessed because it is a human soul. For it does not need to have complicated ideas about the means which the Saviour will use to bring His person, His merits, His humanity, His bodily consanguinity to the heart. Rather it is sufficient that each one of us declares himself when He brings it about in us.

We are unconcerned how He accomplishes this among the heathen; we are too remote from the heathen and leave them to the missionaries among them. We are people who hear His name mentioned every day. There are many millions of people in Europe who hear of Him and have His history and the books which contain it. To their hearts He draws near and makes use of their various situations as an introduction, and thus it takes place under different circumstances, be they as they may: it may begin with sorrow or with joy, with distress or with pleasure; it may happen directly or indirectly; a person may begin to feel this right in the midst of his sins or during a sermon. But in what form does He always come to His "Christians"? I answer, never in any other than His suffering form. All meditations upon the Godhead, upon the omnipotent Being, upon the original Loving-being, yes, even upon the virtuous and wonderful life of the Saviour when He is in our thoughts and minds as the Son of God, as God of God and Light of Light, nicely orthodox, and true enough — all this is, however, nothing more than a refined, reasonable Methodism,[11] just a little bit better than pure morality. For there is no other indisputable criterion by which a man can be assured that he is now standing at the point of being saved, that now his period is here, that his time for being saved has come, than the Saviour's appearing in His suffering form before his heart: when the words which he has heard innumerable times concerning the passion of the Saviour, the torments of God, effectively constrain him either to sorrow over his sins, or to misgivings, or even to a half-desperation at his faithlessness, at his ungodliness, at his wicked actions, provided that it does not happen because he is afraid of hell or because he cannot come to heaven in such a condition, but rather because he has sinned against his Creator.

It is true: sin has provoked God to such anger, His floods have risen so high, His rods have so scourged, that they have lacerated, furrowed

---

11 Zinzendorf uses the term *Methodismus*.

throughout, mutilated, pierced through, and tortured the Creator Himself to death. But by this even the remembrance of sin is blotted out in the tribunal of God; for no longer will a single human soul be damned because Adam has fallen; not a single human creature needs to look pained because Adam has fallen. For all at once all sin is atoned for on the Cross, the entire Fall is erased, and the whole obligation to Satan and the entire sentence passed upon the fall of Adam is torn up, cancelled, and annulled by the nails of Jesus, so that on our side there is not the least question regarding this: "As in Adam all die, so in Christ are all made alive" (I Cor. 15:22) — all who nevertheless go to the devil, all who nevertheless go to hell, not excepted. On the wood of the Cross the world was saved all at once, and whoever is lost loses himself, because he will not receive the Saviour, because he falls again and repeats the fall of Adam, because from a certain opposition and hostility toward his Reconciler he takes the side of his enemy, who is still alive, who is still active, who is still unbound, and who is still trying the very same thing on each soul that he tried on the first man. And if men consider their own particular cases, they will find their own and Adam's circumstances so parallel, if they should be called to account, that they would have to give the very same answer he did. This is also the true reason, which Luther gives, why so many men die before they reach the age of reason; why, in all probability, so many millions of men are not born into the world alive: because the souls have all been saved on the wood of the Cross, and because God, for hidden reasons (to pry into them with our mind and reason about them would be insolence), wants to spare them the danger of passing through the course of time — for He will be the richest, for, if we count at all, He will have immensely more in His blessed freedom than His enemy in his dark prison. It is therefore a false notion that most souls are lost, for taken all together most human souls are saved.

If we restrict our consideration to the present world and claim that most of the men who are alive at present are lost, that may well be. But this does not correspond to the whole truth; this says nothing about that place where everything is brought together, where all threads, all guideropes, all rays of the entire universe and all courses of time converge at one point. There the almighty grace of the atonement, the incontestable council of the atonement, is triumphant, and as long as a soul has not attained to thinking, to reflecting, to bidding and bargaining, it goes straight into the Saviour's arms. All souls are His; this principle, the basic principle, is settled. The exception which the devil makes to this rule in our realm depends on two circumstances, which belong to the other part of my lecture.

My friends, I have spoken of a supposition on which one is saved, and it is simply this: to receive, to receive the Saviour, to feel an inclination within oneself: I want to have Him! If I only had Him! He is coming!

Welcome! When these thoughts are united — He is coming! Welcome, a thousand times welcome, dearest Lamb! Come, do come soon, my Bridegroom! — then salvation is real and incontestable.

Yes, someone says, in this way there is still an order of salvation. For because there is a *formido oppositi*,[12] because it is to be feared that unless I do everything just right, I will not be saved, at least not at this time, not on this day, not this year, but rather perhaps next year or many years from now, perhaps so unfortunately and disappointingly only at the last moment of my life — because of this, therefore, there is a certain compulsion and order to it after all. My reply is that this is a reasoning contrary to all nature and against men's own insight. Who in all his life, though of the most rebellious disposition, ever denied that a country is free because it has laws, because there are national constitutions; a republic or a mixed form of government is not considered suppressed, it endures without all infringement by despotism and tyranny if it has submitted to certain orders in external things. What reasonable person views it as a sign of absolute freedom if there is no order and system of government in a country? Who claims that anyone should be permitted to be in a trade and carry on a profession who in his entire life has never had the least knowledge of the business? Who claims that anyone should choose an office for himself, whether he understands it or not? Who says that any one should move into whatever house he pleases and take possession of as many goods as he likes? These would be freedoms with which the republic could not endure; therefore there must be a certain order in all things. The savages themselves could not survive their freedom, were there not a kind of order suitable to their situation among them. Order and despotism, or arbitrary power, are not correlates; but rather order is the soul of freedom; it places freedom in its true light, in its brightness and happiness, and keeps it there. Therefore, that there is an order in spiritual matters, that, if I may speak this way, salvation presupposes something, this of itself has nothing to do with compulsion; however, this certain something is not the ground of salvation. The presupposition, if one wants to be saved, consists in nothing that is to be done or observed by us. Indeed, in republics one is obligated to pay for a thing the amount due; to qualify for a matter one must wait many years until one can attain something; one is subjected to the order of succession, of rank, and of precedence, and nobody has any right to complain about this state of affairs. But even this is not the question in connection with salvation; there is no active condition at all, no, nothing to which a man is to contribute a grain of reason, skill, or his own power, for then he would always have an excuse. On the contrary, the condition is passive and presupposes only that something which is completely in our power

---

12 Fear of the opposite.

be avoided. If we only abstain in fact from all action, contrary resolution and opposition, if we only are passive and gladly passive to let good be done to us, then there is no difficulty in obtaining salvation. What then at last is the condition? None other than believing in Him; not looking upon the Saviour as an imposter and upon His teaching as a fable; honoring His suffering and death as a divine truth. He must be to us the Reconciler of our souls as truly as if we had seen Him crucified with our own eyes, as if the spectacle of His crucifixion and His agony unto death had happened at the present time before our very eyes and we, for this reason, had saved our natural life.

This is believing, and it all depends on this: "To all who believed in His name, He gave power to become children of God" (John 1:12), to them He gave the charter, the privilege, or rather granted them the deed to it; He put them in possession of a thing already gained, already earned, and already belonging to them; He only invested them with it: I give you this sign, this certitude, the paper with which you can prove your identity. What kind of a deed is this then, properly speaking? (I will say it only in passing), what kind of note or certificate is this really, with which souls can prove their identity as children of God? It is nothing other than the frank and free testimony from their own hearts: "I believe that my Creator is my Saviour"; I believe that He who made me is my Husband; I believe that my Husband, by His own blood, by His real death on the tree of the cross, has placed me in a privileged position; I believe that there is a point in time when my Creator Jesus Christ will wed me, body and soul. Those other situations are much different. There one must buy an article or be obliged to earn it at a dear and expensive price; one must work and serve forty or fifty years on land and sea; one must brave a hundred deaths; and finally there is only one among many thousands who receives the treasure or the office, who carries off this or the other object of his labor as a spoil, during which time, as may be easily imagined, such a person is encamped among a hundred uncertainties. Whereas to attain salvation and moreover to become the Saviour's own soul, to share in His eternal grace and His eternal kingdom without end, to come into His arms to rest eternally, and for each one among all to attain as much as the other and for no one to attain more than all the rest, for all this nothing is required other than believing that another has paid for me, that another has worked for me, labored for me, allowed Himself to be tormented for me to death itself, has been taken down from the Cross for me, and had His pale corpse laid in the grave and reckoned among the dead for me, that I may live, that I may be at rest.

Now to believe this, that is the whole point which makes us at the same time forget and slip away from the entire world and all dangerous involvements with it. And if anyone would say, my circumstances prevent me from doing this, my affairs and my position prevent me from it; I am a soldier, I cannot; I am a merchant, I am a scholar, and I cannot; I am plagued with so many earthly things day and night; then I reply, why then can't poor beggars believe? Why can't those who have been bed-ridden for thirty years and have had nothing to do with the world, who were politically dead and scarcely knew any more that there is such a thing as a city in the world, that there are still people in the world? Why can't those who have been dying for years and have nothing else to think about but their souls? I repeat once again, why then can't they believe? Ah! There is no other reason why this easy thing cannot be done, why it cannot be believed that another has suffered in one's stead, that another has obtained our salvation with tears and agony, than the enmity toward such suffering, death, and merit, than the Belial's [13] pride which lies in the heart and which makes one think this: If He would command me to go some place, let it be anywhere at all, I would do it; but that I should be saved without having to contribute anything myself, without having given even a stiver beforehand, without having even the slightest right to it, just out of sheer grace, as a beggar — this is no natural thing for the human spirit, whose freedom has degenerated into impudence.

But just this is the condition: Gladly would I save you, gladly would I make you a child of God, gladly would I see the new spirit begotten in you; my father would very gladly beget you for his child and transform you into my image. But your soul must come crawling to me; you must receive this upon your knees, like a beggar, in complete poverty of spirit; you must neither be able to do nor have done the least thing for it, but I alone must be the one who helps you towards it; "I will help you to me, all you who are weary and heavy laden" (Matt. 11:28, alt.); I will find a way. Counsel me according to your heart, O Jesus, Son of God! Our self-sufficiency is the only dividing wall between God and us.

No human soul, as such, need be lost in the entire world; a pure, simple man would certainly be saved. But he who has allowed Satan to put the notion in his head of being a fool, of one who wants to be like God, who has allowed Satan to flatter him into a kind of deification, an idolatry of himself, and to make him a self-idolator, a person who is in love with himself, who admires himself, who wants to balance accounts with God Almighty, who wants to measure himself by Him, who would gladly conclude an agreement with Him for salvation — whoever has allowed Satan time to build such castles in the air is not a simple man, no plain human soul; rather he is pregnant with demonic ideas; he participates in the spirit of Satan; he is spiritually possessed.

And so it is with all human souls who do not want to be saved by the

---

13 The spirit of evil personified. Cf. I Samuel 2:12, II Corinthians 6:15.

merits of Jesus, who do not want to be saved solely by the crucified One and His wounds, who still have the most trifling doubt rising up against this, who quarrel with faith but write and read books on a hundred other matters which they have never seen, yet are prepared to persuade other people to accept. But when it comes to believing their own wretchedness and His grace, they are obstinate and adverse to throwing themselves into their bridegroom's arms, to commit themselves willingly with body and soul as creatures to His wounds.

They are people who look upon the few parentheses of the apostles concerning morality as the main point and upon their proclamation concerning grace, merit, and the blood and wounds of Jesus (which fill almost every line) as the parentheses, as mere ejaculations, as perhaps the effects of an overheated imagination. Such people are in reality spiritually possessed. Since the cross of Jesus, no human soul is damned, except those so obstinately possessed. And therefore the Saviour says, "The unclean spirit must depart from every man" (Luke 8:29, alt.); there is no other remedy. Exorcism must be pronounced over every soul that is seduced and, on account of His atonement, on bad terms with the Saviour. This soul must be exorcised, be it doctor or idiot, emperor or beggar; there is simply no other remedy. And when such an exorcism is applied to the soul by the Holy Spirit and the unclean spirit has departed from it, so that the soul can think of the passion of Jesus with feeling[14] and rejoice in this passion, so that it can love the torments of Jesus and wish for no other salvation than that which comes through Jesus' merits, then the word *gratis* occasions no reluctance; on the contrary, it is most agreeable to the soul, whose joy is to be saved by grace. "I can love a great deal, for a great many sins have been forgiven me" (Luke 7:47, alt.); I can love astonishingly, because I do not know how I came to grace; I can enjoy in amazement, for salvation costs me nothing; I can, even now while in this bodily tent,[15] be contained body and soul in my Reconciler; I cannot live without Him; I am occupied with Him day and night; He possesses me, because He laid down His life for me.

It is this connection which makes it necessary to say that the soul has a free will and that, if it keeps to itself, then it will be saved; only it may not allow itself to be possessed, and if it is possessed, it must acknowledge the possession and be willing to allow itself to be exorcised. It must say: "Ah, for God's sake! I should really be saved, but I cannot perceive any right will. Satan must have possessed me; he must have captivated my heart, I must be under a foreign power; I must be under the law of sin and death. Wretched man that I am, who will deliver me from the body of this death! Although I want to believe, I cannot. There is a sort of half a will present, but I don't know; something is opposing me."

---

14 *Gefühl*.
15 *Hütte*.

But this is a remedy which only those who are possessed need, which only deists need — such people as are disconcerted by the God on the Cross; to them He says, "Oh, you poor people, you will never manage; come to me." He commands the teachers, "Send the possessed one to me. Satan knows me; as soon as my name is called for them, I will stretch out my invisible hand of blessing over them, and as soon as Satan sees my wounded hand, he retreats, and the soul does not know how it comes to freedom. But the soul also scarcely knows how it came to its former obstinate recalcitrance, to mutter against the way and manner of its becoming saved; it reads the texts, it hears the sermon, it sings the hymns, and it feels as if it were hearing them for the first time in its life.

> The blood of Christ, His righteousness:
> This its jewels and wedding dress
> In which it stands before the Lord.

Thus will the Christian denominations, thus will the human souls in them be united. That is, "Preach the gospel to the whole creation" (Mark 16:15b); do not exclude a single human soul, for they all have their right to it. Among them there are possessed ones, people who are wedded to Satan; they are there by the thousands. But he must let them go also; if one refers him, with all of his claims, to the little Lamb, then the most wicked spirit flees.

PRAYER

Dear and faithful Lamb! We entreat you, for your wounds' sake, to remember the entire human race incessantly before your Father and never to forget your flesh and blood. For the sake of men, for the sake of the souls present here, we say this, that at the same time you may, moreover, come to them and they join their sighing with our sighing.

O dear Lamb! Entreat your Father for your wounds' sake that in these days He increases His procession of souls a thousand, a million times and from the kings of the earth down to their lowest subjects. Entreat your Father that in this great city of God, from the sanctified person of our dear King George down to the meanest and most despised creature in the hospitals, from the most venerable heads among the exemplary citizens down to the very unworthiest, most loathsome creature rotting in the deepest distress on the dunghill, that your blood, which was poured out on the Cross, may speak for them, that they may attain to the freedom of thinking as they ought and, of their own accord, but in deepest recognition of their unworthiness, at the same time with your faithful hearts may think and lay themselves into your arms. The souls are surely all yours. Amen.

Lecture VII

On the Essential Character and Circumstances of the Life of a Christian

Preached in the Brethren's Chapel in London, September 25, 1746

TEXT: John 21:16. *"Do you love me?"* (RSV)

MY PURPOSE is to make clear from these words what constitutes the essential Christian.

These are common book titles and especially in England very much in style: *The Almost Christian; The Christian; The True Christian; The Christian's Journey to Eternity.*[1] Thus almost nothing more stale and threadbare can be mentioned than such a subject, or rather such a wording of the subject, as when one says, "I will set forth the true, the essential Christian." But I will, nevertheless, say something rather new.

We want to look first at the essential character of a Christian, and secondly we will consider the circumstances of his life.

The genuine[2] character of a Christian consists absolutely in this: when he speaks with the Saviour, when he speaks with his brethren, when he has anything to straighten out with God the Father, when he needs the

---

1 *The Gentleman's Magazine* (Vol. 16, 1746), published in London, listed in its July issue the following items as "recent publications" under the heading of Divinity: *Infidelity Scourged; or, Christianity Vindicated,* by J. Bate; *The Reasonableness of the Christian Religion, as Delivered in the Scriptures,* by G. Benson. The August issue listed: *A Vindication of Some Truths of Natural and Revealed Religion* by John Brine; *The Christian Life in Divers of its Branches Described and Recommended,* by B. Wallin.

2 *Naturelle.*

ministry of angels, when he shall present himself on the day of the Lord to join in judgment over the living and the dead — then he absolutely does not appeal to his religious denomination, but rather to his nature, to his descent. For the most serious objection on that day will be, "I do not know you nor where you come from" (Luke 13:25).

This is the *Crinomenon*,[3] which decides on that day and in all similar circumstances and upon which it depends, that one is received and the other cast away. The Saviour does or does not call a person to mind. "I will acknowledge him; I will say, 'I know you'" (Matt. 10:32, alt.).

Therefore, it is a rule belonging absolutely to the character of the true Christian that, properly speaking, he is neither Lutheran nor Calvinist, neither of this nor the other religious denomination, not even Christian. What can be said more plainly and positively? What reformer, be it Hus or Luther or Wycliffe, or whatever his name might be, would be so presumptuous as to maintain that men are saved because they are his followers? For Paul excludes Christ Himself when he says, "Not of Paul, not of Cephas, not of Apollos, not of Christ" (I Cor. 1:12, alt.).

It is really a great misfortune that people read the scriptures but read them without the proper attention and that such main passages are not noticed. For seventeen hundred years men have written this for all the world to see, *Christianus sum*,[4] and for as many centuries have put this into the mouths of all the martyrs, *Christianus sum*, which is contrary to the plain words of the apostle Paul, who has expressly forbidden that any man call himself "of Christ" or Christian. Let our enemies call us that, let the Turks and pagans, let the Jews call us this in derision: *Vir bonus, sed malus, quia Christianus est*,[5] it is a pity that he is a Christian. But we must not speak this way. To be sure, the ancient fathers have themselves given occasion to this confusion: Prudentius says, "*Secta generosa Christi nobilitat Viros*," i.e., the noble, the excellent religion of Christ makes people even more noble than they were before.

Who directed the people to do this? Who directed them to make a religion out of the family of Christ, in direct contradiction to the Holy Scriptures? It does not matter that men have confessions of faith; it does not matter that they are divided into religious denominations; they may very well differentiate themselves according to their *Tropo Paedias* (form of doctrines). An upright Christian man can say, I side with Calvin; an upright Christian man may also say according to my judgment I rather side with Luther. But this gives neither the one nor the other the least warrant, the least right to salvation; this only distinguishes him according to his insight and

---

3   From *krino*, "to judge."
4   I am a Christian.
5   He is a good man, and bad because he is a Christian.

as an honest man among the faithful; it entitles him not to be arbitrarily judged in his manner of acting, in his form, his method of treating souls, and in the outward appearance of his worship. Each thing has its peculiar external form, its external shape, and everything does not look alike. No man has the same point of view as another, and by this means he distinguishes himself innocently and inoffensively. For as soon as anyone appeals to the fact that he does not hold with another's logic, in that moment the other's right to censure him ceases. And it is a vulgar, mean disposition of mind when people of one religious denomination take pleasure in opposing people of another, or when on that account they show enmity toward each other. For as soon as someone says that he is of a persuasion different from mine, then he has taken away my spiritual right over him to censure him.

Now thus far it is good that we have many religious denominations; up to this point I am in agreement, so much so that I despise anyone who, without the deepest and most thoroughly examined reason, changes over from one denomination to another; so much so that nothing sounds more ridiculous to my ears than a proselyte. Only with the greatest difficulty can I make myself deal with such a person, when I become aware that he has left his former denomination, especially among the Protestants, who all take the Scriptures as the guiding principle of faith. Therefore, frivolity should not govern denominational matters. The differences in religious denominations are important and venerable concerns, and the distinction of religious denominations is a divine wisdom. No peculiarity should cause a disturbance. But all of these ideas still betray their human origin, of which it may be said that three hundred, five hundred, a thousand years ago things were not yet conceived in this way. There is only one of whom it may be said, "Yesterday, today, and forever He is ever still the same" (Heb. 13:8, alt.);

> And His church stands as she has stood,
> Jehovah the Father is her God;
> She still retains her very first dress:
> Christ's own blood and righteousness.

Now then, I have said what a Christian is not, what a person must not presume to comprehend under the name of Christians, in what respect a person must not boast of Christ, what a Christian upon occasion must consider entirely as *skybala,* as refuse, as Paul calls it (Phil. 3:8, RSV), whenever it tends to interfere with the foundation, with the main point, even were it good and real in itself or could in a certain sense be valid.

Now, what then is the proper character of a Christian? Take notice, my dear friends, for here we must in advance set aside the common word as it is used in all languages, except the German, which has something special in its usage.

In all languages one says, a Christian, and in our German alone one says, *ein Christ*, and that is the right word.[6] "All things are yours; and you are Christ's" (I Cor. 3:22b–23a, RSV); you belong to Christ, you are His heirs, you are His family. And in another place it is also put quite "germanly": "You are bone of his bone and flesh of his flesh," and this refers to Genesis 2:23. "She shall be called Woman [*Männin*], because she was taken out of Man [*Mann*]" (Gen. 2:23b). All the prophets make allusion to this when they say, "Those who are called according to my name" (Isa. 43:7). In no way are we called by the name of Jesus or Christ in the sense of a religious denomination, as if Christ were our teacher, as if Christ were our prophet, our lawgiver, as if He were the founder, the author of our religion, as it is sometimes expressed by a pagan historian, as for example in Lucian. "The founder of this religion was crucified."[7] In this sense we are not Christians. Rather, we are Christians in the same way that, in our European countries, a wife takes the name of her husband and afterwards is called not by her maiden name but by her husband's name. Thus every soul who has the right to call herself by this name, "because she was taken out of Man" (Gen. 2:23) belongs to Christ, is Christian.[8]

Now whoever will not grasp this and has no other support for himself than that he has read the teachings of Jesus and industriously given lectures on it, that he can recount this teaching, and that he is established in its principles according to his religious denomination; such a person can be considered nothing more than one of those Christianly-religious people.[9] And even though he discharges all the duties according to his religious denomination, so that there can be no objection to him, yet he cannot on that basis lay claim to this: "O Lamb of God, you who take away the sin of the world (John 1:29), acknowledge me!" Rather, whoever wishes to claim this, he must be christened in his heart, as here in England it is said of one who is baptized, "He is christen'd";[10] he must be made a Christian; he must be of the bone and spirit of Christ; he must in truth take pride in this: "My Maker is my husband" (Isa. 54:5, alt.); He has not only created me, and He is not only the potter of my clay, but "He is the husband of my soul, who has betrothed Himself to me for ever and has betrothed

6 Zinzendorf compares the German words *Christianer* and *Christ*.
7 Lucian, "The Passing of Peregrinus," in *The Works of Lucian* 8 vols. (Cambridge: Harvard University Press, 1936), 5:13. "The man who was crucified in Palestine because he introduced this new cult into the world."
8 *Christin* is the female form of Christian.
9 *Christianischen Religions Leute*.
10 Zinzendorf gives this sentence in English.

Himself to me in grace' and mercy, yet, has betrothed Himself to me in faith"[11] (Hos. 2:19f, LT, alt.). I am certain who my Husband is; I know Him.

Thus far I have spoken about the character of a Christian, of a man who can call himself Christian without being a liar or a foolish, stupid person who does not know what he is saying.

Now I come to the other part of my discourse, to the chief circumstances which are found in the case of such a Christian.

The character of a Christian, the entrance into this state, and the entire progress in it as well are based on the text which I have read: "Do you love me?"

First of all, it is undeniable that if a person had no other certainty concerning the Saviour than what the school teacher dictated to him about Him in his youth, he would certainly be in bad shape. For then this objection might be raised against him: "Who knows? If you had been born a Jew, then you would have believed what the rabbi had taught you; if you had been born a Turk, then you would have believed what the Mullah had taught you; if you had been born in a pagan religion, you would have believed what the bonze or the lama or some other pagan priest had taught you." And not much of a reply can be made to that.

Therefore there must necessarily be something which gives us more certainty than do all the achievements of our understanding, something which gives us a firm footing and enables a person to maintain in the face of everyone, "Yes, I still would have been a Christian even though I had been born a Jew. I still would not have remained a Turk or pagan, even though I had been born a Turk or a pagan."

But what is the special factor which so distinguishes us from all the religions, from all the persuasions and opinions, that every reasonable person must admit it? It is just that very thing which the Apostle Paul calls the folly of his preaching.

Here one would like for God's sake to beg all theologians, if they would only listen, not to take such pains constantly to represent our religion as agreeing with reason, as being common sense. If writings of this kind are assigned to pamphlets, by which people earn a living for themselves, then it may pass. But as soon as it is taken seriously, as soon as they want to demonstrate to atheists and common deists and people like that that our religion is a wisdom rooted in their heads, a discernment which they can take in their own way, then they are obviously threshing empty straw, according to all instruction of the Scripture.

This position is false from the very start, for Paul states positively that there is something foolish in our preaching, and none of the wise ones of

11 RSV "faithfulness."

this world can comprehend it. There is no ear that can hear our language; there is no eye that can see our concerns; there is no sight sharp enough, no natural understanding sufficient to penetrate our matters, and one must be prepared for this. As it is said in the Acts of the Apostles, *tetagmenoi*, "as many of them were ordained for eternal life" (Acts 13:48); there the work had been done, their head, their mind and their heart had been set straight, they could apprehend these things as wisdom, as wisdom in spite of everything. "Teach me wisdom in my secret heart," said David, "You purge me, you wash me, you make my bones rejoice, which before were broken, and you give me a ready spirit" (Ps. 51:6b–10, RSV, alt.); you give me ideas quite different from those I had before, and you do this, your wisdom in my secret heart does this. This is the wisdom in I Corinthians 1, which none of the wise people of this world were able to reach or obtain; and if a bet be made, says Paul, if there are contrasting opinions on how the Gospel shall be propagated, how the teaching of Jesus shall grasp the hearts, and an honorable man says, "Our wise, our understanding people will do this; the vulgar certainly will not comprehend it, but if it comes first to the learned, wise and devout people, they will understand it," — then Paul tells them to their faces: now we do have Christianity, and we do have an example, a congregation of God; now, good friend, where are the wise, where are the intelligent, where are the nobles? Well? Show them to me.

This is the plain, true, and genuine meaning of all that Paul says in the place cited. This is to prove nothing else but that the ordinary means do not suffice, that the ordinary frame of mind is not enough, that the understanding of man, as man, is as insufficient for grasping our matters as is the understanding of a poor animal for comprehending our geometric or algebraic propositions. It is undeniable; it must first be given to us. I said in my last Sunday's sermon that He gives power (John 1:12); it must be given, and those to whom it has not yet been given ought by rights to say, "This is too profound a wisdom; we have not yet advanced so far." They ought to say what Aristotle said, when he threw himself into the Euripus: "O you being of all beings! *Eleeson*." [12] They ought to say, "I am too stupid, too inept." Or as David, "I am a *Behema*, [13] a dumb animal before you; I cannot penetrate into the depths of things" (Ps. 73:22, alt.).

Instead of this the proud spirit of man, that presumptuous creature, which, however, is only a poor wretched human being says in a quarrelsome way to its Creator, "It is foolishness, nonsense; it is enthusiasm; it is good for fanatics." This is quarreling and striving against the Creator; for the people who say this have our Bible as well as we do; they read it, they print

---

12 Have mercy.
13 Beast (Hebrew).

it, and they circulate it among men as God's Word. What right do they have to call these same Biblical truths foolishness, just because they do not understand them? They have most certainly no right, but it is their pleasure. Every man loves to maintain his own assertion; every man is so disposed that if there is something he does not have, the other person shall not have it either, and what the other person does have is nothing at all, is not even worth the effort. Therefore I cannot help it: our theology, our mysteries, our Christianity I must let pass as foolishness for them, with the protestation that it is nevertheless wisdom for those who understand it; in this sense of it I will now mention what it is all about.

My friends, I will not dispute about how one enters into the state of being a Christian. Words are spoken, there is preaching; fine hymns and texts on glorious things contribute and are means to it, yes, may even be vehicles of it. But they are not the whole, not even the central concern. Then what is the central concern? My friends, it is this: whoever will answer Yes to the Saviour's question, "Do you love me?" must have caught sight of the Saviour when the Saviour looked into his heart for the first time. This is the order: First the Saviour looks at us, and we perceive him; at that moment we have the matter in hand, and the Christian is ready.

My friends, not even a quarter of an hour, not even a minute, not even as much time as it takes to stop to think must intervene between the point when the Saviour looks at us and when we perceive Him. Afterward we again stop seeing; then we believe, and then it is the constant and unceasing act of the Saviour to be looking at us: "His eyes remain open day and night toward us" (II Chron. 6:20, alt.). "I will counsel you with my eye upon you" (Ps. 32:8b, RSV).

I want to explain these two points a little more closely. When a person becomes a Christian [ein Christ], when the Saviour receives him, when a person is admitted to the power to be a child of God, then it happens this way: for a moment the Saviour becomes present to him in person. In an hour, in a moment (it may be in an indivisible point of time which cannot be compared with any measure of time that we have, including moments themselves), a person comes into the circumstances in which the apostles stood when they saw Him.

I do not pretend that we see a body with our corporeal eyes; I do not desire that the mind try to imagine a body or try to conceive a representation of it, or that the mind look into itself or turn its thoughts in toward itself until it sees a form standing before it. But I do ask for the essential in this, and that is that a person who has seen abstractly and purely must in the next moment realize that he has actually seen; that a person must know as certainly that his spirit has seen, that his heart has seen and felt, as when in ordinary human life one can be certain that he has seen or touched something. In the moment when this happens he does not need to have a sense-experience or see something visible (this cannot be excluded with any certainty, but neither is it essential); it is only necessary that afterward the essential effect remain, that one can say not only, "I have seen, I have heard"; but rather, "Thus have I seen it, and thus have I heard."

The Scripture says that our entire work of the Gospel is to portray Jesus, to paint Him before the eyes, to take the spirit's stylus and etch — yes, engrave — the image of Jesus in the fleshly tablets of the heart, so that it can never be removed again.

Now the only question is, "In what kind of a form does one see the Saviour?" In the Old Testament it was said, "You shall not make yourself a graven image or likeness" (Exod. 20:4), for this reason: in all your life you have never seen a likeness nor any original, and therefore you cannot make a copy. For I will not have my religion, my worship, profaned with masks and illusions; cherubim you may make, for you have seen some of them. But you shall make no god, for in your entire life you have never seen one.

In the New Testament this commandment is at an end: we have seen. Therefore the Lutherans are right in leaving this commandment out of the catechism,[14] for it no longer has any relation on earth to us. This makes the particular distinction between us and the Reformed,[15] for they combine the ninth and tenth commandments to make room for the commandment forbidding images, which we Lutherans, according to our understanding, leave out of the Decalogue. We do not hold that a person should make himself no picture or image in the New Testament; a person may make an image, no, he should. It is a part of the Christian religion to form for oneself a picture of that God who took a body upon Himself. Augustine wishes to see *Jesum in Carne*, Jesus in the flesh; and because I cannot do this, he said, He stands before my eyes as if I saw Him being crucified.

Some of the theologians have wanted to find the whole suffering form of the Saviour in the Song of Songs, in the bride's description of her beloved, "This is my beloved" (Song 5:26, RSV), and think that there He is painted piece by piece, as His figure was on the cross. I do not want to enter into this discussion at present. But this is certain, that Christians can rightly, by divine right, sing:

> In that form appear to me
> As, for my great distress,
> Upon the Cross so tenderly
> You did bleed to death.

---

14 Zinzendorf refers to the fact that in the Lutheran version of the Ten Commandments the reference to the graven images is omitted.

15 *Reformierten*, the German term for the followers of the Calvinist Reformation.

This they may claim; they have a right to speak this way, and all men, all souls have a right to say what Thomas said, "Unless I see in his hands the print of the nails, and place my finger in the mark of the nails, and place my hand in his side, I will not believe" (John 20:25, RSV).

And this is the advice which I give to all hearts. If anyone asks me about his salvation, I say to him, "Do not believe, if you do not want to be deceived, do not believe until you see the prints of the nails and place your finger in the prints of the nails and place your hand in His side: then believe."

But who must see? It is the heart which must see at least once. Afterward it goes on believing until it shall see Him again. I must freely concede that this advice does not at first sight seem to conform to the advice of the Saviour, "Blessed are those who have not seen and yet believe" (John 20:29b, RSV). Now how shall I reconcile my advice with the words of the Saviour? Nothing is easier: there is a seeing and a not seeing. The Scripture shows that this is possible: "They have eyes and do not see, they have ears and do not hear" (Jer. 5:21, alt.). Therefore a person may also not seem to see and yet be seeing; a person may not seem to hear and yet be hearing; a person may not seem to feel and yet be feeling. And so it is, "as dying, and behold we live" (II Cor. 6:9). According to the external senses and the human disposition we neither see, hear, nor feel the Saviour. But why then does He so often say, "I will manifest myself" (John 14:21)? Why does He say, "He who has ears to hear, let him hear" (Mark 4:9)? And that He did not say this only to those people who were speaking with Him is made clear in that He repeated in the Revelation of John to those people who did not see Him, "He who has ears to hear, let him hear" (Rev. 3:22, alt.). Why does the apostle say, "You should seek Him until you feel Him" (Acts 17:27, alt.)? All His arrangement in the whole world was made for this purpose, that people may obtain a feeling [16] of Him (Acts 17:27). And from where comes the testimony of the apostle, "When it pleased God to reveal His Son in me, I set out immediately" (Gal. 1:15–16, alt.)? And from where comes the constant witness of all the other apostles concerning the direct and immediate special relationship with Him?

Once one is involved in the Spirit, one comes into that extraordinary state concerning which John expresses himself thus, "I was in the Spirit on the Lord's day" (Rev. 1:10a, RSV). And this may happen with more or less sense experience, with more or less distinctness, with more or less visibility, and with as many kinds of modifications as the different human temperaments and natural constitutions can allow in one combination or another. One person attains to it more incontestably and powerfully, the

---

16 *Gefühl.*

other more gently and mildly; but in one moment both attain to this, that in reality and truth one has the Creator of all things, the fatherly Power, the God of the entire world, standing in His suffering form, in His penitential form, in the form of one atoning for the whole human race — this individual object stands before the vision of one's heart, before the eyes of one's spirit, before one's inward man. And this same inward man, who until now has been under the power of the kingdom of darkness, as soon as he catches sight of his Deliverer, this Deliverer reaches out His hand to him and plucks him immediately out of all corruption; He pulls him out of the dungeon of his prison and places him in the light before His face: "Take heart, my child, your sins are forgiven (Matt. 9:2, RSV); I will make a covenant with you, that you shall be mine (Jer. 31:33?); I will be your advocate in judgment, and you shall be allowed to appeal to me; but, will you have me?" That is the *Crinomenon*, the deciding factor. Do you want me? Do you receive me? Do I suit you? Am I acceptable to you? Do I please your heart? See, here I am! This is the way I look. For your sake I was made to be sin (II Cor. 5:21), and for your sake I was made a curse (Gal. 3:13); for the sake of your sins I was torn, beaten, and put to death. I have sweated the sweat of fear and anguish, the sweat of death, the sweat of the strife of penance; I have laid down my life for your sake. I have been laid into the dust of the grave for your sake. Does this suit you? Is this important to you? Are you satisfied with me? Do I in this way please you? Do I please you better in the idea of a mangled slave who is thrown to the wild beasts in the circus, or in the form of the emperor who sits high on the throne and takes pleasure in the destruction of the poor creature? How do I please you the best?

He who in this moment, in this instant, when the Saviour appears to him and when He says to him, as to Peter, "Do you love me in this figure?" — he who can say, "You know all things; you know that I love you"; he who in this minute, in this instant, goes over to Him with his heart, passes into Him, and loses himself in His tormented form and suffering figure — he remains in Him eternally, without interruption, through all eons; he can no longer be estranged[17] from Him. No possibility can be imagined, though the whole universe should join together, that any thing could separate him from that friendship which is formed at the moment of His bloody appearing.

Now this is the entrance to this state, that one receives Him at that moment, looks at Him longingly, and falls in love with Him; that one says, "It is true; now I can do nothing more, now I want nothing more. Yes, God Creator, Holy Spirit! My eyes have seen your *soterion*[18] (Luke 2:30),

---

17 *Entfremdet.* This word is used by Luther in his translation of *apallotrioomai* in Ephesians 4:18. WA 70,202 New Testament, 1522.
18 Salvation.

they have seen your little Jesus; my heart wept for joy when His nail prints, His wounds, His bloody side stood before my heart. You know this."

Then our perdition is at an end; then flesh and blood have lost. Satan, who had already lost his case in court, really lays no more claim on such a soul; and it is just as if a man, who had sold himself to Satan, gets back his promissory note, as if the slip of paper came flying into the meeting, torn to pieces. The signature, the note, says the apostle, is torn up and fastened to the cross, pounded through with nails, and forever cancelled; and this is registered at the same time, that is, we are set free; we are legally acquitted. When the books are opened, so it will be found.

What is called repentance in the world, what is called conversion, this David describes thus: "As the eyes of the servants look to the hand of their master, as the eyes of a maid to the hand of her mistress" (Ps. 123:2, RSV), so the eyes of the sinner look for Him until He appears before them. Then a person begins to look and to listen in the hope of finding the Saviour as his Creator in His true, human suffering form, with His corpse wounded for us, before our eyes. When that has happened, then the person has seen Him and now believes continually, no more desiring to see and never again in his whole life losing the look of the tortured Saviour; He remains engraved in one's heart. One has a copy of this deeply impressed there; one lives in it, is changed into the same image, and every year, I might say every day, is placed into a greater light streaming from the wounds: it looks more and more reddish around such a person, as the prophets express it (Isa. 1:18); he appears more and more sinful; as we express it, he keeps to the point of His sufferings. Then one can no longer fluctuate. One knows of no other presence of the Creator than in the beauty of His sufferings.

But what kind of authority, what kind of eternal and incontestable effect on our heart does His perpetual look have afterward? This belongs to our progress. Here there is no need to tell people, do not steal, do not get drunk, do not lead a disorderly life, do not be so fond of the creature, do not set your heart on this and that, do not be hostile. Now there is no need to preach one point of morality after the other at a person, not even of the most refined and subtle. Even though a person were to be most adept in the matter and become an example to the whole country, still there would be no need for reasoning. For every loving look from the Saviour indicates our morality to us throughout our whole life: one dissatisfied, one sorrowful, one painful look from the Saviour embitters and makes loathsome to us everything that is immoral, unethical, and disorderly, all fleshly-mindedness, as often as it is necessary.

I suppose that we remain men; it is a part of the state of sin not to think more highly of ourselves. But we shall succeed, if our Head but look now and then, at some interval, upon us.

We are not people who from the first moment of our spiritual life until into eternity itself remain unassaulted[19] and unattacked. From a distance something comes at us; there is something in our own selves which we cannot name, to which we have as yet been unable to give the right name, until the proper position of the soul has been determined. This must be handled with great caution and watched over carefully; and even if it should stick in the deepest recesses of the mind, even if it is also lying imprisoned, so that it is actually not able to block our course in following Christ, yet it is still there, and no reading, no hearing, no moral doctrine guards against it. For the only remedy against all such alluring demands, gross or subtle, is the doubtful glance of the Saviour, when the form of Jesus does not seem so pleasing, so joyful to our hearts, when He seems to us to be no longer so sweetly before our hearts as usual.

People who have murdered someone have said that the person and image of the murdered one always hovered before their eyes; they have neither been able to bear it nor escape from the sight of it. We also say of people who are very important to us, I see him as clearly as if he were here; I could paint him right now. This David applies to his Saviour, "I have placed Him so directly before my eyes that I will never lose Him from my thoughts, from my point of view; I need only look up, and I have Him immediately there" (Ps. 139). Suppose, then, that one might fall into all sorts of questionable situations, if possible to go astray in something, to allow oneself to be implicated in something by one's thoughts, to wander from the Saviour with one's senses. The Saviour need only look at one, even though one does not look towards Him, and the glance of His eyes goes through one like a flame of fire: one is transparent, known throughout by Him; He knows the moment when He is to look at us, and He also knows how He is to look at us, for He has read our thoughts before they have formed themselves. When Judas came and betrayed Him, He preached him a sermon: "My friend, you give me a kiss and betray me." When Peter denied Him, He spoke no words but rather looked upon him. In the case of Judas the sermon availed nothing; the look had this effect on Peter: "He went out and wept bitterly" (Matt. 26:75); he bathed himself in tears. What kind of tears? Tears of love. He wept for love, for he had not owned, confessed, or affirmed his Master, for he had not risked his life for Him. And when the Saviour said a few days later, "Do you love me?" the answer was, O dear Lord! I appeal to you; you have looked upon me: you have seen not only the faithful Nathanael under the fig tree, but you have also seen me, an unfaithful heart. You do know what your look has effected; you know indeed how your look operated upon my heart; my eyes were

---

19 *Unangefochten.*

wet with tears; it went through body and soul. Yes, the Saviour was obliged to say, it is true; you already have the right doctrine, and you are a good theologian; you know what you shall set forth to the church; you shall be a bishop. Point your diocese only toward my merits; point them only toward this method of coming to love me, toward this method which I have used, the method which you have experienced, which immediately brings a person out of all labyrinths into the right way. "Strengthen your brethren" (Luke 22:32) with the example of your conversion by the glance of my eyes.

It is this also, beloved in the Lord, which we have to wish each other at the end of this discourse, that we may be looked upon by the Saviour so graciously, so powerfully, so essentially; and that at the same time we may be so blessed, so happy that we turn away our view and our eyes from everything which otherwise seemed to us proper or improper and turn them toward Him with no desire to look at or into anything else; that our eye may not be able to throw a glance anywhere else but to this point.

And when you have once caught sight of the beauty of His suffering, so that in all your life you will not be able to get rid of that sight, then He conducts you with His eyes wherever He will have you; then with His eyes He teaches you what good and evil is. Your knowledge of good and evil lies in His eyes, not in the tree from which Adam poisoned himself, from which Adam ate his curse. But rather in the eyes of the tortured Lamb, there lies your blessed, happy knowledge of good and evil. As far as this same image looks upon you, into the midst of your mortal bodies, so far shall you be changed, pervaded, captivated by the person of Jesus, so that your other brethren perceive you no longer as a man in your denomination, as a brother of the same persuasion only, but rather as a consort, as a playmate for the marriage-bed[20] of the blessed Creator and eternal Husband of the human soul.

PRAYER

My dearest Saviour! We beg of you this same blessed look, this same irresistible look, which You always know to fix upon the souls who like to look upon You, who like to receive You, who, when You come, are ready to pass over into Your heart and wounds, to whom the touching of Your corpse is important, for whom the first savour of Your corpse can

---

20 *Gespielen Zum Ehe-Bett.*

banish all curse and guide them even to the sight of Your wounds. And to this look help, according to Your wisdom, all souls, high and low, rich and poor, in all the circumstances they are in, at the moment of their willingness. In the meantime let us witness so long and, as far as possible, propagate our testimony among mankind so long, until You have gradually accomplished the number of those who want to and will see Your saving Cross's image here in time, and until nothing more is remaining which pertains to election, so that Your witnesses, before they rest, may be able to bring You the answer: Lord, what You have commanded is done, and there is still room.

Lecture VIII

Concerning the Blessed Happiness of Sincere and Upright Hearts

Preached in the Brethren's Chapel in London, October 2, 1746

TEXT: Psalm 32:2. *"Blessed is the man to whom the Lord imputes no iniquity, and in whose spirit there is no deceit."* (RSV)

THE MAN HAS an upright heart: this is a common saying. It is also not unusual to draw this conclusion: that man has an upright heart; therefore God will be gracious to him. That man was saved. Why? He had an upright heart. I would not guarantee that those servants of the Lord, who in these days work, and rightly so, utterly to extirpate all self-righteousness so that He Who is our righteousness may have due homage paid Him by all His souls whom He has purchased with His blood — I would not guarantee that those servants would not gladly admit that a man is saved because he has an upright heart. Presumably they might dispute it; but they would do it because of a misunderstanding. Nobody can dispute the salvation of one who has an upright heart; that matter is settled. But there is an equivocation in the terms which no one would suspect there and of which one is not aware when one speaks in this manner. Holy Scripture grants nobody a heart but those who are already saved. It absolutely excludes all men from that which is called a spiritual heart; it will not even allow them a heart of flesh, as Scripture phrases it, a flexible heart, a heart that can be dealt with. Rather, it declares that at the place where the heart should be everything is petrified in man; in that place he is dead, even though he is alive according to nature.

This assertion of Scripture has given rise to a great controversy among the several sects of the Protestant church: Are men completely dead? Or do they still have a little bit of spiritual life? Or do they have absolutely no spiritual faculty? Or do they have some small portion of it before the Saviour turns toward them and they are regenerated?

Thus, if anyone says, that man has an upright heart, we must first hear how he means it. If he understands by this expression that which Jude (Jude 19) and the other apostles of the Lord call spirit, even that which the English Bible renders "spirit" in the very section of the 32nd Psalm which I have just read to you in the German version — if he means this by it, then there are no other people with upright hearts, except the children of God. "For the others have no spirit" (Jude 19); they do not have this spirit. "Create in me a new heart, O God, and give me a new, trustworthy spirit, a willing spirit" (Ps. 51:12, alt.), *Spiritum voluntarium*, that sovereign spirit, that spirit which can will, that spirit which is capable of making a covenant, which of itself can dispose, as it is so beautifully explained in the 6th and 7th chapters of the Epistle to the Romans: "To whomever you yield yourselves as servants" in obedience, with whomever you sign a contract, "you are his servants" (Rom. 6:16). As soon as you are given your freedom, as soon as you are delivered from the power of Satan and have become your own masters, then you must dispose yourselves and effectually declare whether you will keep to the Saviour. For between the service of Satan and the being engaged to the Saviour there is on our side a shorter or longer interval during which men may choose their own future condition. If at that time they do not choose the Saviour, if their thoughts and reasonings venture into other matters, and if they do not look for their husband, their future lord, the future head of their family in the Lamb, in the suffering form of Jesus, then a soul cannot remain free, but rather then, as the Saviour says, the former master comes again, "brings seven other spirits," and takes possession of the house he had left (Luke 11:24–26). And this results in people who have twice died, the desperately godless people; they come from among those who at one point have taken time to deliberate about themselves, who at one point have had the freedom to leave Satan, but who have deliberated too long and finally looked cross-eyed back again to their old situation.

Now it is indeed true that nobody can own himself. There is something in the whole situation of man, in the nature of such a creature, which makes it impossible for him to own himself. He must have a lord, either sin unto death or the bloody righteousness, the Lord who is our righteousness, unto eternal life.

What then is the reason why, after the removal of the ambiguity of the word "upright," one may very well say that an upright heart, or an upright mind (if we wish to avoid the word heart), an upright soul — as we ordinarily say — must be saved? The proposition in itself is right. An upright soul will certainly be saved; no upright soul will be lost; for all men who do perish are never upright. But then being upright does not mean to acquit oneself well, to go through the world honestly, to be reliable in all one's dealings, to be a faithful, dependable friend, a man of his word, to do more than one promises but never to promise more than one keeps. All this falls far short of "upright," if the ground from which this honesty proceeds is not settled beforehand. If such honesty is accompanied by the most minute secondary, the most subtle subsidiary aim and is not the pure impulse of the heart, not a universal plan which such a person has laid down for himself without any further reason than that it is universal for him, then he may perhaps behave honestly toward all mankind; he will perhaps never grieve a child; perhaps he will consider it a sin to trample down a small flower without reason, or to allow a crumb of bread to be wasted; he will be just and reasonable toward all creatures. And yet with all this he will have a faithless and false heart toward his Creator.

It is for this reason that eternal blessedness, heaven and its glory, and the Creator Himself in His loving kindness are invisible. Some day when he shall become visible, we may be assured that no natural man will be able to love Him. As He is described in Isaiah 53, no man would desire Him. Why? Because the Creator absolutely refuses to be loved for any other reason than because one does love; because one is so inclined to Him; because one is so astonishingly delighted with Him; because His intrinsic worth gives Him preference over all other things that can be named; because His grace and mercies, His merits and infinite faithfulness which He has shown to us do not make Him better, but rather make us better; and He always remains the only man worthy of our love, the only good, the only tender, the only faithful man, worthy of all devotion in time and eternity.

Now in order that souls may not be inclined to be led into loving Him with an insidious and designing heart because of His miracles, His glory, and His benefits, He therefore is invisible. Therefore He does not bestow His benefits so richly upon some; therefore He suffers so many people to be poor; therefore He suffers many things to go contrary to the wishes of men: He suffers people to be sick, who would like to be well; to those who would like to live a life of ease He permits a life of troubles; in matters of faith He lets them remain in a sort of Babel, in a kind of uncertainty with regard to opinions; He suffers so amazingly many dubious ideas to gain the upper hand among men. All this He does so that all human means which could induce one to love Him for subsidiary aims may be entirely cut off, so that every person who comes to love Him nevertheless can allege nothing else than this: "Once He gave me a kiss of peace, and immediately I could not, I would not live any more without Him; nothing delights and satisfies me except Him; all other things are but trifles to me." He who is to be blessedly happy must be able to say, "When it pleased Him to reveal

Himself to my heart, I liked it immediately; I deliberated no longer, for He pleased my heart, and we became one."

In all speeches I always presuppose that we ourselves never take the first step toward becoming blessedly happy. At times we do take the first step in becoming weary of our troublesome life; we do at times take the first step being cloyed with the misery of sin; we take the first step being in consternation at our own condition. But we never of ourselves take the first step thinking about blessed happiness; for as to that which from time to time comes into our memory out of books, out of discourses, out of sermons, and out of those matters which we have heard from infancy, all this did not grow in our soil, and thus it is also not to be credited to our account.

We never initiate thoughts of our blessed happiness; we are never the first to fall in love with His wounds, through the narration, through the description by others. This affects the blood, this touches some springs of nature, but there it remains: there is no channel from there to the heart; one may weep a thousand times, but not a drop of it comes out of the heart; and as soon as the tears are wiped from the cheeks, it is all gone. Therefore if something real is to reach our heart, if we are to love our Creator in the beauty of His suffering, for the sake of His merits, then He must necessarily (as I have always said hitherto) appear before the heart; He must show Himself. "Had I not been pursued by you alone, I would never have gone looking for you on my own." Paul speaks this way, as do all the disciples of Jesus; Matthew must speak this way, and Peter must speak this way, and Nathanael must speak this way, indeed we all must speak this way.

With this presupposed, that thus He alone takes the first step, observe, my dear hearts, where uprightness is to be sought, namely here: where a man, when the Lord Jesus appears before his heart, when he can believe and feel, "I am now entering into the class of people of whom the Scripture says, their Creator, their Saviour is close at hand (as it often occurs in the prophets, "Draw near to me, draw near to my soul" [Ps. 69:18, alt.]) — where this man also says, "This same thing is happening to me; something of those matters which I have always heard preached comes close to my heart; my heart is beginning to open; I am beginning to notice something in my spirit, in my ordinary inward man, which I never in all my life noticed or felt there, something which I also did not feel, when in the greatest natural emotions I was arrested by something good." Here is an upright heart; here is an upright man who at this point thinks neither of wife nor child, neither of father nor mother, neither of money nor possessions, neither of flesh nor blood, neither of his best things nor even of his own weakness, sin or misery. But rather in this very moment, without any further reflection, without all elaborate refinements of reason and thoughts, but with the greatest speed he follows this pulling from the Lamb, to his Creator who purchased him. "I set out immediately" (Gal. 1:16). It is said of Mary, that when Martha told her, the Master calls you, she "rose quickly" (John 11:29) and immediately ran to seek the Master. And of Peter, that great sinner, it is said, that when there was again news of his Saviour, he ran, he so ran that he outstripped the others (Luke 24:12).

Falseness of mind and the artifices of the heart first disclosed our father Adam in his entire sinful nature, with all his misery and corruption. "Where are you?" (Gen. 3:9). "I heard your voice and hid myself, because I was naked." "Who told you this? Who made you believe this? How have you become so modest? This is not the first time I have seen you" (Gen. 3:10–11, alt.). Take note; this gives a clear insight into the modesty, the self-righteousness, the equity, the humility present when a person, out of great discretion and with ever so many compliments and an exaggeration of his misery, wants to evade the Saviour; an insight into these things as seen through the eyes of God. These things pertain to the artifices of the depraved mind of man, to the malice of the human heart, to the same bad qualities which exclude a person from the honest society of the children of God and thus from their Head as well, so that these qualities cannot be incorporated into that blessed body. No! For once one must approach just as one is. "When I wanted to keep silent, then my bones wasted away" (Ps. 32:3, LT); then I fell into cries and weeping and came into confusion, into pressure, and into anxiety; I did not know what to do, and I fell into the struggle of repentance.

But what is the cause of this? It is given in the very psalm from which I just read: my sins are too heavy and too great; I do not dare to appear before the almighty God; I would like to be better first; I would like to please Him first, and I would like to bring a holy heart along with me. This is not really true, but only a mere compliment. I just did not like to acknowledge that I am a sinner; I would like to conceal it from Him. I set about contriving, devising, thoroughly studying an excuse; I wanted to see whether I could think up something which justified me a little better and left me with some good; I wanted to hide myself. Then I was overcome by confusion, yes, a spiritual confusion, and this spiritual confusion is that very struggle of repentance, the same absurd, odd situation which makes men a spectacle for a time and has brought Christians under suspicion, as if they were some kind of fanatics and fools. But nobody must attribute this to the manifestation of Jesus Christ in His bloody form before our hearts; rather, this comes from the cunning and malignity of the heart, which would like to gain time to reach an agreement with Him and yet knows neither how to handle itself nor how to bring it about. And this perplexity, in which one talks as if he would gladly come to the Saviour and yet at the bottom of his heart has many or perhaps few excuses to call to mind and conditions to make, this perplexity finally breaks out into a spiritual convulsion, into a standstill and an impatient outcry, into a futile emaciation, into a torment of the mind, and then into a melancholy, at first natural and then affected, or vice versa, so that when this has lasted for some time, one finally persuades oneself that it is true. A man may drag on this way for one, two, three, ten, twenty years, especially when the so-called spiritual guides come to his assistance and confirm him in it and represent it to him as indeed a quite weighty matter and tear several passages out of their context of the Bible in order to find a point parallel to his condition.

In all these things we take no part, neither the Saviour nor His witnesses; all of it is vexation of one's own making. "Let no one say," when he is plagued and driven, "when he is tempted," when he comes into provoking circumstances, "that he is tempted by God" (James 1:13). Rather, this is actually the situation: when God pulls on the one side, and our own egotism pulls on the other, when one eye is kept on God and the other on our subsidiary matters, and one cannot resolve to approach, to disentangle oneself at once from all things, and to throw oneself into the open arms of the Saviour, then one is consequently reduced to one's own contrivances: one's own desires, one's own self-will produces such a temptation.

Blessedly happy is therefore the man who has an upright heart; who takes things as they are; who, not without concern, looks upon himself as dead as long as he is dead and, in that moment when he begins to feel life in himself, is glad to live; who, in the moment when he begins to live, looks around and, when he becomes aware of his Creator in the beauty of His suffering, immediately and without deliberating on it rushes into His arms. Blessedly happy is this man! And though he had been sitting in eternal chains of darkness, they are at that very moment broken apart; and though he had been lying under the feet of the enemy, soon he is soaring above his head; and though he had been stuck in sin, in the slavery of sin, in the distress of sin, yes, stuck in the love of sin up to his neck, yet in the moment when his Reconciler, his Redeemer, his eternal and lawful Husband, who made him, who bought him back again with His own blood, in the moment when He sees him and lets Himself be seen by him, and he believes in Him and comes to love Him and gives himself to Him — then in this very same moment he is delivered from the power of sin, from the fear of sin, from the inclination for sin. Then he is delivered from all attachment to sin and stands there like a newborn child, as a new creature, as a creature which had not been before, as it is written concerning the Creator, "He calls into existence the things that do not exist" (Rom. 4:17b, RSV). There the Creator has again called a soul into the light; there He has again secured Himself a person from among mankind.

The Saviour does this; this is His concern;[1] this is the work of the Holy Spirit. He can pursue a soul for ten years, go around it, come before and behind it, and can perfectly time the happy moment for it, the right time, as it is written in our 32nd Psalm and expressed in the English translation, "in a time when Thou mayest be found" (Ps. 32:6, King James); that point of time when God and man agree to speak together, when the Holy Spirit begins so maternally to act in us that nothing can stand in our way except our own malicious heart.

He who has experienced in his heart that of which I have spoken can easily comprehend it. And he who has not experienced it may still hope to do so, provided that he is disposed to present himself, not as he would wish to be, but as he actually is, before those eyes, which see everything anyway, to present himself with delight and a certain joy within, because he is known. For no sooner is he known, openly and upright just as he is, than he immediately learns to know and understand the great salvation, his Redeemer, his Helper, the Husband who can forever save all those who come to God through His wounds.

This is the goal of all speeches and sermons and of the more detailed commentaries on a text of Scripture which may be clear and edifying of itself: that among men several kinds of thoughts are stimulated, others are taken away, and sometimes thoughts that were already there are renewed, and thus the work of the Holy Spirit is continually pointed to. All this is done so that the two hearts in love with the human soul, namely, the Saviour and His Spirit, once experienced the moment, the instant, when the outward word that is preached amid their continual cooperation and the drawings of the Father to Himself — when this and the personal presence of the bleeding Redeemer before the heart converge at one point at the same time, to the mutual joy of teacher and hearer. This is the goal of preaching.

The apostle Paul speaks of it this way: the word and faith blend with one another, pull toward each other like two sparks of fire, like two flames. The word goes out of the teacher's mouth, and love, desire, longing, and faith come from out of the hearer's heart; and these things become one. The Father holds His hand over this; this the Holy Spirit embraces; then in that very moment the bleeding Husband forms Himself in the innermost part of the soul. Then the heart stands full of Jesus, full of His wounds and His sores, full of the Merits of the Lamb. Then the Redeemer extends Himself over heart and body, as Elisha did over the boy (II Kings 4:34), and His agonizing sweat bedews our body and soul. Then the soul is set for time and eternity. Blest is the man who has an upright heart; all sins are forgiven him.

---

1 German: *das ist seine Sache*, which means "this is his thing." Zinzendorf actually means what this term has come to mean in contemporary America.

PRAYER

Heart with us! Faithful and merciful Redeemer! Let your great objective, which is the deliverance and redemption of us all, in regard to this city also, constantly remain upon your heart. Continually call to mind those souls in whom so much preparation has been made by your Father and the Holy Spirit, in some by day and night for many years toward that blessedly happy moment when you would pass into them and become one heart and soul with them.

Let not only this assembly, but all assemblies of this city and of the whole realm, from the head to the lowest member, lie upon your heart and remain continually in your remembrance, until, at that moment when their thoughts are upright, when they think honestly, when they think without ambiguity, you can take them into your arms and carry them away upon your shoulders with joy. Do this for the sake of your wounds. Amen!

Lecture IX

That which, Properly Speaking, can Secure Us from all Fear, Danger, and Harm

---

Preached in the Brethren's Chapel in London, October 16, 1746

TEXT: Acts 23:11. *"The following night the Lord stood by him and said, 'Take courage.'"* (RSV)

I BELIEVE that when the really important matter comes up — as has happened occasionally in the lectures which for some time have been delivered here — namely, that our Saviour's simple gaze has such an astonishing effect upon the heart, it happens that some think, yes, those were happy days, when people were able so to talk with the Saviour in person, when He could look upon someone in such a way. Jesus *in Carne:* [1] What blessed happiness!

Now at this point I do not want to appeal to the passage where the Lord Jesus says, "I am with you always, to the close of the age" (Matt. 28:20, RSV), for I realize that this passage is subject to interpretation, i.e., present through His Spirit and gifts. But I have other passages for your comfort, one being the text which I have just read and on which I shall base my lecture; it is clear and expressive. "The Lord stood by him." As he at one point was looking around during the night, our Lord stood before him and said, "Take courage."

We have additional instances; we have that well-known case when He appeared to Paul and cried, "Why do you persecute me?" (Acts 9:4, RSV).

---

1 "In the flesh."

We have the remarkable, great, and long instance in the Revelation of John and such an ample discourse, such a detailed appearance, that John has described His clothes, His countenance, and the whole man from head to toe (Rev. 19:11–16). But all these instances will be looked upon as extraordinary events which do not happen nowadays.

But my text presents itself so simply and without any extraordinary occasion: "The Lord stood by him." And elsewhere Paul cites a similar instance: the Lord came to me and told me this and this (e.g., I Cor. 11:23, or II Cor. 12:9). If we take two things together: (1) another passage of Scripture, and (2) an insight universally received among Christians, then we will have the whole picture.

The passage of Scripture is this: "So the Lord opened the eyes of the young man, and he saw the entire mountain full of fiery horses and chariots" (II Kings 6:17, alt.).

The second point is that article, accepted throughout all Christendom, at least by all reasonable persons, concerning the communion of the invisible Church: "I believe in the communion of saints."

Not every man is so foolish that he restricts the communion of saints, the invisible Church, to the case of the person who, belonging to the Anglican, the Lutheran, or any other church, travels to Paris and there remains in his spirit in communion with his Anglican or Lutheran church. There are indeed such absurd teachers, who do restrict it to this; but they are not so respected that they are able to adulterate the general interpretation, which is that in all nations and even in the erroneous religious denominations themselves God has His own people; "The Lord knows His own" (II Tim. 2:19). However, by this it is not confirmed that one can be saved in all religions; by this it is not confirmed that one is able to get along quite well with all notions and opinions. For this doctrine does not signify that; it does not say that the souls which the Saviour has all over the world cannot be wrong in their principles; one is not to be indifferent to doctrine. Rather, it is presupposed that they are preserved through a particular grace of the Saviour in that which is essential to salvation. And this we believe of the darkest and most obscure eras, that the souls who were saved have always had a sufficient light, a clarity adequate for themselves which distinguished them from the general darkness. Whoever reads their writings, whoever considers their sayings, considers their sufferings themselves, will find that they had quite another idea in matters which bring redemption, in the points relating to salvation, than did the common people and the clergy around them in those darkened eras; they are called witnesses of the truth. But besides these witnesses to the truth there still are the quiet ones in the land of whom we see and hear nothing and who yet enjoy the very same blessed happiness.

Now what does this position imply? What does the instance which I have cited suppose? That the eyes of that man were opened? I answer that the instance implies that there are many things which are not perceived, which, if one's eyes were opened, would disclose an indescribable splendour, so that one would be astonished at things which are daily around and near, but, indeed, invisibly. But what does the universal position concerning the invisible Church imply? It assumes an invisible Head; it assumes an invisible intimate association of the Head with His invisible members, a walking with His invisible body, the revelation and manifestation of which depends every moment upon the bidding and will of its Head. And note, my beloved, that this is what I should very much like here, this is my great aim and my sole purpose, that this principle, "Send my children and the work of my hands to me" (Isa. 45:11), which the Saviour delivered through the mouth of the prophets and palpably intended of and undeniably centered in His own person, may be deeply established in the hearts of all, particularly the hearts of the children of God.

It is far too precarious, far too vexatious and unsafe an affair if one is obliged to stake his salvation, his being kept and preserved on any external circumstance whatsoever. If I am to place my salvation and the preservation of my salvation on the good and sound understanding which Almighty God has given me, then as long as God lets me have the use of my understanding, I will not think differently. But what if I should lose my understanding? As long as I can use my five senses, I shall never conceive these matters differently. But what if I can no longer use my five senses? As long as I still have the Word of God, the Bible, I would still have its consolation in view. But if I no longer had the Bible, would the great, the profound words remain in my memory? But what if I lose my memory? As long as I still have a good friend, he will remind me of it; certainly there will always be at least one person who will care about me. But what if there is no one? Then I will reflect until I am again able somehow to aid myself. But what if you are no longer able to think reflectively? These are all things which are possible, which do happen. To presuppose the absence of such things has the most miserable effect: an insecurity, an uncertainty, an unreliability in the whole matter of religion. From this come all the laments of the apostles, when they say, "After my departure," after I have turned my back, after I am called home, "fierce wolves will arise from among your own selves, not sparing the flock" (Acts 20:29, alt.); and then they will start sects, and a great number of the people of our congregations will go into these seductive sects; it will be terrible. This literally came to pass. But why? Must it perhaps be so? Are these cases absolutely necessary? Are these unavoidable misfortunes? In effect they are, but they have no foundation in the nature of the thing. For if souls were reconciled with this matter, so that they would hold fast to their only, inward, true, chosen, and necessary Friend, who is from their point of view indispensably necessary to them and who again for His person neither can nor will subsist without them; who is so affected, as we say, that He cannot leave the souls, that He cannot do without the souls who have cost Him His own blood and life; who would have to forget and deny Himself, if He wanted to deny and lose the great pains He took for the sake of these souls — would souls hold fast to Him, then they would be safe. That they do not hold fast to Him, this is the fault. A close connection, an inseparable friendship must be established with the Lamb, with the slaughtered Lamb, with that sinner executed for mankind, Jesus Christ, with Him in Whom the whole world was absolved; and this is the goal of all our lectures. The Saviour must be able to look upon souls as He did upon Peter; He must be able to stand by them, so that if they opened their eyes, they would see Him, so that if only they could open their eyes, they would see Him standing before them. In the meantime His soul must continually associate with them, and they must not be able to conceive even a moment when He would not be near them; for so says the apostle, "Yet he is not far from each one of us" (Acts 17:27).

It would be right if every one of us would base all his association with people, all love toward people, all brotherly love solely on this principle — that these others are also my Lord's people; they are my brothers and sisters; we are the children of one Father; they all have the same blessed happiness that I have; they enjoy what I enjoy; they are just as favored as I am and just as redeemed; they are destined for the same glory to which I am called through grace. All love and affection toward one another should derive from this fact, even the friendship occasioned by consanguinity, by like dispositions of mind, or by being schoolmates. And as souls advance in the experience, in the insight, in the feeling and love of the Saviour, such affection and intimacy would grow in its extensiveness. But as high as heaven is from the earth, as far as the thoughts of God are from ordinary, human thoughts, so far must the preference which a person gives his Lamb, his Husband, his Creator, the Surety crucified for our debt, his Redeemer and Saviour, transcend everything which one owes all one's fellow creatures, all one's fellow men, yes, all one's fellow Christians, so that it is not even possible to make a comparison.

If our whole world should die away, if all of our brothers and sisters should be lost, if all of our intimate friends should be taken away, if we should come into such a condition that we could find no more resources in or outside of ourselves, that the favors and the recreation which the faithful and wise Father has laid in men's own nature, in their own favored heart, all fell away or became useless in the distress we would still miss nothing; as long as we had the Saviour, we should remain as blessedly happy, as complete, as unharmed, as we were in the very first moment of our spiritual life, in the first moment of our absolution and acceptance into grace. Only let us spare ourselves that amazing confusion of conceiving the look of the Saviour at some mathematical distance from us; for this is the greatest spiritual absurdity that can exist. The shirt on our back is not nearer to us than He is; the heart in our body is not nearer to us than He is. And when David said, "If my body and soul waste away, still I have something" (Ps. 73:26, alt.), if I have You, then I do not lack comfort, either he was saying something that had neither sense nor meaning — speaking nonsense — or else with the loss of life and limb and of all the powers of mind and soul everything cannot yet be lost, as long as one still has and knows his Saviour.

For that reason the Saviour says so well: "If a man were to gain the whole world and suffer the smallest detriment to his soul, the loss would be irreparable" (Mark 8:36–37, alt.). And yet He can also say, whoever would lose his soul for My sake, he for the first time finds it truly; for the first time he has brought it to safety; only then has he helped it along. But these would be contradictory sayings, if the Saviour were not still beyond the soul itself, if He were not nearer to us than our own soul is to ourselves. "In Him we live and move and have our being" (Acts 17:28, RSV); He is the true element in which the children of God subsist. "I have ceased to live," says Paul, "but Christ lives in my place, and the life I still live in the flesh," what remains of this weak, earthly life in this bodily tabernacle, what can still be seen of this outward humanity, "this is all transferred by faith into the Son of God, who loved me and gave Himself for me, so that I no longer know whether I also am still living, or He alone in me" (Gal. 2:20, alt.).

If only we had that at all times; if the blessed minutes and hours, during which, in this present clay of ours, we feel, perceive, and become aware of nothing but Him, were uninterrupted, then we would have everlasting life here and would need no other. But this is the misfortune of the present course of things: as long as we here in our body cannot follow where He is (He can follow us everywhere, though we cannot follow Him), so that for hours, moments, seconds, or even imperceptible intervals, we may be said to be *apontes*,[2] so that we seem to ourselves to be absent from Him, so that we can forget ourselves — as is said in ordinary life, he forgets himself — as long as this happens, one can also forget his Lord. For a moment one can be disturbed and confused in his mind; and if Satan can succeed in making it last for hours and days, then he has gained so much, that, as Paul says, a person becomes deranged and agitated, that one is disturbed in his spiritual faculty, that one may no longer be considered a spiritual man in a regular state, but rather a man in an extraordinary condition,

---

2 Greek: absent (e.g. 1 Corinthians 5:3).

a man in confusion. Then Satan takes particular delight in us; and even though he neither can nor is allowed to come quite near to us, though he can do us no essential damage, yet he still has his fun, and we grieve and lament over the derangement and disturbance in our hearts, in which no one can pacify us.

But here is the shortest and best remedy, that in one moment we may turn around and return again to where we were. This was won for us on the Cross: that in the very middle of such confusion, such perplexity, in the very middle of such distress, just as we are, we may sit or lay ourselves before Him and say, there You have me, as I am. As little ceremony as a sick person or one who has fainted can make, as little as such a person can consider in whose hands he is or how well he is dressed, as little as a person in excruciating pain can think about the posture in which he finds himself at that moment, but rather lets himself be seen just as he is and helped as help can be given even so must we be completely unable to reflect upon our condition or want first to make it better. We must not want to try to repair anything in ourselves, so that it might have a better and nobler appearance. Rather, we must come to Him entirely natural, in the most wretched form in which we happen to find ourselves, pleading His blood, His faithfulness, and His merits, and reminding Him that we men are the reward of His suffering, that we are His people, and that He has promised Himself to us for eternity. Then immediately He is as good as His word, and His mere presence, his mere approach drives our enemies out of our sight and away from our borders:

> Send with his pretended claim
> The worst of spirits to the Lamb:
> It quickly flies.

But if this often happens, if we have many times fallen fainting and poor at the Saviour's feet unaccustomed to the spiritual life and thus in various confusions, but yet have always recollected ourselves to a point and regained our senses to the extent that we said, where can my Saviour be? where is my Redeemer? my heart, where is Jesus? — if Satan has had to experience it ten, twenty times, that we again have the Saviour with us immediately; then he finally becomes tired out, gives up, and keeps away from us. Not due to our own courage or power, not due to our own virtuous dispositions, perfection, goodness, beauty, or holiness, but rather because Satan stands in fear of his Creator, we finally reach the point when he no longer comes near, when he gets out of our way. We still remain people whom he could toss, sift, and prostitute, people in whom he could perpetrate his evil inclinations; for we are flesh. But his political shrewdness does not allow it; his Satanical understanding does not admit of it; he does not stand to win enough by it, but he sees how much he might lose; he sees a soul come nearer and nearer to its Saviour: it is more and more united with its Head, and it cries more and more for His heart. So Satan thinks, what good does my work do me? I only drive the souls more and more into Jesus, and that I will not do.

What is then the best way to get rid of him, as John expresses it, "So that the evil one no longer comes near one" (I John 5:18, alt.), so that he no longer even desires to come near? The best way is that the soul be near its Head. But as long as a soul and the Saviour remain separated, the soul may be as Christian, as perfect, as devout, as watchful, as diligent in prayer as it will, or have a great hatred of evil — yet all these efforts are only games for Satan, rather, inducements for him to perpetrate his evil inclinations in us and, because he is not able to draw us to himself, at least to scourge, afflict, beat, and harass us (Paul says [II Cor. 12:7], a gnawing worm has been inflicted upon me, which has plagued me more than enough). A certain self-conceit on the part of the soul, a sort of high opinion of itself, or even only the fear that it might come to such a thing, has done Satan the service: a subtle removal from the Saviour.

As long as something can still separate us from the Saviour; as long as the most trifling thing can remain between us and the Saviour; as long as one soul in the world — be it the dearest brother or sister or even a spiritual father — still claims or seems to have in effect the most minute but nevertheless more intimate right to us than does our Redeemer, whose blood we have cost, and Who is our true and eternal Husband — as long as this is the case our whole Christianity while not actually deception and fantasy (in the end we will certainly not fall into destruction) yet our entire blessed happiness at present, our whole glory, and all the majesty of our state is a fickle and inconstant thing. One cannot proceed in one's course and toward one's destiny with cheerfulness, joyousness, and liveliness of heart; rather, we are obliged to stand in continual ghostly fear of Satan. It is true that we do not love him; he is like a spectre to us; but yet it is true that we are afraid. Therefore by faith and love we must so enter into the Saviour,[3] that we can no longer see or hear anything else above or beyond Him, that we and He remain inseparably together. "I will know Him, as I am known by Him" (I Cor. 13:12, alt.). He knows me so well; He knows my hours and days; He knows my motions and emotions; He knows my abilities and inabilities; He knows my inclinations and my fears; He knows my danger and my security; in short, I can be nowhere better than in His arms.

---

3 Zinzendorf says: *Darum muss man sich in den Heiland so hineinglauben, so hineinlieben.*

PRAYER

And to this end, my atoning Lamb, I commend myself and all these souls to you. Do not allow us for even a moment to leave that near and blessed intimacy with you which is our surest defence against sin and Satan. Only remain all things to us, our very life and our only strength, and let us believe and sink so deeply into you, that you may be infinitely dearer to us than we are to ourselves, that you may be much closer to us and much more depended on by us than we can or shall be to ourselves in time and in eternity. Amen.

Bibliography

I. *Primary Sources*

Zinzendorf, N. L. *Acta Fratrum Unitatis in Anglia.* London, 1749. (Many pieces from the hand of Zinzendorf.)

———. *Allen Teutschen Eltern . . . Welche Ihre Kinder . . . Besorgt Sähen.* Germantown, Pa.: Christoph Saur, 1742.

———. "Die ältesten Berichte Zinzendorfs über sein Leben, sein Unternehmungen und Herrnhuts Entstehen." Ed. J. Th. Müller. *Zeitschrift für Brüdergeschichte,* V, 1 (1911), pp. 92–116; VI, 1 (1912), pp. 45–118; VI, 2 (1912), pp. 196–217; VII, 1 (1913), pp. 114–120; VII, 2 (1913), pp. 171–215.

———. "Aus Zinzendorfs Briefwechsel vom 8. April bis 29. Juli, 1716." Zinzendorf an seine Mutter, 8. April, 1716; Zinzendorf an Walbaum, 8. April, 1716; Walbaum an Zinzendorf, 27. Juni, 1716; Zinzendorf an Walbaum, 4. Juli, 1716; Walbaum an Zinzendorf, 18. Juli, 1716. *Zeitschrift für Brüdergeschichte,* I, 2 (1907), pp. 192–203.

———. *Auszüge aus des Seligen Ordinarii der Evangelischen Brüder-Kirche Herrn Nikolaus Ludwig Grafens und Herrn von Zinzendorf und Pottendorf sowol ungedrukten als gedrukten Reden über die vier Evangelisten.* 6 Vols. Ed. Gottfried Clemens. Barby: H. D. Ebers, 1766–1792.

———. *Auszüge aus des Seligen Ordinarii der Evangelischen Brüder-Kirche sowol ungedrukten als gedrukten Reden über biblische Texte . . .* 3 Vols. Ed. Gottfried Clemens. Barby, 1763–1765.

———. *B. Ludwigs Wahrer Bericht.* De dato Germantown den 20. Febr. 1740, an seine liebe Teutsche, und wem es sonst nützlich zu wissen ist, wegen Sein und seiner Brüder Zusammenhanges mit Pennsylvania, zu Prüfung der Zeit und Umstände ausgefertiget; nebst einem P. S. de dato Philadelphia den 5. Martii; und einigen Unsre Lehre überhaupt und dieses Schriftgen insonderheit. Erläuternden Belagen. Philadelphia: Benjamin Franklyn, 1742.

———. Beilage "Zinzendorfs Instruktion für Wittenberg," *Zeitschrift für Brüdergeschichte,* II, 2, (1908), pp. 118–129.

———. *Berliner Reden an die Frauen.* Berlin, 1738.

———. *Berliner Reden an die Männer.* ("Inhalt dererjenigen Reden, Welche zu Berlin vom 1. Januarii, 1738, biss 27. Aprilis in denen Abend-Stunden sonderlich für die Manns-Personen gehalten worden.") Berlin, 1738.

———. *Büdingische Sammlung eineger in die Kirchen-Historie einschlagender, sonderlich neuerer Schriften,* I–III. N. L. von Zinzendorf Ergänzungsbände. Eds. Erich Beyreuther and Gerhard Meyer. Hildesheim: Georg Olms Verlagsbuchhandlung, 1966, Vols. VII, VIII, IX, X.

————. *A compendious extract* containing the chiefest articles of doctrine and most remarkable transactions of Count Lewis of Zinzendorf and the Moravians. Together with the most natural objections of some of their antagonists. Collected from the German. Intended for a summary of that controversy, which at present is a matter of universal speculation, in this part of America . . . Philadelphia: A. Bradford, 1742.

————. *Deutsche Gedichte, N. L. von Zinzendorf Ergänzungsbände.* Eds. Erich Beyreuther and Gerhard Meyer. Hildesheim: Georg Olms Verlagsbuchhandlung, 1964, Vol. II, pp. 1–368.

————. *Diarium des Jungerhauses von 1747–1760.* (Manuscript). Herrnhut: Unitäts-Archiv.

————. *Diejenigen Anmerkungen, Welche der Herr Autor des Kurzen Extracts, etc. von dem Herrn v. Thurnstein, d. z. Pastore der Evangel. Luth. Gemeine Jesu Christi zu Philadelphia in der Vorrede seiner Schrift freundlich begehret hat* . . . Philadelphia: Isaias Warner, 1742.

————. *Ein und zwanzig Discurse Über die Augspurgische Confession gehalten vom 15. Dec., 1747 bis zum 3. Mart., 1748. N. L. von Zinzendorf Hauptschriften.* Eds. Erich Beyreuther and Gerhard Meyer. Hildesheim: Georg Olms Verlagsbuchhandlung, 1963, Vol. VI, pp. 1–366.

————. *Eine Sammlung Öffentlicher Reden, von dem Herrn der unsere Seligkeit ist, und Über die Materie von seiner Marter. N. L. von Zinzendorf Hauptschriften.* Eds. Erich Beyreuther and Gerhard Meyer. Hildesheim: Georg Olms Verlagsbuchhandlung, 1963, Vol. II, pp. 1–238, 1–324.

————. *Eines abermaligen Versuchs zur Übersetzung der historischen Bücher Neuen Testaments unsers Herrn Jesu Christi aus dem original, erste probe zweyte Edition. N. L. von Zinzendorf Hauptschriften.* Eds. Erich Beyreuther and Gerhard Meyer. Hildesheim: Georg Olms Verlagsbuchhandlung, 1963, Vol. VI, pp. 1–97.

————. *Einige Reden des seligen ordinarii fratrum Herrn Nicolaus Ludwig Grafens und Herrn von Zinzendorf und Pottendorf, mehrentheils auf seinen Reisen im Jahr 1757 gehalten.* Barby: H. D. Ebers, 1768.

————. *Ergänzungsbände.* 12 Vols. Eds. Erich Beyreuther and Gerhard Meyer. Hildesheim: Georg Olms Verlagsbuchhandlung, 1964–1972.

————. *Etliche zu dieser Zeit nicht unnütze Fragen über Einige Schrift-Stellen.* Welche von den Liebhabern der lautern Wahrheit Deutlich Erörtert zu werden gewünschet hat Ein Wahrheitforschender in America, im Jahr 1742, so deutlich und einfältig erörtert als es ihm möglich gewesen ist; und in folgender klaren und bequemen Form herausgegeben von einem Knecht Jesu Christi. Philadelphia: B. Franklin, 1742.

————. *Every man's right to live. A sermon on Ezek: XXXIII. 2. Why will ye die?* Preached at Philadelphia, by the Rev. Lewis of Thurenstein, deacon of the ancient Moravian Church. Translated from German into English. Philadelphia: B. Franklin, 1743.

————. *An Exposition, or True State of the Matters Objected in England to the People Known by the Name of Unitas Fratrum.* London, 1755.

————. *Die gegenwärtige Gestalt des Kreuz-Reichs Jesu in seiner Unschuld.* Büdingen: Stohr, 1746.

————. *Gewisser Grund Christlicher Lehre* (Katechismus). Görlitz. 1735.

————. *Haupschriften.* 6 Vols. Ed. Erich Beyreuther and Gerhard Meyer. Hildesheim: Georg Olms Verlagsbuchhandlung, 1962.

————. *Herrnhuter Diarium* (Manuskript). Herrnhut: Archiv des Brüderunität.

————. *Kleine Schrifften, I–XIII.* Frankfurt, 1740.

————. "Kurz Mitteilungen: Der Parther." [A weekly journal published anonymously by Zinzendorf, Dresden, 1725.] *Zeitschrift für Brüdergeschichte,* 1 (1910), pp. 124–128.

————. *A Letter from Lewis Thurenstein, deacon of the Moravian Church, to people of all ranks and persuasions, which are in Pennsylvania; but more especially to those who are not bigotted by any particular opinion.* Translated from the Latin by Philip Reading. Philadelphia, 1743.

————. *Letzte Privat-Erklärung für Pennsylvania, über Jemands Bericht, Der sich nicht nur über eine unter seinem Namen, ohne sein Wissen und Willen, und noch dazu Unganz gedruckte Schrift beschweret; Sondern auch über die Gemeine des Herrn das Urtheil Spricht.* Philadelphia: Benjamin Franklin, 1742.

————. *Londoner Predigten von 1754. N. L. von Zinzendorf Hauptschriften.* Eds. Erich Beyreuther and Gerhard Meyer. Hildesheim: Georg Olms Verlagsbuchhandlung, 1963, Vol. V.

————. *Ludovici a Thürenstein in Antiquissima Fratrum Ecclesia ad taxin kai Euschemosynen diaconi Constituti,* et. h. t. Ecclesiae, Quae Christo Philadelphiae inter Luteranos Colliquitur, Pastoris, ad Cogitatus Ingenuos Pium Desiderium, h.e. Epistola ad Bonos Pennsylvaniae Cives Christo non inimicos, ob conversationis difficultatem toliter qvaliter Latino Idiomate conscripta, Et dexteritati cordati interpretis, duce providentia pie con credita. Philadelphia: Ex officina Frankliniana, 1742.

————. *Ludwig von Zinzendorf Peri Eautou. N. L. von Zinzendorf Ergänzungsbände.* Eds. Erich Beyreuther and Gerhard Meyer. Hildesheim: George Olms Verlagsbuchhandlung, 1964, Vol. 4, pp. 1–364.

————. *Maxims, Theological Ideas and Sentences, out of the Present Ordinary of the Brethren's Churches.* His Dissertations and Discourses From the Year 1738–1747. Extracted by J. Gambold. London: J. Beecroft, 1751.

————. *Nine Publick Discourses upon Important Subjects in Religion.* Preached in Fetter-Lane-Chapel at London, in 1746. London: James Hutton, 1748.

————. *Oratio.* Philadelphia: B. Franklin, 1742.

————. *Peremptorisches Bedencken.* London, 1753.

————. "Rede am Kirchweyh-Feste der Märischen Brüder, den 12. May, 1745." *Zeitschrift für Brüdergeschichte,* III, 2 (1909), pp. 207–238.

————. *The Remarks which the Author of the* Compendious Extract, *etc. in the Preface to his book, has friendly desired of the Rev. of Thurenstein, for the Time Pastor of the Lutheran Congregation of J. C. in Philadelphia.* Philadelphia: B. Franklin, 1742.

————. *Des seligen Grafen Nicolaus Ludwig von Zinzendorf Gedanken über verschiedene evangelische Wahrheiten, aus dessen Schriften zusammengezogen.* Gnadau: H. F. Burkhard, 1840.

————. *Sixteen Discourses on the Redemption of Man by the Death of Christ.* [Preached at Berlin.] London, 1740.

————. "Stammtafeln. Die von Grafen v. Zinzendorf, der Zelkingsche Zweig." *Zeitschrift für Brüdergeschichte,* I, 2 (1907).

————. *Summarischer Unterricht in Anno 1753 für Reisende Brüder.* London, 1755.

————. *Theologische und dahin einschlagende Bedenken. N. L. von Zinzendorf Ergänzungsbände.* Eds. Erich Beyreuther and Gerhard Meyer. Hildesheim: Georg Olms Verlagsbuchhandlung, 1964, Vol. IV, pp. 1–206.

————. *Vorschlag zur Errichtung einer Deutschen Schule.* Germantown: Christoph Saur, 1742.

————. *Die wichtigsten Missionsinstruktionen Zinzendorfs.* Ed. O. Uttendörfer, *Hefte zur Missionskunde.* Herrnhut: Missionsbuchhandlung, 1913, Vol. XII.

————. *Wundenlitanei, 1747. N. L. von Zinzendorf Hauptschriften.* Eds. Erich Beyreuther and Gerhard Meyer. Hildesheim: George Olms Verlagsbuchhandlung, 1963, Vol. III, pp. 1–399.

————. *Zeister Reden. N. L. von Zinzendorf Hauptschriften.* Eds. Erich Beyreuther and Gerhard Meyer. Hildesheim: Georg Olms Verlagsbuchhandlung, 1963, Vol. III, pp. 1–454.

————. "Zinzendorfs Tagebuch 1716–1719." Eds. G. Reichel und J. T. Müller. *Zeitschrift für Brüdergeschichte.* I, 2 (1907), pp. 113–191; II, 2 (1908), pp. 81–117; IV, 1 (1910), pp. 5–97.

————. *Zwei und dreissig einzelne Homiliae in den Jahren 1744-1746 gehalten.* Görlitz Marche, 1749.

Zinzendorf-Gedenkjahr. Hamburg: Ludwig Appel Verlag, 1960. (Herrnhuter Hefte 16.)

II. *Secondary Sources*

Aalen, Leiv. "Evangeliet og nademidlene, et bidrag til rettferdiggorelseslaeren pa bakgrunn av luthersk laeretradisjon." *Tidsskrift for Teologi og Kirke,* I–II (1947), p. 71.

————. "Kirche und Mission bei Zinzendorf." *Lutherische Rundschau,* V (1955–1956), pp. 267–281.

————. "Die Theologie des Grafen von Zinzendorf." *Gedenkschrift für Werner Elert.* Ed. Friedrich Hübner. Berlin, 1955, pp. 220 ff.

————. *Die Theologie des jungen Zinzendorf.* Berlin: Lutherisches Verlagshaus, 1966.

————. *Den unge Zinzendorfs Teologi.* Oslo: Lutherstiftelsens Forlag, 1952.

Addison, W. G. *The Renewed Church of the United Brethren 1722–1930.* New York: Macmillan, 1932.

Akten aus dem Herrnhuter Archiv Aarau und Aargau betreffend 1740–1775. Not printed.

Aland, Kurt. Spenerstudien (Arbeiten zur Geschichte des Pietismus I). Berlin: W. de Gruyter, 1943.

Allison, William H. *Inventory and Unpublished Materials for American Religious History in the Protestant Church Archives and Other Repositories.* Washington: Carnegie Institution, Publication No. 137 (1910), pp. 147–165.

Alt und neuer Brüdergesang. London, 1753.

Althaus, Paul. *Forschungen zur evangelischen Gebetsliteratur.* Gütersloh: C. Bertelsmann, 1927.

Amerikanische Provincial Synoden, 1748–1835. 20 Vols. Bethlehem Archives Mss. Original Minutes and Documents of the American Church North.

Anonymous. *Abbildung des Grafen von Zinzendorff, Haupt der neuen Sekte der Herrnhuter nach der Natur: nebst der Abbildung eines Christen nach der heiligen Schrifft.* Hutter: Frankfurt/Main, 1749.

Anonymous [John Wesley]. *Queries Humbly Proposed to the Rt. Rev. and Rt. Hon. Count Zinzendorf.* London: J. Robinson, 1755.

Antes, Heinrich. *Herrn Pyrlaei Ausruf-Zeddel an die Einwohner in Pensilvanien, dass Diejenige, so Herrn Grafen von Zinzendorf noch einmal wolten predigen hören, sich melden solten.* Germantown, Pa.: Christoph Saur, 1742.

Arndt, Johann. *Des weiland Hocherleuchteten Theologi, Herrn Johann Arndten. . . . Sämtliche Geistreiche Bücher vom Wahren Christenthum. . . . Mit einer Vorrede.* Ed. J. F. Buddeus. Frankfurt: Reinhard Eustachius Müller, 1733.

Arnold, Gottfried. *Die erste Liebe. Das ist: wahre Abildung der ersten Christen, nach ihrem lebendigen Glauben und heiligen Leben.* Frankfurt and Leipzig, 1712.

———. *Theologia Experimentalis.* Frankfurt: J. D. Zunners and J. A. Jung, 1715.

———. *Unparteyische Kirchen und Ketzerhistorie, von Anfang des Neuen Testaments biss auff das Jahr Christi 1688.* Vols. I–IV. Frankfurt: Thomas Fritsch, 1699–1700.

Aspacher, Dekan. "Pietisten und Herrnhuter in Prichsenstadt, 1717–1756." *Zeitschrift für Brüdergeschichte,* X (1916), pp. 1–31.

Aufrichtige Anzeige, was es mit des Grafen Ludwigs von Zinzendorf Conduite in ansehung des Reichs und der Sache Christi für einen Zusammenhang hat (R 20 A 1). Herrnhut: Archiv der Brüderunität.

Banyas, Frank A. *The Moravians in Colonial Pennsylvania.* Masters thesis, Ohio State University, 1940.

Barth, Karl. *Die protestantische Theologie im 19. Jahrhundert.* Ihre Vorgeschichte und ihre Geschichte. 2nd ed. Zurich: Evangelischer Verlag, 1947.

"Karl Barth, der Graf und die Brüder." *Deutsches Pfarrerblatt,* 5 (1962).

Baudert, S. "Zinzendorf's Thought on Missions Related to His Views of the World." *International Review of Missions,* 21 (July 1932), pp. 390–401.

Baumgart, Peter. *Zinzendorf als Wegbereiter historischen Denkens.* Lübeck: Matthiesen Verlag, 1960. Vol. 381, *Historische Studien.*

Baumgarten, Siegmund Jacob. *Theologische Bedencken I.* 2nd ed. Halle, 1744.

Bayer, Siegfried. "Nikolaus Ludwig Graf von Zinzendorf. Ein echter Ökumeniker im 18. Jahrhundert." *Ökumenische Profile, I* (1961), pp. 119–128.

Becherer, Johann Georg. *Nöthige Prüfung der Zinzendorfischen Lehr-Art von der Heil. Dreyeinigkeit.* Frankfurt/Main, 1748.

Bechler, Theodor. "Christian David (1690–1751). Der Erbauer Herrnhuts." *Lebensbilder aus der Brüdergemeine,* IV (1922).

———. *200 Jahre ärztliche Missionsarbeit der Herrnhuter Brüdergemeine.* Herrnhut: Verlag der Missionsbuchhandlung, 1932.

———. *Ortsgeschichte von Herrnhut mit besondere Berücksichtigung der älteren Zeit.* Herrnhut: Verlag der Missionsbuchhandlung, 1922.

———. *Wie es zur Gründung Herrnhuts kam.* Herrnhut: Verlag der Missionsbuchhandlung, 1922.

———. "Einzelbekehrung und Volkskirche nach den Erfahrungen der Brüdermission." *Die Einwurzelung des Christentums in der Heidenwelt.* Ed. P. Jul. Richter. Gütersloh: Bertelsmann, pp. 87–145.

———. *Graf Zinzendorf. Jugendschriften.* No. 1. Herrnhut: Missionsbuchhandlung, 1907.

Becker, Bernhard. "Schleiermacher und die Brüdergemeine." *Monatshefte der Comeniusgesellschaft,* III (1894), pp. 47 ff.

———. "Zinzendorfs Beziehungen zur römischen Kirche." *Theologische Studien und Kritiken* (1891), pp. 321 ff.

———. *Zinzendorf im Verhältnis zu Philosophie und Kirchentum seiner Zeit.* Leipzig: J. C. Hinrichs Verlag, 1886. (Geschichtliche Studien VIII.)

Becker, John. "Goethe und die Brüdergemeine." *Zeitschrift für Brüdergeschichte,* III (1909), pp. 94 ff.

Bemman, Herbert. *Die soziologische Struktur des Herrnhutertums.* Heidelberg, 1921.

Bender, Wilhelm. *Johann Konrad Dippel. Der Freigeist aus dem Pietismus. Ein Beitrag zur Entstehungsgeschichte der Aufklärung.* Bonn: E. Weber, 1882.

Bengel, Johann Albrecht. *Abriss der Brüdergemeine.* Stuttgart: J. B. Metzler, 1751.

Benham, Daniel. *Memoirs of James Hutton: Comprising the Annals of His Life, and Connection with the United Brethren.* London: Hamilton, Adams, and Co., 1856.

———. *The Memorial Days of the Renewed Church of the Brethren.* London, 1895.

Benner, D. Johann Hermann. *Die gegenwärtige Gestalt der Herrnhuterey in ihrer Schalkheit.* Giessen: J. P. Krieger, 1746.

Benz, E. and Renkewitz, Heinz. *Zinzendorf-Gedenkbuch.* Stuttgart: Evangelisches Verlagswerk, 1951.

III

Beonar, F. "Ecumenical Idea in the Czech Reformation." *Ecumenical Review*, 6 (1954), pp. 160–168.

Bettermann, W. "Das Los in der Brüdergemeine." *Zeitschrift für Volkskunde*, III, 3 (1931), pp. 284 ff.

———. "Die Bedeutung des 13. Aug. 1727 für die evangelische Christenheit." *Wochenblatt "Herrnhut,"* 30–31 (1927).

———. "Die Geschichte der Konfirmation in der Brüdergemeine." *Monatsschrift für Gottesdienst und Kirchliche Kunst*, 2–3 and 9–10 (1929).

———. "Grundlinien der Theologie Zinzendorfs." *Zeitschrift für systematische Theologie*, XI (1934), pp. 3 ff.

———. *Theologie und Sprache bei Zinzendorf.* Gotha: Leopold Klotz, 1935.

———. "Vorläufiges über Zinzendorfs Stellung zur Mystik." *Zeitschrift für Kirchengeschichte*, III (1933), pp. 599 ff.

———. "Zinzendorfs Lied 'Abendmahlsgedanken', 25. Sept. 1718 in Wittenberg." *Zietschrift für Kirchengeschichte*, XIV (1918), pp. 128–133.

———. "Zinzendorf, Nikolaus Ludwig." *Die Religion in Geschichte und Gegenwart.* Eds. Hermann Gunkel and Leopold Zcharnack. Tübingen: J. C. B. Mohr, 1931, Vol. 5, pp. 2217 ff.

Beyreuther, Erich. *August Hermann Franke 1663-1727.* Marburg: Verlag der Francke-Buchhandlung, 1956.

———. *A. H. Francke und die Anfänge der ökumenischen Bewegung.* Hamburg-Bergstedt: Herbert Reich Evangelisches Verlag, 1957.

———. "Christozentrismus und Trinitäts-Auffassung bei Zinzendorf." *Evangelische Theologie*, 21 (1961), pp. 28–47.

———. "Ehe-Religion und Eschaton bei Zinzendorf." *Kerygma und Dogma*, 6 (1960), pp. 276–305.

———. *Der Junge Zinzendorf.* Marburg: Francke-Buchhandlung, 1957. Vol. I of *Nikolaus Ludwig von Zinzendorf.* 3 Vols.

———. "Lostheorie und Lospraxis bei Zinzendorf." *Zeitschrift für Kirchengeschichte*, 71 (1960), pp. 262–286.

———. "Mission und Kirche in der Theologie Zinzendorfs." *Evangelische Missions-Zeitschrift*, 17 (1960), pp. 65–76, 97–113.

———. *Nikolaus Ludwig von Zinzendorf in Selbstzeugnissen und Bilddokumenten.* Hamburg: Rowohlt, 1965.

———. "Pietistische Erlebnistheologie-Existenzialtheologie von heute." *Evangelische lutherische Kirchenzeitung*, 1 (1952), pp. 4 ff.

———. *Studien zur Theologie Zinzendorfs.* Neukirchen: Neukirchener Verlag, 1962.

———. "Der Ursprung des Pietismus und die Frage nach der Zeugenkraft der Kirche." *Evangelische Theologie*, 11 (1951–52), pp. 137 ff.

————. "Zinzendorf und das Judentum." *Judaica*, 19 (1963), pp. 193–246.

————. "Zinzendorf und der deutsche Osten." In *Jahrbuch der Schlesischen Friedrich-Wilhelms-Universität zu Breslau*, 7 (1962), pp. 130–151.

————. *Zinzendorf und die Christenheit 1732–1760*. Marburg: Francke-Buchhandlung, 1961. Vol. III of *Nikolaus Ludwig von Zinzendorf*. 3 Vols.

————. *Zinzendorf und die sich Allhier Beisammen Finden*. Marburg: Francke-Buchhandlung, 1959. Vol. II of *Nikolaus Ludwig von Zinzendorf*. 3 Vols.

————. "Zinzendorf und Luther." In *Luther-Jahrbuch*, 28 (1961), pp. 1–12.

————. *Zinzendorf und Pierre Bayle*. Hamburg: Ludwig Appel, 1955.

Beyreuther, Gottfried. *Sexualtheorien im Pietismus*. München, 1963.

Bienert, Walther. *Der Anbruch der christlichen deutschen Neuzeit dargestellt an Wissenschaft und Glauben des Christian Thomasius*. Halle: Akademischer Verlag, 1934. (Theologische Arbeiten zur Bibel, Kirchen und Geistesgeschiehte II).

Binöder, Carl. *Zur soziologischen Bedeutung der Herrnhuter Brüdergemeine*. Ph.D. dissertation, Erlangen, Germany, 1956.

Blanckmeister, Franz. *Aus dem Leben V. E. Löschers, Beiträge zur sächsischen Kirchengeschichte*. Leipzig, 1893.

————. *Der Prophet von Kursachsen, Valentin Ernst Löscher und seine Zeit*. Dresden: F. Sturm and Co., 1920.

Blanke, Fritz. *Zinzendorf und die Einheit der Kinder Gottes*. Basel: Mojer, 1950.

Böhm, B. *Socrates im 18. Jahrhundert*. Leipzig: Quelle and Meyer, 1929.

Bötticher, Walter von. *Geschichte des Oberlausitzer Adels und seiner Güter*. Görlitz: Oberlausitzer Gesellschaft der Wissenschaften, 1912.

Böttinger, Karl Wilhelm. *Geschichte des Kurstaates und Königreiches Sachsen*. 4 Vols. Gotha: F. A. Perthes, 1867–1873.

Bogatzky, Karl Heinrich von. *Tägliches Haus-Buch der Kinder Gottes bestehend in erbaulichen Betrachtungen und Gebeten auf alle Tage des ganzen Jahres*. 2 parts. Halle: Verlag des Waisenhauses, 1773.

Bornkamm Heinrich. *Mystik, Spiritualismus und die Anfänge des Pietismus im Luthertum*. Giessen: A. Töpelmann, 1926. (Vorträge der theologischen Konferenz zu Giessen.)

Bovet, Felix. *Le Comte de Zinzendorf*. Vols. I–II. Paris: Grassart, 1860.

Bowman, E. J. "Efforts to Christianize the Indians of Pennsylvania in Colonial Times." *Lutheran Church Quarterly*, 2 (1929), pp. 190–222.

Bready, J. Wesley. *England: Before and After Wesley*. London: Hodder and Stoughton, 1938.

Brennecke, R. H., Jr. "Culture of Missionary Interest; a study of the source of Moravian missionary spirit." *Mission Review*, 40 (1917), pp. 608–610.

Brian, B. M. "[Zinzendorf] Father of Modern Missions." *Missionary Review of the World*, 23 (1900), pp. 329–340.

Brock, Peter. *The Political and Social Doctrines of the Unity of Czech Brethren in the Fifteenth and Early Sixteenth Centuries*. The Hague: Mouton and Co., 1957.

Der Brüder Bote. Herrnhut: Unitäts Buchhandlung, 1827–1891.

Brüder-Gesangbuch, das Kleine. 5th edition. Barby, 1772.

Brunner, Peter. "Zinzendorfs Spiritualismus." *Theologische Literaturzeitung*, LXXIV, 8 (1949), pp. 469–476.

Burkhardt, Guido. *Die Brüdergemeine*. Vol. I. Gnadau: Verlag der Unitäts-Buchhandlung, 1905.

————. "Einige Gedanken über die vom Grafen Zinzendorf ausgegangenen Anregungen auf liturgischem Gebiet." *Monatsschrift für Gottesdienst und Kirchliche Kunst* (April, 1901), pp. 118 ff.

Carpenter, S. C. *Eighteenth Century Church and People*. London: John Murray Publishers, 1959.

Carpzow, J. G. *Religions-Untersuchungen der Böhmischen und Mährischen Brüder, von Anbeginn ihrer Gemeinen bis auf gegenwärtige Zeiten*. Leipzig: Breitkopf, 1742.

Cate, G. "De Herrenhuttersche Gemeente te Akkrum." *Doopsgezinde Bijdragen* (1885), pp. 68–90.

Christelijke Encyclopaedie voor het Nederlansche Volk. Kampen, 1925, Vol. I, pp. 379–384; 1929, Vol. V, pp. 807–808.

Clarke, W. K. Lowther. *A History of the Society for Promoting Christian Knowledge*. London: S.P.C.K., 1959.

————. *Eighteenth Century Piety*. London: S.P.C.K., 1944.

Comenius, Johann Amos. *De Bono Unitatis et Ordinis Disciplinae et Obedientiae*. Amsterdam: Christopheri Cunradi, 1665.

————. *Kurzgefasste Kirchen-Historie der Böhmischen Brüder*. Schwabach: Enderes, 1739.

————. *Ratio Disciplinae Ordinisque Ecclesiastici in Unitate Fratrum Bohemorum*. Amsterdam: Christopheri Cunradi, 1660.

Correll, Ernst. "Ehe." *Mennonitisches Lexikon*. Frankfurt und Weierhof: Pfalz, 1922.

Cranz, David. *Alte und Neue Brüder-Historie oder Kurz gefasste Geschichte der Evangelischen Brüder-Unität*. 2 Vols. Barby: C. F. Laux, 1772.

————. *The Ancient and Modern History of the Brethren*. Translated by La Trobe. London: W. & A. Strahan, 1780.

Cröger, E. W. *Geschichte der alten Brüderkirche*. Gnadau (Leipzig): H. Schultze, 1865.

————. *Geschichte der erneuerten Brüderkirche*. Gnadau (Leipzig): Kummer, 1852–1854.

Croll, P. C. "Oley Conference; a rare pamphlet, published by B. Franklin in 1742, with translation." *Lutheran Quarterly*, 56 (January, 1926), pp. 84–108.

Curnock, Nehemiah, ed. *The Journal of the Rev. John Wesley*. 8 Vols. London: Epworth Press, 1938. Bicentenary Standard Edition.

Cysarz, H. *Deutsche Barockdichtung*. Leipzig: H. Haessel Verlag, 1924.

Dalman, Gustav. "Zinzendorf und Lieberkühn." *Schriften des Institutum Judaicum*, 32 (1903).

Dannenbaum, Rolf. *Joachim Lange als Wortführer des Halleschen Pictismus gegen die Orthodoxie*. Dissertation, Göttingen, 1952.

David, Christian. *Beschreibung und Zuverlässige Nachricht von Herrnhut in der Ober-Lausitz, Wie es erbauet worden, und welcher Gestalt nach Lutheri Sinn und Meinung Eine recht Christliche Gemeine sich daselbst gesammelt und eingerichtet hat*. Leipzig, 1735.

Deghaye, Pierre. *La Doctrine Esoterique de Zinzendorf*. Paris: Klincksieck, 1969.

Delius, R. V. *Gedichte des Grafen von Zinzendorf*. Berlin: Furche Verlag, 1920.

Dibelius, Franz. *Gottfried Arnold*. Berlin: Hertz, 1873.

Dilthey, Wilhelm. *Gesammelte Schriften*. Leipzig: B. G. Teubner, 1921. Particularly: Vol. II, *Weltanschauung und Analyse des Menschen seit Renaissance und Reformation*. Leipzig, 1914, and Vol. III, *Studien zur Geschichte des deutschen Geistes*. Leipzig, 1927.

———. *Leben Schleiermachers*. Vol. I. Berlin: G. Reimer, 1870.

Dirks, J. "De Hernhuttersche Gemeente te Akkrum in 1797." *De vrije Fries*, XV (1882), pp. 265–274.

Dober, Martin. *Beschreibung und zuverlässige Nachricht von Herrnhut*. Leipzig: Samuel Benjamin Walther, 1735.

Dobias, F. M. "Ecumenical motifs in the theology of the Unity of Bohemian Brethren." *Ecumenical Review*, 12 (1960), pp. 455–470.

Dodwell, C. R., ed. *The English Church and the Continent*. London: Faith Press, 1959.

Dorner, Joh. August. *Geschichte der protestantischen Theologie*. München and Oldenburg: J. G. Cotta, 1867, pp. 629 ff.

Duyckinck, Gerardus. *A Short though true account of the establishment rise of the Church so called Moravian Brethren, under the protection and administration of Nicholas Lodewyck, Count of Zinzendorf. By which it plainly appears that they are not of that church of the ancient United Moravian and Bohemian Brethren. The Same is taken out of their own writings, and some observations on it*. New York: Henry DeForeest, 1744.

Eberhard, Samuel. *Kreuzes-Theologie. Das reformatorische Anliegen in Zinzendorfs Verkündigung*. München: Christian Kaiser Verlag, 1937.

Eck, Samuel. *Über die Herkunft des Individualitäts-Gedankens bei Schleiermacher*. Universitäts-Programm Giessen, 1908.

———. *Zinzendorf und seine Nachwirkung in der Gegenwart*. Leipzig: Grunow, 1890.

Eckerlin, Israel. *Ein Kurtzer Bericht von den Ursachen warum die Gemeinschaft in Ephrata sich mit dem Grafen Zinzendorf und seinen Leuten eingelassen. Und wie sich eine so grosse Ungleichheit im ausgang der Sachen auf beyden Seiten bekunden.* Germantown, Pa.: Christoph Saur, 1743.

Eckstein, Fritz, ed. *Comenius und die Böhmischen Brüder.* Zürich: Insel Bücher, 1939.

Ehmann, K. Chr. Eberh. *Friederich Christoph Oetinger, Leben und Briefe als urkundlicher Commentar zu dessen Schriften.* Stuttgart: J. F. Steinkopf, 1859.

van Einem, J. A. C. *De oude en hedendaagsche Kerkelijke Geschiedenissen, van wijlen den hooggeleerden J. L. Mosheim Kanselier der Hooge School te Göttingen, van den aanvang der tegerwoordige eeuwe tot aan het zes en zeventigste jaar derzelve, vervolgd.* Of Proeve eener volledige Kerk Historie der Achttiende eeuwe. Utrecht, 1779.

Eitle, Johannes. *Der Unterricht in den einstigen württembergischen Klosterschulen von 1556–1806.* Berlin: Weidmann 1913. (Zeitschrift für Geschichte der Erziehung und des Unterrichts, Supplement 3.)

Eloessen, A. *Die deutsche Literatur vom Barock bis zur Gegenwart.* Berlin: B. Cassirer, 1930–1931.

van Emdre, S. *Historisch Bericht van alle de Gezinthenden, die, buiten onze Gereformeerde Kerke, in ons Vaderland vrijheid van openbaare Godsdienstoeffening hebben, waar in Kortelijk derzelven Leerstukken en Kerkelijke Plegtigheden worden opgegeven.* Utrecht, 1784.

Engelhardt, Moritz von. *Valentin Ernst Löscher nach seinem Leben und Wirken. Ein geschichtlicher Beitrag zu den Streitfragen über Orthodoxie, Pietismus und Union.* Stuttgart: S. G. Liesching, 1856.

Erbe, Hans Walther. *Zinzendorf und der fromme hohe Adel seiner Zeit.* Leipzig, 1928.

Erbe, Helmuth. *Bethlehem, Pa.: Eine Herrnhuter-Kolonie des. 18. Jahrhunderts.* Herrnhut: Gustav Winter, 1929.

Ermatinger, E. *Barock und Rokoko in der deutschen Dichtung.* Leipzig: B. G. Teubner, 1928.

Evenhuis, R. B. *De Biblicistische-Eschatologische Theologie von Johann Albrecht Bengel.* Wageningen, 1931.

Fendt, Leonhard. "Die Theologie des jungen Zinzendorf." *Theologische Literatur-zeitung,* 10 (1954), pp. 593 ff.

Feuerbach, Ludwig. *Schriften zur Ethik und Nachgelassene Aphorismen.* Ed. Friedrich Jodl. Stuttgart: Fromman Verlag, 1960.

Fleischmann, Max. *Christian Thomasius.* Hallische Universitätsreden 39, Halle: M. Niemeyer, 1929.

Förster, Erwin. "Diakonie in der Brüdergemeine." *Die Innere Mission,* L, 5 (1960).

Forell, Mary Elizabeth. *Zinzendorf's Journey to America.* Senior thesis, Yale University, Department of Religious Studies, 1971.

Fousek, M. S. "Perfectionism of the early Unitas Fratrum." [15th Century.] *Church History,* 30 (1961), pp. 396–413. Bibliography, pp. 410–413.

Francke, August Hermann. *Busspredigten.* Vols. I–II. Halle: Waisenhausbuchhandlung, 1745.

——. *Sonn-Fest-und Apostel-Tags-Predigten.* . . . Vols. I–III. Halle: Waisenhausbuchhandlung, 1746.

——. *Sonn-und-Fest-Tags-Predigten.* . . . Halle: Waisenhausbuchhandlung, 1745.

Fresenius, Johann Philip. *Bewährte Nachrichten von Herrnhutischen Sachen.* Frankfurt,
Andreasche Buchhandlung, 1747–1751.

Freylinghausen, Johann Anastasius. *Geistreiches Gesang-Buch.* Halle: Verlegung des
Waysenhauses, 1741.

Freytag, Gustav. *Bilder aus der deutschen Vergangenheit.* Vol. IV. Leipzig: S. Hirzel,
1897–1898.

Frick, R. "Weltlogsigkeit und Weltoffenheit des christlichen Glaubens." *Zeichen der
Zeit,* 11 (1950).

Fries, Adelaide L. *The Moravians in Georgia, 1735–1740.* Raleigh, N. C.: Edwards
and Broughton, 1905.

Fries, Adelaide L., and Pfohl, J. K. *The Moravian Church, Yesterday and Today.* Raleigh,
N. C.: Edwards and Broughton, 1911.

Froereisen, Johann Leonhard. *Vergleichung des Graf Zinzendorfs mit dem Mahomet.* Frankfurt, 1748.

Frohberger, Christian Gottlieb. *Briefe über Herrnhut und die Brüdergemeine.* Barby:
Schöps, 1797.

——. *Reise durch Kursachsen.* Barby: Schöps, 1909.

Funk, Theophil. *Die Anfänge der Laienmitarbeit im Methodismus.* Bremen: Anker Verlag,
1941.

Gärtner, Friedrich. *Die Gemeinde Zwischen Religion and Atheismus.* Hamburg: Ludwig
Appel Verlag, 1956. (Herrnhuter Hefte 10.)

——. *Karl Barth und Zinzendorf.* Munchen: Kaiser, 1956. (Theologische Existenz
heute, N. F. 40.)

Gass, W. *Geschichte der protestantischen Dogmatik in ihrem Zusammenhang mit der Theologie
überhaupt.* Berlin: G. Reimer, 1862. Vol. 3.

Die Gedenktage der alten Brüderkirche, nebst einem Anhang. Gnadau: Verlag der Buchhandlung der Evangelischen Brüder Unität, 1821.

Geiges, Robert. "Aus dem Stammbuch eines schwäbischen Herrnhuters." *Blätter
für württembergische Kirchengeschichte* (1927), pp. 41–60.

——. "Die Auseinandersetzungen zwischen Chr. Fr. Oettinger und Zinzendorf.
Zur Geschichte des württembergischen Pietismus im 18. Jahrhundert." *Blätter
für Württembergische Kirchengeschichte,* XXXIX (1935), pp. 131–148; XL (1936), pp.
107–135.

——. "Herrnhut und Württemberg. Die Verhandlungen zwischen Zinzendorf und der württembergische Kirche 1745–1750." *Blätter für Württembergische Kirchengeschichte* (1930), pp. 211–269.

———. "Johanne Conrad Lange und die Anfänge der herrnhutischen Gemeinschaftspflege in Württemberg." *Zeitschrift für Brüdergeschichte*, VII, 1 (1913), pp. 1–65.

———. "Württemberg und Herrnhut im 18. Jahrhundert. Johann Albrecht Bengels Abwehr und der Ruckgang des Brüdereinflusses in Württemberg." *Blätter für württembergische Kirchengeschichte*, XLII (1938), pp. 28–88.

———. "Zinzendorf und Württemberg." *Blätter für württembergische Kirchengeschichte* (1913), pp. 52–78, 138–152.

Geistliche Lieder für Mitglieder und Freunde der Brüdergemeine. Bunzlau, 1827.

Geller, Fritz. *Gotteshaus und Gottesdienst in den Herrnhuter Brüdergemeinen.* Herrnhut: G. Winter, 1929.

Das Gesangbuch der Gemeine in Herrn-Huth. Herrnhut, 1732.

Gichtel, J. G. *Theosophia Practica.* Berlin: Wever, 1768.

Gloege, Gerhard. *Zinzendorf und das Luthertum.* Jena, 1950.

Goebel, Max. *Geschichte des christlichen Lebens in der rheinischwestphälischen evangelischen Kirche.* 3 Vols. Coblenz, 1849, 1852, 1860.

Goethe, J. W. *Bekenntnisse einer schönen Seele. (Wilhelm Meisters Lehrjahre.)* Stuttgart: Cotta, 1857.

Götz, W. *Zinzendorfs Jugendjahre.* Leipzig: F. Jansa, 1900.

Goll, Jaroslav. *Quellen und Untersuchungen zur Geschichte der Böhmischen Brüder.* 2 Vols. Prague, 1878, 1882.

Gollin, Gillian Lindt. *Moravians in Two Worlds.* New York: Columbia University Press, 1967.

Gottschick. "Ehe, christlich." *Realencyklopädie für protestantische Theologie und Kirche.* Leipzig: J. C. Hinrichs, 1898. Vol. 5, pp. 182–198.

Gradin, A. "De ecclesia unitatis fratrum bohemico-moravica." *Acta historicoecclesiastica*, XIV (1750). (Weimar.)

———. *A short history of the Bohemian-Moravian protestant church of the United Brethren.* London, 1743.

———. *til Herrnhutiska Partiets Seder och Forsvar emot Inledningen angaende Herrnhutiska Secten.* Stockholm: A. I. Beckman, 1749.

Great Britain, Parliament, House of Commons. "Report of the Committee on United Moravian Churches." London, 1749.

Greenfield, John. *Methodists and Moravians.* Nazareth, Pa., 1907.

———. "Some Fruits of the Moravian Revival." *Biblical Review*, 14 (1929), pp. 227–244.

Gross, Andreas. *Erste und letzte Antwort auf die sogenannte Erklärung des Herrn Grafen Nicol. Ludwigs von Zinzendorff.* Frankfurt: Andreasche Buchhandlung, 1742.

————. "Herrn A. G. vernünfftiger und unpartheyischer Bericht an einen guten Freund über die neuaufkommende Herrnhutische Gemeinde." Anhang III, *Geheimer Briefwechsel.* Frankfurt, 1741. Pp. 401 ff.

Grosser, Johannes. *Studie über Friedrich von Watteville.* Dissertation, Halle, 1914.

Gruber, Johann Adam. *Eines Geringen Bericht, was sich zwischen ihm und Herrn Ludwig und andern seiner Zugehörigen, in der Herrnhuter Sache in Jahr und Tag begeben 1743, samt den nöthigen Belegen.* Germantown: Christoph Saur, 1743.

Grünberg, Paul. *Philipp Jakob Spener.* 3 Vols. Göttingen: Vandenhoeck und Ruprecht, 1893, 1905, 1906.

Grund der Verfassung der Evangelischen Brüder-Unität Augsburgischer Confession. Barby, 1789. (Also known as *Ratio Disciplinae Unitatis Fratrum A. C.*)

Günther, Hans R. G. "Psychologie des deutschen Pietismus." *Deutsche Vierteljahrsschrift für Literaturwissenschaft und Geistesgeschichte,* IV (1926), pp. 144 ff.

Günther, W. "Diaspora als Daseinsform der Gemeinde." *Civ. Praes.,* II (1959).

Hadorn, W. *Geschichte des Pietismus in den Schweizerischen Reformierten Kirchen.* Konstanz und Emishofen: C. Hirsch, 1901.

Hagen, F. F. *Old Landmarks: or Faith and Practice of the Moravian Church at the time of its Revival and Restoration in 1727, and twenty years after.* Bethlehem, Pa., 1886.

Hamilton, John Taylor. *A History of the Church Known as the Moravian Church or the Unity of the Brethren, During the Eighteenth and Nineteenth Centuries. Transactions of the Moravian Historical Society.* Vol. VI. Bethlehem, Pa.: Times Publishing Co., 1900.

————. *A History of the Missions of the Moravian Church, During the Eighteenth and Nineteenth Centuries.* Bethlehem, Pa.: Times Publishing Co., 1901.

Hamilton, Kenneth Gardiner. "The Resources of the Moravian Church Archives." *Pennsylvania History,* XXVII (1960), pp. 263–272.

————. *The Bethlehem Diary.* Vol. I, *1742–1744.* Archives of the Moravian Church, Bethlehem, Pa., 1971.

Hammer, Herbert. *Abraham Dürninger.* Berlin: Furche Verlag, 1925.

Hanstein, A. von. *Die Frauen in der Geschichte des deutschen Geisteslebens des 18. und 19. Jahrhunderts.* 2 Vols. Leipzig: Freund und Wittig, 1899–1900.

Hark, F. S. "Der Konflikt der Kursächsischen Regierung mit Herrnhut und dem Grafen von Zinzendorf 1733 bis 1738." *Neues Archiv für sächsische Geschichte,* III, 1.

Harnack, Theodosius. *Die Lutherische Kircke Livlands und die Herrnhutische Brüdergemeine.* Erlangen, 1860.

Hartog, J. *De spectatoriale geschriften van 1741–1800.* Utrecht: Gebr. van der Post, 1872. Pp. 234–237.

Hasse, E. R. *Die Brüder in England.* Hamburg: Appel Verlag, 1951.

————. *The Moravian Church.* London: Moravian Publication Office, 1906. (Brief historical information.)

————. *The Moravian Church.* Sermon at celebration of 450th anniversary of the Moravian Church, Fetter Lane Chapel, London, March 10, 1907.

————. *The Moravians.* Intro. The Bishop of Durham. London: F. B. Meyer, 1912. (Leaders of Revival Series.)

Haupt-schlüssel zum Herrnhuterischen Ehe-Sacrament. Jena: Hartung, 1755.

Hennig, Liemar. *Kirche und Offenbarung bei Zinzendorf.* Dissertation, Zürich, 1939.

Henry, James. *Sketches of Moravian Life and Character.* Philadelphia: J. B. Lippincott, 1859.

Heppe, Heinrich. *Geschichte der quietistischen Mystik in der Katholischen Kirche.* Berlin: Hertz, 1875.

Hermelink, Heinrich. *Geschichte der evangelischen Kirche in Württemberg von der Reformation bis zur Gegenwart. Das Reich Gottes in Württemberg.* Stuttgart: R. Wunderlich, 1949.

Herpel, Otto. *Zinzendorf über Glaube und Leben.* Berlin: Furche Verlag, 1925.

Herzfeld, M. "Die Aussenhandelslehre des Grafen Karl Zinzendorf; eine deutsche Freihandelslehre aus dem 18. jahrhundert." *Schmollers Jahrbuch,* 43 (1919), pp. 1365–1393.

Herzog, Heinrich. "Die rechtliche Sonderstellung der Oberlausitz in der sächsischen Landeskirche." *Herbergen der Christenheit*, ed. Franz Lau. Leipzig: Koehler und Amelang, 1957.

Heuler, A. *Das Erlebnis in der Lyrik J. Chr. Günthers.* Würzburg, 1925.

Heyd, Wilhelm. *Bibliographie der württembergischen Geschichte.* Stuttgart: W. Kohlhammer, 1895.

Hickel, Helmut. *Das Abendmahl zu Zinzendorfs Zeiten.* Hamburg, 1956. (Herrnhutter Hefte 9.)

Hijmans, L. "Graaf Zinzendorf en de Zending." *Lichtstralen op den Akker der Wereld,* III, IV (1900).

Hinrichs, Carl. *Friedrich Wilhelm I. Jugend und Aufstieg.* Hamburg: Hanseatische Verlagsanstalt, 1941.

————. "Der Hallische Pietismus als politisch-soziale Reformbewegung des 18. Jahrhunderts." *Jahrbuch für die Geschichte Mittel-und Ostdeutschlands,* II (1953), pp. 177 ff.

————. *Ranke und die Geschichtstheologie der Goethezeit.* Göttingen: Musterschmidt, 1954. (Göttinger Bausteine zur Geschichtswissenschaft 19.)

Hirsch, Emmanuel. *Geschichte der neuern evangelischen Theologie im Zusammenhang mit den allgemeinen Bewegungen des europäischen Denkens.* 5 Vols. Gütersloh: C. Bertelsmann, 1949–1954.

————. "Zum Verständnis Schwenckfelds." *Festgabe für K. Muller.* Tübingen, 1922.

Hirzel, Stephan. *Der Graf und die Brüder.* Gotha: Leopold Klotz, 1935.

Hoffmann, Georg. *Die Lehre von der fides implicita.* 3 Vols. Leipzig: A. Pries, 1903–1908.

Hoffmann, Heinrich. "Die Frommigkeit der deutschen Aufklärung." *Zeitschrift für Theologie und Kirche,* XVI (1906), pp. 234 ff.

Hök, Gösta. *Die elliptische Theologie Albrecht Ritschls nach Ursprung und innerem Zusammenhang.* Leipzig: O. Harassowitz, 1942.

————. *Herrnhutisk Theologi I Svensk Gestalt.* Uppsala: A. B. Lundequistska Bokhandeln, 1950.

————. *Zinzendorfs Begriff der Religion.* Uppsala: A. B. Lundequistska Bokhandeln, 1948.

Holl, Karl. *Gesammelte Aufsätze zur Kirchengeschichte.* Tübingen: I. C. B. Mohr, 1928–1932.

Hollatz, D. *Examen Theologicum Acroamaticum.* Leipzig: Breitkopf, 1763.

Holloway, Mark. *Heavens on Earth: Utopian Communities in America, 1680–1888.* New York: Library Publishers, 1951.

Holmes, John B. *History of the Protestant Church of the United Brethren.* 2 Vols. London: Bradford, 1825–1830.

"How Moravian Missions Began." *Missionary Review of the World,* 26 (1903), p. 381.

Hutton, Joseph E. *History of the Moravian Church.* London: Moravian Publications Office, 1909.

————. *A History of the Moravian Missions.* London: Moravian Publications Office, 1923.

————. "Moravian Contribution to the Evangelical Revival in England, 1742 to 1755." *Owens College History Essays,* pp. 423–452.

————. "Moravian Missions in Moslem Lands." *Muslim World,* 14 (1924), pp. 125–130.

Huober, Hans-Günther. *Zinzendorfs Kirchenliederdichtung.* Berlin: Dr. E. Ebering, 1934. (Germanische Studien, 150.)

Hymnal and Liturgies of the Moravian Church. Bethlehem, Pa.: Moravian Publications Office, 1920.

Ihmels, Ludwig. *Fides implicita und der evangelische Heilsglaube.* Leipzig: A. Deichertsche Verlagsbuchhandlung, 1912.

Jacobsson, N. *Den svenska Herrnhutismens uppkomst.* Uppsala: W. Schultz, 1908.

Jahrbuch der Brüdergemeine. Vols. I–IV. Herrnhut, 1906–1961.

Jannasch, Wilhelm. "Christian Renatus Graf von Zinzendorf." *Zeitschrift für Brüdergeschichte,* II, 2 (1908), pp. 45 ff., III, pp. 61 ff.

————. "Erdmuthe Dorthea Gräfin von Zinzendorf, geborene Gräfin Reuss zu Plauen." *Zeitschrift für Brüdergeschichte,* VIII (1914), pp. 1–448.

Jecht, Walther. *Untersuchungen zur Gründungsgeschichte der Stadt Görlitz und zur Entstehung des Städtewesens in der Oberlausitz.* Görlitz, 1919.

Jeschke-Dobias. "Unitas Fratrum." *Aufsätze zur Theologie und Religionswissenschaft*, 12 (1960). (Berlin.)

Jordan, J. W. "Moravian Immigration to Pennsylvania." *Pennsylvania Magazine of History and Biography*, III (1879), pp. 528–537.

Jung, Johann Heinrich. *Theobald oder die Schwärmer*. Frankfurt and Leipzig, 1785.

Jung, W. F. *Der in dem Grafen Zinzendorf noch lebende und lehrende Luther*. Leipzig: Kummer, 1752.

Jursch, Hanna. *Schleiermacher als Kirchenhistoriker*. Buch I. Jena: Verlag der Frommannschen Buchhandlung, 1933.

Kantzenbach, Friedrich Wilhelm. "Das Bild des Grafen. Ein Literaturbericht zur Zinzendorfforschung." *Lutherische Monatshefte*, 1 (1962), pp. 384–391.

Keller, E. F. "Die Buttler'sche Rotte, ein merkwürdiges Seitenstück zu den neu entdeckten Muckern in unseren Tagen." *Zeitschrift für die historische Theologie*, 4 (1845), pp. 74–153.

Kersten-Thiele, Wilhelm. *Die Kirchengeschichtsschreibung Valentin Ernst Löschers*. Halle: Fricke Verlag, 1937.

Kirchenordnung der Evangelischen Brüder-Unitat in Deutschland vom Jahre 1935. Gnadau: Unitäts Buchhandlung, 1935.

Kleinschmidt, E. A. "De Broedergemeente." *Kerk en Secte*, III, 10 (1909). (Baarn.)

———. "Geschiedenis van het Zeister Zendingsgenootschap." *Berichten vit de Heidenwereld*, 1893, p. 52; and 1918, pp. 129–166.

Klepper, Jochen, ed. *Der Soldatenkönig und die Stillen im Lande. Begegnungen Friedrich Wilhelms I. mit August Hermann, August Gottlob Francke, Johann Anastasius Freylinghausen, Nikolaus Ludwig Graf von Zinzendorf*. Berlin: Eckart Verlag, 1938.

Kluckhohn, Paul. *Die Auffassung die Liebe in der Literatur des 18. Jahrhunderts und in der deutschen Romantik*. Halle: N. Niemeyer, 1931.

Knapp, Albert. *Geistliche Gedichte des Grafen von Zinzendorf*. Stuttgart and Tübingen: Cottaische Buchhandlung, 1845.

Knothe, Hermann. *Die Stellung der Gutsuntertanen in der Oberlausitz zu den Gutsherrschaften von der ältesten Zeit bis zu den Ablösungen der Zinsen und Dienste*. Berlin, 1851.

Knox, Ronald A. *Enthusiasm: A Chapter in the History of Religion, with Special Reference to the Seventeenth and Eighteenth Centuries*. London: Oxford University Press, 1950.

Koch, Eduard Emil. *Geschichte des Kirchenliedes und Kirchengesangs, mit besonderer Rücksicht auf Württemberg*. Stuttgart: Belser, 1847, Vols. 1, 2.

Kölbing, Friedrich Ludwig. *Die Gedenktage der alten und der erneuerten Brüderkirche*. Gnadau: Verlag der Missionsbuchhandlung, 1821.

Kölbing, Paul D. "Zinzendorfs Verhältnis zur Aufklärung." *Theologische Studien und Kritiken*, (1911), pp. 60–88.

———. "Zur Charakteristik der Theologie Zinzendorfs." *Zeitschrift für Theologie und Kirche*, 10 (1900), pp. 245–283.

122

Kölbing, Wilhelm Ludwig. *Die Geschichte der Verfassung der Evangelischen Brüderunität in Deutschland mit besonderer Berücksichtigung der kirchenrechtlichen Verhältnisse.* Leipzig: Jansa, 1906.

Koepp, Wilhelm, and Arndt, Johann. *Eine Untersuchung über die Mystik im Luthertum.* Berlin: Trowitzsch & Sohn, 1912. (Neue Studien zur Geschichte der Theologie und der Kirche, XIII.)

Körner, Ferdinand. *Die kursächsische Staatsregierung dem Grafen Zinzendorf und Herrnhut bis 1760 gegenüber.* Leipzig: B. Tauchnitz, 1878.

Kohnova, Marie J. "The Moravians and Their Missionaries, a Problem in Americanization." *Mississippi Valley Historical Review,* XIX (1932), pp. 348–361.

Kolb, Christoph Adolf. *Die Anfänge des Pietismus und Separatismus in Württemberg.* Stuttgart: W. Kohlhammer, 1902.

Konrad, Johanna. "Das Prinzip der Anschauung in Zinzendorfs Religionsmethode." *Zeitschrift für Theologie und Kirche,* 1922, pp. 203 ff.

Korff, Hermann August. *Geist der Goethezeit Versuch einer ideellen Entwicklung der Klassischromantischen Literatur-Geschichte.* Vols. I–IV. Leipzig: J. J. Weber, 1923–1953.

Korschelt, G. *Geschichte von Berthelsdorf.* Leipzig: Kummer, 1852.

————. *Geschichte von Herrnhut.* Leipzig: Kummer, 1853.

————. *Geschichte von Oderwitz.* Neu-Gersdorf: Trommer, 1870.

Kortz, Edwin W. "The Liturgical Development of the American Moravian Church." *Transactions of the Moravian Historical Society,* Vol. XVIII, Part 2. Nazareth, Pa.: Whitefield House, Laros Publishing Co., 1962, pp. 267–382.

Kramer, Gustav. *August Hermann Francke. Ein Lebensbild.* Vols. I–II. Halle: Buchhandlung des Waisenhauses, 1880, 1882.

————. *Beiträge zur Geschichte August Hermann Franckes.* Halle: Buchhandlung des Waisenhauses, 1861.

————. *Neue Beiträge zur Geschichte August Hermann Franckes.* Halle: Buchhandlung des Waisenhauses, 1875.

————. "Zur Jugendgeschichte Zinzendorfs." *Kirchliche Monatsschrift,* IV (1884).

Kramer-Wendell, Barlow. *Criteria for the International Community: A Study of the Factors Affecting the Success and Failure in the Planned, Purposeful, Cooperative Community.* PhD. dissertation, New York University, 1955.

Kühn, Johannes. *Toleranz und Offenbarung. Eine Untersuchung der Motive und Motivformen der Toleranz im offenbarungs-gläubigen Protestantismus.* Leipzig: F. Meiner, 1923.

Kurzgefasste historische Nachricht von der gegenwärtigen Verfassung der evangelischen Brüderunität augspurgischer Confession. Frankfurt and Leipzig, 1774.

Laag, Heinz. "Der Pietismus ein Bahnbrecher der deutschen Aufklärung." *Theologische Blätter* III (1924), pp. 269 ff.

Lang, Gustav. *Geschichte der württembergischen Klosterschulen von ihrer Stiftung bis zu ihrer endgültigen Verwandlung In Evangelischtheologische Seminare.* Stuttgart: Kohlhammer, 1938.

Lange, Joachim. *Abgenöthigtes abermaliges Zeugnis der Wahrheit und Unschuld gegen Hrn. D. V. E. Löschers zweyten Theil seines sogenannten Vollständigen Timothei Verini.* Halle, 1722.

————. *Abgenötigte völlige Abfertigung des sogenannten vollständigen Timothei verini Hrn. D. V. E. Löschers in der Lehre von der Erleuchtung und zugehörigen Materien, auch vom Indifferentismo.* Halle: Waisenhausbuchhandlung, 1719.

————. *Erläuterung der neuesten Historie bei der evangelischen Kirche von 1689–1719. ... darin zur erwünschten Endigung des Sectirerischen Fabelwesens vom Pietismo, der also genannte "Timotheus verinus" auf Gutbefinden der fälschich beschuldigten sämtlichen Theologischen Facultät auf der Königl. Preuss. Friedrichs-Universität völlig abgefertiget wird.* Halle: Renger, 1719.

————. *Die Gestalt des Kreutzreichs Christi in seiner Unschuld mitten unter den falschen Beschuldigungen und Lästerungen sonderlich unbekehrter und fleischlich gesinnter Lehrer . . . mit dem Exempel D. V. E. Löschers ausführlich erwiesen und erläutert.* Halle: Waisenhausbuchhandlung, 1713.

Langen, August. *Der Wortschatz des deutschen Pietismus.* Tübingen: N. Niemeyer, 1954.

Langston, Edward. *History of the Moravian Church, the Story of the First International Protestant Church.* London: Georg Allen and Unwin, 1951.

Lederhose, K. F. *Das Leben A. G. Spangenbergs, Bischofs der Brüdergemeine.* Heidelberg: Karl Winter, 1846.

Lederhose, Charles F. *The Life of Augustus Gottlieb Spangenberg.* London: William Mallalieu, 1855.

Leedertz, W. J. "Joannes Deknatel, een Piëtist onder de Doopsgezinden." *Geloof en Vrijheid* (1887), pp. 393–445.

Lehman, H. "Eine offene Antwort auf die offene Frage Dr. Pfisters, zugleich eine Ehrenrettung Zinzendorfs gegen Pfisters Entwertung der Frömmigkeit Zinzendorfs." *Zeitschrift für Religionspsychologie* (1911), pp. 60–65.

————. "Das religionspsychologische Problem Zinzendorf." *Zeitschrift für Religionspsychologie* (January, 1912), pp. 317 ff.

————. "Zinzendorfs Frömmigkeit und ihre Bedeutung." *Zeitschrift für Religionspsychologie* (1910), pp. 285–300.

Leube, Hans. "Pietismus." *Die Religion in Geschichte und Gegenwart.* Ed. H. Gunkel and L. Zscharnack. Tübingen: J. C. B. Mohr, 1930, Vol. IV, pp. 1250–1262.

————. *Die Reformideen in der deutschen lutherischen Kirche zur Zeit der Orthodoxie.* Leipzig: Dörffling und Francke, 1924.

Levering, J. Mortimer. *A History of Bethlehem, Pennsylvania, 1741–1892, with Some Account of Its Founders and Their Early Activity.* Bethlehem, Pa.: Times Publishing Co., 1903.

Lewis, A. J. *Zinzendorf the Ecumenical Pioneer.* London: SCM Press Ltd., 1962.

van der Linde, J. M. "Moravian Church in the World, 1457–1957." *International Review of Missions*, 46 (1957), pp. 417–423.

Lindeboom, J. *Stiefkinderen van het Christendom*. Gravanhage: Nijhoff, 1929, pp. 375–378.

Lindroth, Hj. *Försoningen; en dogmhistorisk och systematisk undersökning*. Uppsala: A. B. Lundequistska bokhandeln, 1935.

Lindström, M. *Philipp Nicolais Kristendomstolkning*. Stokholm: Diakonistyrelses bokförlag, 1937.

The Litany Book According to the Manner of Singing at Present Mostly in Use Among the Brethren. London: 1759.

Loebich (Pfarrer Loebich in Lichtenstein). "Zinzendorf und der Pietismus seiner Zeit." *Zeitschrift für Brüdergeschichte*, VII, 2 (1913), pp. 129–170.

Löscher, Valentin Ernst. *Edle Andachtsfrüchte oder 68 auserlesene Örter Heiliger Schrift. . . . . darinnen die theologia mystica orthodoxa in sechs Teilen vorgetragen wird*. Dresden: Gollner, 1741.

―――. *Vollständiger Timotheus verinus oder Darlegung der Wahrheit und des Friedens in den bisherigen pietistischen Streitigkeiten*. Wittenberg: Universitäts Bibliothek, 1726. 2 parts. Part 1 includes: Briefwechsel mit D. Buddeus, 1715–16, pp. 67–99.

Lohmann, Martin. *Die Bedeutung der deutschen Ansiedlungen in Pennsylvanien*. Stuttgart: Ausland und Heimat Verlags-Aktiengesellschaft, 1923.

Loosjes, J. "De ontvangst der Herrnhutters in de Nederlanded in de 18e eeuw." *Stemmen voor Waarheid en Vrede*, 1922, pp. 880–899.

Lütjeharms, W. *Het Philadelphisch-Oecumenisch Streven der Herrnhutters in de Nederlanden in de achttiende Eeuw*. Zeist: Zendingsgenootschap der Evang. Broedergemeente, 1935.

Lummel, H. B. "Voortgedreven. Nicolaus Ludwig, graaf van Zinzendorf en zijn werk." *Bredee's Bibliotheek voor School en Huis*, V, Rotterdam, 1890.

Luther, Johannes. *Pietistische Streitigkeiten in Greifswald*. Greifswald, 1925.

Mälzer, Gottfried. *Bengel und Zinzendorf*. Witten-Ruhr: Luther-Verlag, 1968.

Mahrholz, Werner. *Der deutsche Pietismus*. Berlin: Furche Verlag, 1921.

―――. *Deutsche Selbstbekenntnisse. Ein Beitrag zur Geschichte der Selbstbiographie von der Mystik bis zum Pietismus*. Berlin: Furche Verlag, 1919.

Maronier, J. H. *Geschiedenis van het Protestantisme van den Munsterschen vrede tot de Fransche Revolutie, 1640–1789*. Leiden: E. J. Brill, 1897.

Martin, John Hill. *Historical Sketch of Bethlehem, Pa.* Philadelphia: Lippincott, 1869.

Marx, Wolf. *Die Saalkirche der deutschen Brüdergemeine im 18. Jahrhundert*. Leipzig: Dieterich, 1931.

Meyer, D. *Das Kirchenlied*. (Eine ästhetische Untersuchung.) Heilbronn, 1892.

Meyer, E. R. *Schleiermachers und C. G. von Brinkmanns Gang durch die Brüdergemeine*. Leipzig, 1905.

Meyer, Gerhard. *Johann Conrad Weiz.* Wuppertal: R. Brockhaus Verlag, 1962.

———. *Zinzendorf.* Hamburg: L. Appel Verlag, 1950.

———. "Zinzendorf als Vertreter des ostdeutsch-schlesischen Frömmigkeitstypus." *Jahrbuch der Schlesischen Friedrich-Wilhelms-Universität zu Breslau*, 5 (1960), pp. 69–96.

Meyer, Henry Herman. *Child Nature and Nurture According to Nicholas Ludwig von Zinzendorf.* London and New York: Abingdon Press, 1928.

Mirbt, Carl. "Pietismus." *Realencyklopädie für protestantische Theologie und Kirche.* Leipzig: J. D. Hinrichs, 1904, Vol. XV, pp. 774–815.

Miskovsky, L. F. "Unitas fratrum." *Bibliotheca Sacra*, 65 (1908), pp. 510–530.

Moeschler, Felix. *Alte Herrnhuter Familien. Die mährischen, böhmischen und österreichischschlesischen Exulanten.* Herrnhut: Missionsbuchhandlung, 1922.

Möller, Grete. "Föderalismus und Geschichtsbetrachttung im XVII und XVIII Jahrhundert." *Zeitschrift für Kirchengeschichte*, 3 (1931), pp. 393 ff.

Moravian Church Southern Province of North America, Provincial Synod. *Guide to the Manuscripts in the Archives of the Moravian Church in America*, Southern Province. Raleigh, N. C., 1942. (Historical Records Survey, North Carolina.)

Moser, Johann Jakob. *Altes und Neues aus dem Reich Gottes.* Frankfurt and Leipzig, 1733.

———. *Sendschreiben von der grossen Gefahr der Heirathen erweckter und wiedergebohrener Personen mit Unbekehrten, nebst Anmerkungen.* Ebersdorf, 1741.

Motel, Heinz. "Grundsätzliche Äusserungen Zinzendorfs zu Missionsfragen." *Evangelische Missions-Zeitschrift*, 13 (1956), pp. 166–177.

———. "Was versteht die Gemeine unter dem Dienst, in dem sie lebt?" *Mitteilungen aus der Brüdergemeine*, 6 (1938), pp. 157 ff.

———. *Zinzendorf als ökumenischer Theologe.* Basel, 1942.

———. "Zinzendorfs Beitrag zur oekumenischen Frage." *Evangelisches Missions-Magazin*, 93 (1949), pp. 71–80, 99–111.

———. "Zinzendorfs Stellung zur Heiligen Schrift." *Evangelische Missions-Zeitschrift*, 7 (1950), pp. 65–73.

Müller, Joseph Theodor. "Die ältesten Berichte Zinzendorfs über sein Leben, seine Unternehmungen und Herrnhuts Entstehen." *Zeitschrift für Brüdergeschichte*, V, 1 (1911) pp. 93–116; VI, 1 (1912), pp. 45–118; VII, 1 (1913), pp. 114–120; VII, 2 (1913), pp. 171–215.

———. "Das Ältestenamt Christi in der erneuerten Brüderkirche." *Zeitschrift für Brüdergeschichte*, I, 1 (1907), pp. 1–32.

———. "Das Bekenntnis in der Brüdergemeine." *Zeitschrift für Brüdergeschichte*, III, 1 (1909), pp. 1–61.

———. "Die Berührungen der alten und neuen Brüderunität mit den Täufern." *Zeitschrift für Brüdergeschichte*, IV, 2 (1910), pp. 180–234.

————. "Die Bilder Zinzendorfs." *Zeitschrift für Brüdergeschichte*, IV, 1 (1910), pp. 98–123.

————. *Die deutschen Katechismen der Böhmischen Brüder. Monumenta Germaniae Paedogogica.* Berlin: Hofmann & Co., 1887. Vol. 4.

————. *Geschichte der Böhmischen Brüder.* Herrnhut: Missionsbuchhandlung, 1931. Vol. 3.

————. "Geschichte und Inhalt der Acta Unitatis Fratrum (sogenannte Lissaer Folianten). *Zeitschrift für Brüdergeschichte*, VII, 1 (1913), pp. 216–231; IX (1915), pp. 26–79.

————. *Hymnologisches Handbuch zum Gesangbuch der Brüdergemeine.* Herrnhut: Verein der Brüdergeschichte, 1916.

————. "Kurze Mitteilungen: O. Pfister, Die Frömmigkeit des Grafen Ludwig von Zinzendorf. G. Reichel, Zinzendorf's Frömmigkeit im Licht der Psychoanalyse. O. Pfister, Hat Zinzendorf die Frömmigkeit sexualisiert? H. Lehmann, Eine offene Antwort auf die offene Frage Dr. Pfisters, zugleich eine Ehrenrettung Zinzendorfs gegen Pfisters Entwertung der Frömmigkeit Zinzendorfs." *Zeitschrift für Brüdergeschichte*, V (1911), pp. 233–240.

————. "Pfarrer Annonis Besuch in Herrnhut 1736." *Zeitschrift für Brüdergeschichte*, V, 1 (1911), pp. 50–92.

————. "Der Waldenserbischof Stephan und die Weihe der ersten Brüderpriester." *Zeitschrift für Brüdergeschichte*, X (1916), pp. 128–144.

————. *Zinzendorf als Erneuerer der alten Brüderkirche.* Leipzig: Friedrich Jansa, 1900.

————. "Zinzendorf und die Brüdergemeine." *Realencyklopädie für Protestantische Theologie und Kirche.* Leipzig: J. C. Hinrichs, 1908, Vol. XXI, pp. 679–703.

Müller, Karl. *Gotteswirklichkeit und Religion. Zinzendorfs Gedanken über Mission in ihrer Bedeutung für die Gegenwart.* Herrnhut: Missionsbuchhandlung, 1932. (Also printed in: *Neue Allgemeine Missionszeitschrift*, 11.)

————. "Melchior Nitschmann." *Lebensbilder aus der Brüdergemeine*, 2 Herrnhut: Missionsbuchhandlung, 1922.

————. *200 Jahre Brüdermission, Das erste Missionsjahrhundert.* Herrnhut: Missionsbuchhandlung, 1931.

Müller, Lydia. "Der Kommunismus der Mährischen Wiedertäufer." *Schriften des Vereins für Religionsgeschichte*, 45, 1 (1927). (Leipzig.)

Müller, Th. *Een Blik in de Geschiedenis der Evangelische Broedergemeente.* Zeist: Van Lenkhuyzen, 1925.

Mulert, Hermann. *Schleiermachers geschichtsphilosophische Ansichten in ihrer Bedeutung für seine Theologie.* Giessen: A. Töpelmann, 1907.

Natzmer, Gneomar Ernst von. *Die Jugend Zinzendorfs im Lichte ganz neuer Quellen.* Eisenach: W. Wilckens, 1894.

————. "Zinzendorf." *Lebensbilder aus dem Jahrhundert nach dem grossen deutschen Krieg.* Gotha: F. A. Perthes, 1892, pp. 297–408.

Neisser, Georg. *A History of the Beginnings of Moravian Work in America*. Bethlehem, Pa.: Archives of the Moravian Church, 1955.

Neisser, Liselotte. *Christian Thomasius und seine Beziehungen zum Pietismus*. München: Weiss'che Universitätsbuchhandlung, 1928.

Nelle, W. *Geschichte des deutschen evangelischen Kirchenliedes*. Hamburg: G. Schloessman, 1904.

Nelson, Vernon H. *Christian David, Servant of the Lord*. Bethlehem, Pa.: Archives of the Moravian Church, 1962.

van Nes, H. M. *De Graaf van Zinzendorf*. Nijkerk: G. F. Callenbach, 1903.

Nebauer, E. "Die Begriffe der Individualität und Gemeinschaft im Denken des jungen Schleiermacher." *Theologische Studien und Kritiken*, 1923, pp. 1 ff.

Nicolai, R. *Benjamin Schmolck*. Leipzig, 1909.

Nielsen, Sigurd. *Der Toleranzgedanke bei Zinzendorf*. Hamburg: Ludwig Appel Verlag, 1952–1960. (3 Parts.)

Nordmann, Walter. *Die Eschatologie des Ehepaares Petersen, ihre Entwicklung und Auflösung*. 1930.

————. *Die theologische Gedankenwelt in der Eschatologie des pietistischen Ehepaares Petersen*. Naumberg (Saale), 1929.

————. "Im Widerstreit von Mystik und Föderalismus Geschichtliche Grundlagen der Eschatologie bei dem pietistischen Ehepaar Petersen." *Zeitschrift für Kirchengeschichte*, III, 1 (1931), pp. 146 ff.

Nuelsen, J. L.; Sommer, J.; Mann, Theophil. *Kurzgefasste Geschichte des Methodismus von seinen Anfängen bis zur Gegenwart*. Bremen: Verlagshaus der Methodistenkirche, 1929.

Oetinger, Friedrich Christoph. *Kurzgefasste Grundlehre des berühmten Würtenbergischen Prälaten Bengels betreffend den Schauplatz der Herabkunft Jesu zum Gericht des Anti-christs vor dem jüngsten Tag samt den mitverbundenen letzten Dingen*. Nürnberg, 1769.

Oppel, Arnold. *Das Hohelied Salomonis und die deutsche religiöse Liebeslyrik*. Berlin: W. Rotschild, 1911. (Inaugural dissertation, Freiburg.)

Pennsylvänische Synoden Verlass, 1742–1748. Bethlehem Archives Mss., 12 Vols. (Reports and Proceedings of Zinzendorf's attempt to unite the German Protestant sects into a single Church.)

Peschke, Erhard. *Die Böhmischen Brüder im Urteil ihrer Zeit*. Stuttgart: Calwer Verlag, 1964.

————. *Studien zur Theologie August Hermann Franckes*. Berlin: Evangelische Verlagsanstalt, 1964.

————. *Die Theologie der Böhmischen Brüder in ihrer Frühzeit*. Stuttgart: W. Kohlhammer, 1935.

Petersen, Johannes Wilhelm. *Lebens-Beschreibung*. Frankfurt, 1719.

Petersen, Peter. *Geschichte der aristotelischen Philosophie im protestantischen Deutschland*. Leipzig: F. Meiner, 1921.

Peterson, Erik. "Das Problem der Bibel-Auslegung im Pietismus des 18. Jahrunderts." *Zeitschrift für systematische Theologie* (1923), pp. 468–481.

Pettenegg, Ed. Gaston Grafen von. *Ludwig und Karl, Grafen und Herren von Zinzendorf.* Wien: Wilhelm Braumüller, 1879.

Pfister, Oskar. *Die Frömmigkeit des Grafen Ludwig von Zinzendorf. Eine psychoanalytische Studie.* Wien: F. Deuticke, 1925. (Schriften zur angewandten Seelenkunde 8.)

——. *Die Frömmigkeit des Grafen Ludwig von Zinzendorf, ein psychoanalytischer Beitrag zur Kenntnis der religiösen Sublimierungsprozesse und zur Erklärung des Pietismus.* Leipzig and Wien: F. Deuticke, 1910.

Pillendorf, Nicolaus Freyherr von (pseudonym). *Unvorgreifliche Vorschlaege zu einem dauerhaften Frieden zwischen dem hochgebornen Herrn Nicolaus Ludewig Grafen von Zinzendorf und seinen Anhaengern Eines; und Hochgedachten Herrn Grafens Feinden.* Hammerde, Halle: 1749.

Pinson, Koppel S. *Pietism as a Factor in the Rise of German Nationalism.* New York: Columbia University Press, 1934.

Plitt, Hermann. *Zinzendorf's Theologie.* 3 Vols. Gotha: F. A. Perthes, 1869–1874.

Plitt, Johannes. *Denkwürdigkeiten aus der Geschichte der Brüder-Unität.* Herrnhut: Unitätsarchiv, 1828–1840, Nos. 1–12. (Handwritten.)

——. *Geschichte der erneuerten Brüder-Unität.* Herrnhut: Unitätsarchiv, 1829. (Handwritten.)

Posselt, Ingeborg. *Die Verfassung der Brüdergemeine 1727–1775. Mit besonderer Berücksichtigung des Verhältnisses zur sächsischen Landeskirche.* Dissertation, Tübingen, 1949.

Pressler, Woldemar. *Entstehung und Entwicklung der Deutschen Brüder-Unität in Herrnhut (Sachsen), insbesondere ihre Verfassung.* Dissertation, Frankfurt, 1929.

Prince, Isaac. *The Moravians, who they are.* Rossmere, Pa., 1907.

Rade, Martin. *Die Stellung des Christentums zum Geschlechtsleben.* Tübingen: J. C. B. Mohr, 1910.

Raillard, H. "Die Stellung der Moral im Leben des Christen nach Zinzendorf," *Zeitschrift für Theologie und Kirche,* 14 (1933), pp. 236–256.

Ranft, Ruth. *Das Pädagogische im Leben und Werk des Grafen Ludwig v. Zinzendorf.* Weinheim: Beltz, 1958. (Göttinger Studien zur Pädagogik, 3.)

Regent, P. Car. *Unpartheyische Nachricht von der in Laussnitz überhandnehmenden . . . Neuen Sect der so genannten Schefferianer und Zinzendorffianer.* Breslau, 1829.

Reichel, Gerhard. *Die Anfänge Herrnhuts.* Herrnhut: Verlag der Missionsbuchhandlung, 1922.

——. *August Gottlieb Spangenberg, Bischof der Brüderkirche.* Tübingen: J. C. B. Mohr, 1906.

——. "Die Entstehung einer Zinzendorf feindlichen Partei in Halle und Wernigerode." *Zeitschrift für Kirchengeschichte,* XXIII (1902), pp. 549 ff.

————. "Die Geschichte des 13. August 1727." *Mitteilungen aus der Brüder-Gemeine.* Gnadau: Unitätsbuchhandlung, 1927.

————. *Der "Senfkornorden" Zinzendorfs.* Leipzig: F. Jansa, 1914. (Berichte des Theologischen Seminars der Brüdergemeine in Gnadenfeld, 9).

————. *Zinzendorfs Frömmigkeit im Licht der Psychoanalyse.* Tübingen: J. C. B. Mohr, 1911.

Reichel, H. W. "David Nitschmann, der erste Bischof der erneuerten Brüderkirche." *Lebensbilder aus der Brüdergemeine,* 1 (1922), Herrnhut.

Reichel, Levin Theodore. *The Early History of the Church of the United Brethren, Commonly Called Moravians, in North America, A. D. 1734-1748.* Nazareth, Pa.: Whitefield House, 1888. (*Transactions of the Moravian Historical Society,* Vol. III.)

Reichel, William Cornelius. *Memorials of the Renewed Moravian Church.* Philadelphia: Lippincott, 1870.

Reincke, Abraham. *A Register of Members of the Moravian Church and of Persons Attached to Said Church in this Country and Abroad, 1727-1775.* Bethlehem, Pa.: H. T. Clauder, 1873.

Renkewitz, Heinz. "Die Anfange der Gemeindebildung und die sozialen Ordnungen der Brüdergemeine." *Die Innere Mission,* 23 (1928), pp. 107 ff. (Berlin.)

————. *Die Brüdergemeine: Ihr Anftrag und ihre Gestalt.* Stuttgart: Steinkopf, 1949.

————. "Der diakonische Gedanke im Zeitalter des Pietismus." *Das diakonische Amt der Kirche,* ed. H. Krimm, Stuttgart: Evangelisches Verlagswerk, 1953, pp. 258 ff.

————. *Ernst Christoph Hochmann von Hochenau* *(1670-1721).* *Quellenstudien zur Geschichte des Pietismus.* Breslau: Maruschke and Berendt, 1935.

————. *Die Losungen. Entstehung und Geschichte eines Andachtsbuches.* Hamburg: Wittig, 1953.

————. "Luther und Zinzendorf." *Neue Kirchliche Zeitschrift,* 43 (1932), pp. 156-179.

————. "Sozialethik des Pietismus; Sozialethik, Herrnhutter." *Evangelisches Sozial-lexikon,* ed. Fr. Karrenberg, Stuttgart: Kreuz Verlag, 1956, columns 942 ff., and 944 ff.

————. "Die Struktur des Pietismus." *Welt als Geschichte,* II (1936), pp. 577 ff.

————. "War Zinzendorf ein Spiritualist?" *Evangelische Theologie,* 9 (1949-50), pp. 529-558. Also in Benz, *Zinzendorfgedenkbuch,* as "Zinzendorf als Theologe."

————. "Was versteht die Brüdergemeine unter Gemeine?" *Mitteilungen aus der Brü-dergemeine,* 6 (1938), pp. 147 ff. (Herrnhut.)

————. *Zinzendorf.* Herrnhut: Verlag der Missionsbuchhandlung, 1935. (Most recent edition, Hamburg, 1948.)

————. *Zinzendorfs Wort an uns heute.* Hamburg: Appel Verlag, 1952. (Herrnhuter Hefte I.).

Reuber, Kurt. *Mystik und Heiligungsfrömmigkeit der Gemeinschaftsbewegung.* Gütersloh: Bertelsmann, 1938.

Rican, Rudolf. *Die Böhmischen Brüder*. Berlin: Union Verlag Verlin, 1958.

Richter, Julius. "Vier deutsche Missionstheologen." *Festgabe Adolf von Harnack zum 70. Geburtstag*. Tubingen: J. C. B. Mohr, 1921, pp. 243–262.

Richter, Paul Emil, ed. *Literatur der Landes-und Volkskunde des Königreichs Sachsen*. Dresden: A. Huhle, 1919.

Rieger, Georg Konrad. *Die alte und neue Böhmische Brüder, als deren . . . Historie zur Erkenntniss und Wiederholung besonders gegenwärtiger Zeit der Kirchen Gottes wieder nothwendig zu werden scheinet*. Stuttgart: Metzler, 1734–1740.

Rimius, Henry. *A Candid Narrative of the Rise and Progress of the Herrnhuters Commonly Called Moravians or Unitas Fratrum*. London, 1753.

Risler, Jeremias. *Leben A. G. Spangenbergs*. Leipzig: Kummer, 1794.

Rissanen, Eetu. *Kristillinen Palvelu N. L. von Zinzendorfin teologiasso*. (Zusammenfassung: Der Christliche Dienst in der Theologie N. L. von Zinzendorfs.) Dissertation, Helsinki, 1959.

Ritschl, Albrecht. *Geschichte des Pietismus*. 3 Vols. Bonn: A. Marcus, 1880–1886.

Ritter, Abraham. *History of the Moravian Church in Philadelphia*. Philadelphia: Hayes and Zell, 1857.

Ritter, Johann Frch. Wilhelm. *Leben des Frh. Johannes von Watteville und dessen Gemahlin Henriette Benigna Justine, geboren Grafin von Zz*. Hamburg: Kratzsch, 1800.

Römer, Hermann. *Nicolaus Ludwig Graf von Zinzendorf. Sein Leben und Wirken*. Gnadau: Unitäts-Buchhandlung, 1900.

Römer, Karl. *Kirchliche Geschichte von Württemberg*. Stuttgart, 1865.

Roentgen, Ph. H. A. *Kort Overzicht van de geschiedenis en inrichting der Evangelische Broederkerk*. Nijkerk: G. F. Callenbach, 1863.

Rotermund, Hans-Martin. *Orthodoxie und Pietismus*. Berlin: Evangelische Verlagsanstalt, 1959. (Vol. XIII of *Theologische Arbeiten*, ed. Hans Urner.)

Roucek, Joseph S. "The Moravian Brethren in America." *Social Studies*, 43 (1959), pp. 58–61.

Rubriken der Akten des Archives der Brüder-Unität. Herrnhut: Unitätsarchiv.

Ruh, Hans. *Christologische Begründung des ersten Artikels bei Zinzendorf*. Zurich: EVZ Verlag, 1967.

Ruprecht, Rudolf. *Der Pietismus des 18. Jahrhunderts in den Hannoverschen Stammländern*. Gottingen: Vandenhoeck and Ruprecht, 1919. (Studien zur geschichte Niedersachsens, Vol. I.)

Sachsse, Eugen. *Ursprung und Wesen des Pietismus*. Wiesbaden: J. Niedner, 1884.

Samlung der Loosungs-und-Text-Büchlein der Brüdergemeine von 1731 bis 1761. Barby, 1762. (Vol. I, 1731–1740.)

Savory, D. "Five Centuries of the Moravian Church." *Contemporary Review*, 191 (1957), pp. 141–148.

Sawyer, Edwin Albert. *The Religious Experience of the Colonial American Moravians.* Nazareth, Pa.: Laros Publishing Co., 1961. (*Transactions of the Moravian Historical Society,* Vol. XVIII, Part I.)

Schattenmann, Paul. "Zur neuesten Beurteilung des Pietismus." *Evangelisch lutherische Kirchenzeitung,* 5 (1953), pp. 68 ff.

Schauer, H. *Dichtungen des deutschen Barock.* Leipzig: Quelle & Meyer, 1926.

Scheffer-Schwedler-Rothe. *Zeugniss der Wahrheit der Gemeine zu Herrnhut wider Hn. P. Carl Regent, S. J. Missionarii Nachricht von . . . (s.o.) . . . auf vielfältiges Begehren zum Druck befördert von M. Christian Gottfried Marchen.* Herrnhuth, 1730.

Scheffler, Johannes. *Heilige Seelenlust oder Geistliche Hirtenlieder der in ihren Jesum verliebten Psyche.* ed. Georg Ellinger. Frankfurt: Iris-Verlag, 1926.

Schian, M. "Kurtz Mitteilungen: Der Trausermon bei der Trauung des Grafen Zinzendorf." *Zeitschrift für Brüdergeschichte,* V, 1 (1911), pp. 117–119.

———. *Orthodoxie und Pietismus im Kampf um die Predigt.* Giessen: Töpelmann, 1912. (*Studien zur Geschichte des neueren Protestantismus,* 7.)

Schleiermacher, Friedrich. *Aus Schleiermachers Leben.* In *Briefen I–IV,* ed. Ludwig Jonas and Wilhelm Dilthey, Berlin: G. Reimer, 1860–1863.

———. *Der christliche Glaube.* Berlin: G. Reimer, 1835–1836.

———. *Monologen. Eine Neujahrsgabe.* Berlin: G. Reimer, 1822.

———. *Sämtliche Werke in drei Abteilungen.* Berlin: G. Reimer, 1835–1864.

———. *Schleiermacher als Mensch. Sein Werden und Wirken. Familien-und Freundesbriefe I–II.* Ed. Henrich Meisner, Gotha: F. A. Perthes,1922–1923.

———. *Über die Religion. Reden an die Gebildeten unter ihren Verächtern.* Berlin: G. Reimer, 1831.

Schleiff, Arnold. *Selbstkritik der lutherischen Kirchen im 17. Jahrhundert.* Berlin: Junker & Dünnhaupt, 1937.

Schlosser, Manfred. *Genossenschaften in der Grafschaft Ysenburg vom 16. bis 19. Jahrhundert.* Kallmünz: Lassleben, 1956.

Schmid, Heinrich. *Geschichte des Pietismus.* Nördlingen: Beck, 1863.

Schmidt, Gottfried. "Die Banden oder Gesellschaften im alten Herrnhut." *Zeitschrift für Brüdergeschichte,* III (1909), pp. 145 ff.

Schmidt, Gottfried, and Jannasch, Wilhelm. *Das Zeitalter des Pietismus.* Bremen: Carl Schuenemann Verlag, 1965. (*Klassiker des Protestantismus,* Vol. VI.)

Schmidt, Martin. "Das Bild Zinzendorfs in der neueren Forschung." *Evangelisch-Lutherische Kirchenzeitung,* 7 (1935), pp. 340–343, 365–369.

———. *John Wesley.* Zürich, Frankfurt: Crotthelf-Verlag, 1953.

———. "Nachweis der Verwandschaft die zwischen der Grundkonzeption von Speners Pia Desideria und derjenigen von Christian Hoburgs Spiegel der Missbräuche beim Predigtamt besteht." *Theologia Viatorum,* III (1951), pp. 100 ff.

———. "Speners Wiedergeburtslehre." *Theologische Literaturzeitung*, 1 (1951), pp. 17 ff.

Schmidt, Theodor. *Zinzendorfs Soziale Stellung und ihr Einfluss auf seinen Charakter und sein Lebenswerk.* Basel: Basler Buchhandlung, 1900.

Schmidt, W. E. *Neuere Brüdergeschichte rezensiert.* Sitzungsbericht der Kg. Böhm Gesellschaft der Wissenschaften. Vol. III, 1906.

Schmidt, Walther E. "Das religiöse Leben in den ersten Zeiten der Brüderunität." *Zeitschrift für Brüdergeschichte*, I, 1 (1907), pp. 33–92.

Schneider, L. *Johann Leonhard Dober, der erste Missionar der Brüdergemeine.* Herrnhut: Missionsbuchhandlung, 1906.

Schrautenbach, Ludwig Carl Frh. von. *Der Graf von Zinzendorf und die Brüdergemeine seiner Zeit.* Gnadau: F. W. Kölbing, 1851.

Schrenk, Gottlob. *Gottesreich und Bund im ältern Protestantismus vornehmlich bei Johannes Coccejus. Zugleich ein Beitrag zur Geschichte des Pietismus und der heilsgeschichtlichen Theologie.* Gütersloh: C. Bertelsman, 1923.

Schreyer, Paul. *V. E. Löscher und die Unionsversuche seiner Zeit.* Schwabach: J. G. Schreyer, 1938.

Schröder, William von. *Gottfried Arnold.* Heidelberg: Carl Winter Verlag, 1917, (Beitrage zur neueren Literaturgeschichte, 9.)

Schubart, Walter. *Religion und Eros.* München: C. H. Beck, 1941.

Schücking, L. L. *Die Familie im Puritanismus.* Leipzig und Berlin: B. G. Teubner, 1929.

Schütze, J. G. *Herrnhutianismus in Tumore.* Frankfurt & Leipzig, 1748.

———. *Herrnhutianismus in Nuce.* Hamburg, 1750.

———. *Herrnhutianismus in Literis.* Leipzig, 1752.

———. *Herrnhutianismus in Delirio.* Hamburg, 1752.

———. *Herrnhutianismus in Dolo.* Hamburg, 1752.

———. *Herrnhutianismus in Temeritate.* Görlitz, 1759.

Schulze, Ad. "Graf Zinzendorf ein Freund Israels." *Schriften des Institutum Judaicum*, 8 (1907).

———. "Graf Zinzendorf im Verkehr mit Juden." *Schriften des Institutum Judaicum*, 9 (1907).

Schultz, Lic. "Die theoretische Begründung des Begriffs der Individualität in Schleiermachers ethischen Entwürfen." *Zeitschrift für Theologie und Kirche*, V (1924), pp. 37 ff.

Schunke, Siegfried. *Beziehungen der Herrnhuter Brüdergemeine zur Grafschaft Mark.* Ph.D. dissertation, Münster Westfählische Landes Universität, Germany, 1949.

Schuster, Kurt. *Gruppe, Gemeinschaft, Kirche, Gruppenbildung bei Zinzendorf.* München: Kaiser Verlag, 1960. (Theologische Existenz Heute N. F. 85.)

Schwarze, William N. *Early Moravian Settlements in America.* Papers of the American Society Church History, 2nd Series, Vol. VII. New York: G. P. Putnam's Sons, 1923.

De Schweinitz, Edmund Alexander. *The History of the Church known as the Unitas Fratrum, or the Unity of the Brethren, Founded by the Followers of John Hus, the Bohemian Reformer and Martyr.* Bethlehem, Pa.: Moravian Publications Office, 1885.

———. *The Moravian Episcopate.* Bethlehem, Pa.: Moravian Publication Office, 1865.

———. *The Moravian Manual, Containing an Account of the Protestant Church of the Moravian United Brethren or Unitas Fratrum.* Philadelphia: Lindsey and Blakiston, 1859.

Seeberg, Erich. *Gottfried Arnold, Auswahl (Mystiker des Abendlandes).* München: A. Langen, G. Müller, 1934.

———. *Gottfried Arnold, die Wissenschaft und die Mystik seiner Zeit.* Meerane: E. R. Herzog, 1923.

———. "Gottfried Arnolds Anschauung von der Geschichte." *Zeitschrift für Kirchengeschichte*, 2 F. I (1920), pp. 282 ff.

———. *Zur Frage der Mystik.* Leipzig: A. Deichert, 1921.

Sigourney, Mrs. L. H. *Zinzendorf, and other Poems.* New York: Leavitt, Lord and Co., 1836.

Sinning, Waldemar. *Zinzendorf als Prediger.* Münster, 1926.

Sovocol, L. R. "Moravian Missions." *Bibliotheca Sacra*, 89 (1932), pp. 87–90.

———. "Moravians and their Religious Philosophy." *Bibliotheca Sacra*, 88 (1931), pp. 440–464.

Spangenberg, August Gottlieb. *Declaration über die Seither gegen Uns ausgegangene Beschuldigungen.* Leipzig und Görlitz, 1751.

———. *Idea Fidei Fratrum oder kurzer Begrif der Christlichen Lehre in den evangelischen Brüdergemeinen.* Barby: Christian Laur, 1782.

———. *Leben des Herrn Nikolaus Ludwig, Grafen und Herrn von Zinzendorf und Pottendorf.* 8 Vols. Barby, Herrnhut: Verlag der Brüdergemeine, 1772–1775.

———. D. L. Rights, ed. "Moravian Report on John Wesley — 1737: the report sent from Georgia to authorities of the Moravian Church in Herrnhut, Saxony." *South Atlantic Quarterly*, 43 (1944), pp. 406–409.

———. *M. Aug. Gottlieb Spangenbergs Apologetische Schluss-Schrifft, worinn über tausend Beschuldigungen gegen die Brüder-Gemeinen und ihren seitherigen Ordinarium nach der Wahrheit beantwortet werden.* 2 Vols. Leipzig and Görlitz, 1752.

———. *M. Aug. Gottlieb Spangenbergs Darlegung richtiger Antworten auf mehr als dreibundert Beschuldigungen gegen den Ordinarium Fratrum nebst verschiedenen wichtigen Beylagen.* Leipzig and Görlitz, 1751.

Spener, Philipp Jacob. *Consilia et iudicia theologica latina I–III.* Frankfurt: Fleischer, 1790.

————. *Divi Pauli Apostoli Epistolae ad Romanos et Corinthios homiletica paraphrasi illustratae*. Frankfurt, 1691.

————. *Erklärung der Epistel an die Galater*. Frankfurt, 1714.

————. *Erste Geistliche Schrifften*. Frankfurt: Verlag Johann David Zunners, 1699.

————. *Pia Desideria*. Ed. Kurt Aland (Lietzmanns Kleine Texte 170). Berlin: W. de Gruyter, 1940.

————. *Theologische Bedencken I–IV*. Halle: Waisenhausbuchhandlung, 1712–1715.

Spinka, M. "Peter Chelcicky, the spiritual father of the Unitas fratrum." *Church History*, 12 (1943), pp. 271–291.

Stäudlin, C. F. *Geschichte der Vorstellungen und Lehren von der Ehe*. Göttingen: Rosenbusch, 1826.

Stahl, Herbert. *August Hermann Francke. Der Einfluss Luthers und Molinos' auf ihn*. Stuttgart: Kohlhammer, 1939. (Rotermund lists this work as now published as Vol. XVI of *Forschungen zur Kirchen und Geistesgeschichte*.)

Stahl, J. J. "Diary of a Moravian Missionary at Broad Bay, Me., in 1760." *New England Quarterly*, 12 (1939), pp. 747–769.

Stammler, W. *Von der Mystik zum Barock*. Stuttgart: J. B. Metzler, 1927.

Steinberg, H. *Die Brüderkirche in ihrem Werden und Sein*. Herrnhut: Missionsbuchhandlung, 1921.

Steinberg, H. G.; Schütz, H. L. C.; Lutjeharms, W.; and Van Der Linde, J. M. *Zinzendorf*. Essays forming *Boeken der Broeders* No. 1. Nijkerk: G. F. Callenbach, 1960.

Steinecke, O. *Die Diaspora der Brüdergemeine in Deutschland*. Halle: R. Mühlmann's Verlag, 1905–1911. Vols. I–III.

————. *Zinzendorf und der Katholizismus*. Halle: R. Mühlmann, 1902.

————. *Zinzendorfs Bildungsreise. An der Hand des Reistagebuches Zinzendorfs dargestellt*. Halle: R. Mühlmann, 1900.

Stephan, Horst. *Der Pietismus als Träger des Fortschritts in Kirche, Theologie und allgemeiner Geistesbildung. Sammlung Gemeinverständlicher Vorträge und Schriften*, No. 51. Tübingen, 1908.

Sting, Albert. *Graf Nikolaus Ludwig von Zinzendorf. Eine erbcharakterologische Studie*. Dissertation, Tübingen, 1960.

Stolze, Wilhelm. *Friedrich Wilhelm I. und der Pietismus*. Jahrbuch für brandenburg. Kirchen-Geschichte 1908, pp. 172 ff.

Stolzenburg, A. F. *Die Theologie des Jo. Franc. Buddeus und des Chr. Matth. Pfaff. Ein Beitrag zur Geschichte der Aufklärung in Deutschland*. Berlin: Trowitsch & Sohn, 1926. (Neue Studien zur Geschichte der Theologie und der Kirche XXII).

Stoudt, J. J. "Count Zinzendorf and the Pennsylvania Congregation of God in the Spirit." *Church History*, 9 (1940), pp. 366–438.

Stoughton, John. *Religion in England under Queen Anne and the Georges*, 1702–1800. London: Hodder and Stoughton, 1878.

Stromberg, Roland N. *Religious Liberalism in Eighteenth-Century England*. London: Oxford University Press, 1954.

Strupl, M. "Confessional Theology of the Unitas Fratrum (up to the 17th c.)." *Church History*, 33 (1964), pp. 279–293.

Süskind, Hermann. *Christentum und Geschichte bei Schleiermacher*. Tübingen: J. C. B. Mohr, 1911.

Sykes, N. *Daniel Ernst Jablonski and the Church of England*. London: Society for Promoting Christian Knowledge, 1950.

Tacitus, Aletophilus (Pseudonym). *Gedancken ueber die viele, die herrnhuthische Eigentlich aber zu reden die Evangelischen Brueder Maehrischer Unitaet betreffende Streit-Schrifften*. Marche: Leipzig, 1749.

Tagebuch Heinrich XXXI, Reuss, genannt Ignatius. Printed in installments in *Der Brüderbote*, 1883–1884.

Tanner, Fritz. *Die Ehe im Pietismus*. Zürich: Zwingli-Verlag, 1952.

Teufel, Eberhard. "Johann Andreas Rothe, 1688–1758." *Beiträge zur sächsischen Kirchengeschichte*. 30/31 (1917–1918), Leipzig.

Thierstein, Johannes R. *Novalis und der Pietismus*. Philosophy Dissertation, Bern, 1913.

Tholuck, August. *Der Geist der lutherischen Theologen Wittenbergs im Verlauf des 17. und 18. Jahrhunderts*. Hamburg and Gotha: F. & A. Perthes, 1852.

Thune, Nils Brorson. *The Behmenists or the Philadelphians*. Uppsala: Almquist & Wiksell, 1948.

Towlson, C. W. *Moravian and Methodist*. London: Epworth Press, 1957.

Transactions of the Moravian Historical Society. 21 Vols. Nazareth, Pa.: Whitefield House, Laros Publishing Company; and Bethlehem, Pa.: Times Publishing Co., 1876–1966. (Name and place of publication varies.)

Unger, R. *Hamann und die Aufklärung*. Halle: M. Niemeyer, 1925.

Urner, Hans. "Der Pietismus." *Quellen, Ausgewählte Texte aus der Geschichte der christlichen Kirche*, 34 (1961). (Berlin.)

Uttendörfer, Otto. "Abraham Dürningers Anfänge." *Lebensbilder aus der Brüdergemeine*, 5 (1922). (Herrnhut.)

————. *Alt-Herrnhut. Wirtschaftsgeschichte und Religions-soziologie Herrnhuts während seiner ersten zwanzig Jahre, 1722–1742*. (Alt-Herrnhut I.) Herrnhut: Verlag der Missionsbuchhandlung, 1925.

————. "Aus Zinzendorfs Alltagsleben." *Mitteilungen aus der Brüdergemeine*, 3, 4 (1939).

Uttendörfer, Otto, and Schmidt, Walter E. *Die Brüder. Aus Vergangenheit und Gegenwart der Brüdergemeine*. Gnadau: Verlag der Unitätsbuchhandlung, 1922, Vol. III.

136

Uttendörfer, O. "Die Entstehung der 'Beschreibung und zuverlässigen Nachricht von Herrnhut'." *Zeitschrift für Brüdergeschichte*, VI, 2 (1912), pp. 220 ff.

———. "Die Entwürfe Zinzendorfs zu seiner Religionsschrift." *Zeitschrift für Brüdergeschichte*, XIII (1919), pp. 64–98.

———. *Das Erziehungswesen Zinzendorfs und die Brüdergemeine in seinen Anfängen.* Berlin: Weidmann, 1912. (Monumenta Germaniae paedagogica, 51).

———. "Nikolaus Ludwig Graf von Zinzendorf," *Evangelische Gedanken*. Berlin: Christliche Zeitschriftenverlag, 1948.

———. Rezension von W. Jannasch: "Erdmuthe Dorothea Gräfin von Zinzendorf." *Zeitschrift für Brüdergeschichte*, IX (1915), pp. 129–135.

———. "Die schwärmerische Krisis im Seminar." *Zeitschrift für Brüdergeschichte*, XIII (1919), pp. 25 ff.

———. *Wirtschaftsgeist und Wirtschaftsorganisation Herrnhuts und der Brüdergemeine von 1743 bis zum Ende des Jahrs.* (Alt-Herrnhut, Part 2). Herrnhut: Verlag der Missionsbuchhandlung, 1926.

———. "Zinzendorf und die Entwicklung des theologischen Seminars der Brüderunität." *Zeitschrift für Brüdergeschichte*, X (1916), pp. 32–88; XI (1917), pp. 71–123; XII (1918), pp. 1–78; XIII (1919), pp. 1–63.

———. *Zinzendorf und die Frauen.* Herrnhut: Missionsbuchhandlung, 1919.

———. *Zinzendorf und die Jugend.* Berlin: Furche Verlag, 1923. (Bücher der Brüder. 2.)

———. *Zinzendorf und die Mystik.* Berlin: Christlicher Zeitschrift Verlag, 1950.

———. *Zinzendorfs christliches Lebensideal.* Gnadau: Unitätsbuchhandlung, 1940.

———. *Zinzdendorfs Gedanken über den Gottesdienst.* Herrnhut: Gustav Winter, 1931.

———. "Zinzendorfs Pflege des Missionssinnes der Heimatgemeine im Jahr 1758." *Zeitschrift für Brudergeschichte*, VI, 2 (1912), pp. 129–165.

———. *Zinzendorfs religiöse Grundgedanken.* Herrnhut: Verlag der Missionsbuchhandlung, 1935.

———. *Zinzendorfs Weltanschauung.* Berlin: Furche-Verlag, 1929.

———. *Zinzendorfs Weltbetrachtung.* Berlin: Furche Verlag, 1929. (Bücher der Brüder, 6.)

Varnhagen von Ense, Karl, August. *Leben des Grafen Ludwig von Zinzendorf.* Berlin: Reimer, 1846.

Verbeek, Jacob Wilhelm. *Des Grafen Nicolaus Ludwig von Zinzendorf Leben und Charakter.* Leipzig: Kummer, 1845.

Verlässe, und Verhandlungen von, und Mitteilungen aus der Brüderunität. Herrnhut, 1836–1899. (A printed version of the Gemeinnachrichten.)

Viötor, K. *Probleme der deutschen Barockliteratur.* Leipzig: J. J. Weber Verlagsbuchhandlung, 1928.

Voget, Albertus. *Unterscheid der wahren und falschen Gottesgelahrtheit bey Gelegenheit der unter Anführung Herrn Nicol. Lud. Grafen von Zinzendorf und Pottendorf erfolgten Herrnhutischen Bewegungen.* Zürich, 1741.

Volck, Alexander. *Das Entdeckte Geheimnis der Bosheit der Herrnhutischen Secte, . . . vor dem Angesicht der gantzen Christenheit in Gesprächen dargeleget zwischen Timotheo Verino, Politarcho und Alethophilo.* Frankfurt and Leipzig, 1749 and 1751, Vol. 1-7.

Walch, J. G. *Theologische Bedenken von der Beschaffenheit der herrnhutischen Sekte.* ed. Jeh. Philipp Fresenius. Frankfurt, 1749.

Walker, W. "Zinzendorf: Life and Work." *Great Men of the Church.* Chicago: Chicago University Press, 1908, pp. 303-317.

Wat weet gij van de Evangelische Broedergemeente en hare Zending? Zeist: Herrnhutter Zendings-Jubileum-Comite, 1932.

Waver, G. A. *The Beginnings of the Brethren's Church in England.* London, 1901. (Translated from the German *Die Anfänge der Brüderkirche in England.* Leipzig: F. Jansa, 1900–.)

Weaver, G. "Moravians During the French and Indian War." *Church History,* 24 (1955), pp. 239-256.

Wehrung, Georg. "Durchgang Schleiermachers durch die Brüdergemeine." *Zeitschrift für systematische Theologie,* IV (1927), pp. 193 ff.

———. *Schleiermacher in der Zeit seines Werdens.* Gütersloh: C. Bertelsmann, 1927.

Weinlick, John R. *Count Zinzendorf.* New York: Nashville Abingdon Press, 1956.

Weizsäcker, Hugo. *Schleiermacher und das Eheproblem.* Tübingen: J. C. B. Mohr, 1927.

Wendland, Walter. "Die Pietistische Bekehrung." *Zeitschrift für Kirchengeschichte,* I (1920), pp. 193 ff.

Wernle, Paul. *Der schweizerische Protestantismus im 18. Jahrhundert.* 3 Vols. Tübingen: J. C. B. Mohr, 1923.

Westphal, J. *Das evangelische Kirchenlied.* Berlin: Union deutsche Verlagsgesellschaft, 1925.

Westphal, Milton C. "Early Moravian Pietism." *Pennsylvania History,* III (1936), pp. 164-181.

Whitefield, George. *An Expostulatory letter addressed to Nicholas Lewis, Count Zinzendorf, and lord advocate of the Unitas Fratrum* . . . . Philadelphia: Bradford, 1753.

Wieser, Max. *Der sentimentale Mensch. Gesehen aus der Welt holländischer und deutscher Mystiker im 18. Jahrhundert.* Gotha (Stuttgart): Leopold Klotz Verlag, 1924.

———. *Deutsche und romanische Religiosität. Fenelon, seine Quellen und seine Wirkungen.* Berlin: Furche-Verlag, 1919.

Willey, Basil. *The Eighteenth Century Background.* New York: Columbia University Press, 1965. (First Publication 1940.)

Williams, Henry L. *The Development of the Moravian Hymnal. Transactions of the Moravian Historical Society,* Vol. XVIII, Part 2. Nazareth, Pa.: Whitefield House, Laros Publishing Co., 1962, pp. 239-266.

Winter, Eduard. *Die tschechisch und slowakische Emigration in Deutschland im 17. und 18. Jahrbundert.* Berlin: Akademie Verlag, 1955.

Witkop, J. *De Evangelische Broeder-Gemeente der Herrnhutters in oorsprong, aard en werking beschouwd.* Groningen: J. B. Walters, 1841.

Wittern, Max. "Die Geschichte der Brüdergemeine in Schleswig-Holstein." *Schriften des Vereins für schleswig-holsteinische Kirchengeschichte,* 4 (1908).

Woldershausen, Otto Andreas. *Das Leben des Herrn Grafen Nicolaus Ludwig von Zinzendorf.* Wittenberg: Zimmerman, 1749.

―――. *Gegruendete Nachrichten von dem Ursprung Fortgang und Mitteln zur Ausbreitung der herrnhutischen Secte.* Zimmerman: Wittenberg, 1749.

Wolfskehl, Marie Luise. *Die Jesusminne in der Lyrik des deutschen Barock.* Giessen: Münchowsche Universitäts-drukerei, 1934.

Wollstadt, Hanns-Joachim. *Geordnetes dienen in der christlichen Gemeinde.* Göttingen: Vandenhoeck and Ruprecht, 1966. (Arbeiten zur Pastoraltheologie IV.)

Zimmermann, Elizabeth. *Schwenckfelder und Pietisten in Greiffenberg und Umgebung.* Görlitz: Starke, 1939.

Zorb, E. H. "Count Zinzendorf: as 18th century ecumenist." *Ecumenical Review,* 9 (1957), pp. 419–428.